Wine Lover's
DEVOTIONAL

365 Days
of Knowledge, Advice, and Lore for the Ardent Aficionado

Jonathon Alsop

BEVERLY MASSACHUSETTS

QUARRY BOOKS

First published in the United States of America by
Quarry Books, a member of
Quayside Publishing Group
100 Cummings Center
Suite 406-L
Beverly, Massachusetts 01915-6101
Telephone: (978) 282-9590
Fax: (978) 283-2742
www.quarrybooks.com

Library of Congress Cataloging-in-Publication Data

Alsop, Jonathon.
  Wine lover's devotional : 365 days of knowledge, advice, and lore for
the ardent aficionado / Jonathon Alsop.
    p. cm.
  Includes index.
  ISBN-13: 978-1-59253-616-0
  ISBN-10: 1-59253-616-6
  1. Wine and wine making--Miscellanea. I. Title.
  TP548.A43 2010
  641.2'2--dc22

                                                        2010004020

ISBN-13: 978-1-59253-616-0
ISBN-10: 1-59253-616-6

10 9 8 7 6 5 4 3 2 1

Contributing writer: Kristen Hampshire
Design: everlution design
Illustrations: Michael Wanke

Printed in China

"Don't worry if you can't understand wine-speak.
Nobody can. It's a language invented by drunk people."

– JAY FEDIGAN, documentary film maker

This book is dedicated with love, thanks, and more love to my wife Sheleagh Somers, who means literally everything to me, and whose relentless encouragement, faith, and trust made this writing possible.

I could drink a case of you.

contents

A corkscrew collection in a Heuriger, or wine tavern, in
Grinzing, Vienna, Austria

Introduction: Living the Wine Life

When I started writing about wine more than twenty years ago, I was like everyone else: not obsessed with wine, not filling my weekends with wine tastings, and I was not shopping, buying, ordering, cooking with, and thinking about wine all the time . . . yet.

What I was obsessed with at the time was writing. The first time I wrote about wine, it was if I awoke and started seeing and writing about the whole world through the prism of wine. I could write un-sexy corporate collateral material during the day—order now and save!—while tasting wine and calling myself a wine writer by night.

The wine life overtook me, and although I did not know it at the time, I was on a track with millions of other people towards becoming a serious wine lover. As I was discovering that Chardonnay was both the name of a grape and the name of a town in France where they grow, so were millions of others. As I began to like red wine more and more, the taste of millions moved in the same direction.

As you read or browse or study this book, I hope you'll find in it that same arc of discovery that we all travel, whether you're new to wine, experienced with wine, or somewhere in between. Wine itself is just a thing, a great thing granted, but it's tasting wine and sharing wine and thinking about wine daily—living the wine life—that gives wine meaning.

Whether you use this book for a day or a year or forever, remember that the secret of wine is that it's not about the wine—it's about the people, the places, the stories, and everything else behind the wine.

— **JONATHON ALSOP**

How to Use This Book

This book is organized as a day minder, with entries creating a complete year's worth of information. Each of the year's fifty-two weeks has six entries.

You can start reading this book from the beginning, , following the days of the week through the calendar year, reading one entry each day. You can also read from the middle of the book, the end, or skip around from week to week as inspiration strikes. The most important thing to remember is that you can use this book however you want. When you love wine, every day is an opportunity to sample a new vintage. Turn to any page, and you will find another figurative bottle to uncork. Do you have your tried-and-true vino? Bookmark your favorite pages and return time and again.

So, set aside some time and find a quiet place that is yours alone. Sip this book at your own pace, and enjoy the journey through the delicious world of wine!

A Wine Lover's Year

 MONDAYS / The Language of Wine: how we talk about it, how we learn about it

 TUESDAYS / Wine Grapes: the botany of worldwide grape varietals, and how they shape our favorite wines

 WEDNESDAYS / Wine and Food: beyond food pairings, we offer dozens of delicious wine-inspired recipes and recommendations

 THURSDAYS / Geography of Wine: a virtual world tour of wineries, famous wine regions, and places of legend

 FRIDAYS / People Make Wine: profiles of wine-world personalities throughout history and today

 SATURDAYS + SUNDAYS / Weekend Wine Adventures: from vineyard tours to building your own wine cellar

Tasting Wine, Talking Wine

THE LATIN PHRASE *IN VINO VERITAS* captures a peculiar trait of wine known for thousands of years. This phrase does not mean that wine contains an enduring, romantic, artistic truth, but rather that when people drink wine, they tend to talk, sometimes even speaking truths they don't mean, or more accurately, don't mean to say in front of an audience. The active ingredient in wine—alcohol—causes these slips, which is why it is wise to keep your *vino* and your *veritas* in balance.

If you listen closely to what wine lovers say when they talk about wine, most people try to describe that transformative moment when grape juice turns into wine, when its sugar turns into alcohol. For most of human history, people have attributed this to magic or intervention by Dionysus (the Romans called him Bacchus) and his sidekick Silenus. Every time I bow my head to stick my nose into a glass of wine, I think about how wine was once literally considered a god (similar to Zeus and Poseidon) and has been for most of human history. Today, we are wine atheists.

Many wine lovers feel that the *spirit* in wine opens a well of *veritas*, honing their senses' ability to read meaning into and describe wine's exotic flavors. On a biochemical level, it is the alcohol; one alcohol molecule plus one acid molecule equals one ester, a molecule that makes everything aromatic from nail polish remover to brown sugar.

We can smell exotic aromas and taste unexpected flavors in wine because it contains a molecule so similar in chemical structure to the maple syrup ester that it's instantly recognizable. But because these molecules aren't exactly the same, we must keep working hard to put into words how wine tastes and how we feel when tasting it.

Create your own wine lexicon. Buy a small, bound notebook that fits into your pocket or handbag. When you taste a new wine, write down the first word or thought that pops into your mind. As you taste the wine again, ask yourself what you really meant, and jot down more notes.

Pinot Power

European wine grapes of the species *vitis vinifera* are all genetically related and include the Pinots: Pinot Blanc, the white grape; Pinot Noir, the black grape; and Pinot Grigio (or Pinot Gris), a version striped and mottled, neither white nor black, but in between—the wine grape equivalent of gray. *Grigio* means "gray" in Italian; *gris* means "gray" in French.

Pinot Blanc—Pinot Bianco in Italy and Spain— is the lightest expression of Pinot in both color and flavor. These grapes can have extremely thin skin, almost transparent, so you can actually see their white meat. As a wine, Pinot Blanc generally tastes juicy and simple, although several big, ripe, oaky California versions can easily pass for California Chardonnays.

Pinot Grigio, synonymous with Italian white wine, grows up and down the Italian boot. Its styles vary widely depending on location, from the Alpine north to the hot sunny south, but at its core, Pinot Grigio is full-bodied fruit. Mainstream Pinot Grigios represent the most dependably tasty choice for crisp, dry white wine.

Despite its name, Pinot Noir is not black in color, but burgundy, after the eponymous region in France where the most famous and sought-after Pinot Noir grows. This light-red grape typically produces light-red wines with subtle flavors that don't necessarily hit you over the head with power. As a grape, its thin skin makes it physically fragile; as a wine, it's typically delicate and soft-spoken, the kind of wine that grows on you.

Looking for a wine bargain? Pinot Noir is popular, Pinot Grigio is everywhere, but Pinot Blanc is ignored. That's where you may find Pinot value. On the Rhine River's French side, called Alsace, old wine-making families like Hugel, Willm, and Trimbach make deliciously affordable Pinot Blanc. Ditto for Tiefenbrunner (northern Italy) and California's Castoro Cellars and Valley of the Moon.

White Wine with White Food, Red Wine with Red Food

JUST LIKE THERE'S A SPECTRUM OF WINE, there's also a spectrum of food, and understanding how the two align will teach you how to pair them.

Imagine the world of wine as a color continuum. At the extreme left is water—colorless, flavorless, odorless. To the far right is black, opaque India ink. Let Sauvignon Blanc, Chardonnay, Pinot Noir, and Cabernet Sauvignon act as four major reference points on this spectrum.

Sauvignon Blanc is a light, crisp, zippy white wine, with Pinot Grigio, Soave, and dry Riesling as its neighbors. Chardonnay is a heavier white wine with riper, rounder, less spiky flavors. Viognier and semisweet Riesling also fall into this range.

Moving from light to dark, Pinot Noir, with its light-red, sometimes see-through color, comes first. Next is the dark, black Cabernet Sauvignon, followed by some darker, blacker Syrahs and Zinfandels. With this image in mind, you can place almost every wine on this spectrum.

Merlot falls between Pinot and Cab, leaning toward Cab. Chianti, between Pinot and Cab, leans toward Pinot. That crazy Australian Shiraz—so dense it has its own gravitational field—is clearly off the chart.

Do the same exercise with food, laying it over the wine spectrum as if a transparency. Shrimp, shellfish, and light, flaky white fish line up with Sauvignon Blanc. Poultry, pork, and muscular seafood cuts such as shark and swordfish match naturally with Chardonnay or other heavy white wines. Pinot Noir works with chicken, as well as veal, bluefish, and meaty mushroom dishes. Big red wine such as Cabernet Sauvignon goes with big red meat such as lamb, beef, and goat. Outlier foods, including raw-milk blue cheese and stinky Muenster, pair best with outlier wines, including high-alcohol Porto or late-harvest Zinfandel.

13

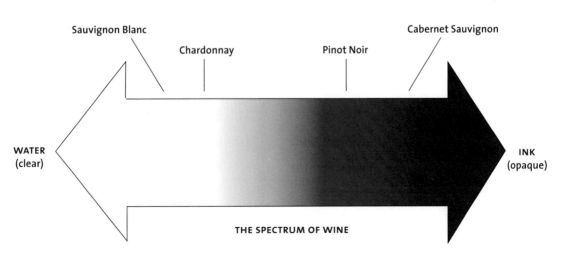

Sauvignon Blanc

Chardonnay

Pinot Noir

Cabernet Sauvignon

WATER (clear)

INK (opaque)

THE SPECTRUM OF WINE

Putting Down Roots

WINE'S SENSE OF PLACE is so strong that the same grape grown in two different places can produce wines that taste almost nothing alike. Just as with twins separated at birth, you expect the unexpected similarities and differences to delight. Yet take two equally valued wines from the same grape but from different circumstances—think French Chardonnay from Burgundy and Australian Chardonnay from halfway around the world—and you taste only the differences.

Although it's unclear exactly how different soils and climates affect a grape's divergent flavors, it shouldn't be surprising that they do. The grape vine needs little to survive—nitrogen, CO_2, and water—and little of each of those.

The roots, meanwhile, live submerged in and surrounded by the soil, awash in comparatively huge amounts of nutrients, minerals, and other substances. After six months, when the grapes are harvested and made into wine, the soil content and quality make a significant, concentrated difference.

Place matters. Just as nowhere else sounds like New Orleans, wine from this hill or that valley has its own unique taste.

SOIL TYPE	MINERAL COMPONENT	FLAVOR ELEMENT
Limestone	Calcium	Chalk, wet sidewalk
Granitic	Quartz	Steely, edgy, intense
Flint	Sedimentary quartz	Smoky
Volcanic	Sodium carbonate	Hot, spicy, smoky
Shale and slate	Diverse clay sediment under pressure	Lean, clear, crisp

Hands-Off Practitioners

THE WORLD'S BEST WINEMAKERS will tell you that wine is made in the vineyard; once they harvest it, they try more than anything else not to screw it up. Between the grape state and the wine state, maybe a dozen good things can go right and thousands can go wrong. Therefore—mathematically, at least—the less you do, the safer you are. The winemaker who does the least often makes the best wine.

Mark Inglis, a winemaker at Brancott-Montana Wines, New Zealand's largest winery, won his job twenty-odd years ago in a competition.

The winery hired a handful of aspiring apprentice winemakers, and gave each a small batch of juice. "They said, 'Here you go, make wine,'" Inglis said. "From there, you could get all the help you asked for, but it was up to you."

Inglis sipped the juice. "It tasted pretty good as it was," he said. "I decided I didn't want to do too much to it." That kind of thinking won him the job, and he helped launch the winery and enunciate its signature style: wines with extreme clarity that illuminate the grapes' character, not the winemaker's presence.

A (Storage) Place for Every Wine

THOSE WITH AN ORGANIZED wine space have an organized, presumably well-focused wine life—good for learning about and enjoying wine. Plus, wine benefits from short-term storage in a cool, dark place. Even a few days stowed under the sink helps a wine settle, knit together, and form a more cohesive, pleasing drink. After a wine rests, it often tastes rested, refreshed, and at its best.

Most of the time, you store wine only briefly before drinking it. You could store it on its head or inside out, and it wouldn't make a difference. Simply keep it off of the radiators and out of the freezer.

Even so, figuring out how and where to store your wine is a process, requiring you try different places until something clicks. The target storage temperature is 55°F (13°C) (and it is a target, not a rule). If it's dark and undisturbed, whether under a kitchen counter or in the corner by some cool exterior wall, it's perfect, whether it's 55°F (13°C) or 65°F (18°C). If you mean business, buy a small digital thermometer for your wine space to keep track of temperature. Here are a few do-it-yourself wine-storage ideas to hold you over until you can excavate your own wine cave.

UNDER THE STAIRS

If your home or apartment has one of those funky, slightly hard-to-use closets beneath the stairs, think about reclaiming it for wine storage.

UNDERGROUND (OR MOTHER EARTH)

For the greenest, least expensive way to store wine, use the Earth's chilly crust to cool your collection. If you have a basement or crawlspace, look for a corner with as many earthen walls as possible.

Stack wine on the floor, placed against the cool wall, with the bottles touching each other. This produces *conductive* cooling off of the earth, and your wine becomes the same temperature as the floor and the wall, almost regardless of outside air temperature.

WINE REFRIGERATORS

Most wine refrigerators fit in a closet or under a counter, meaning maximization of space and good home storage.

STACKED WOODEN BOXES

Most vineyards and wineries store their wines not in ornate cabinetry, but in small piles, with a half-dozen bottles stacked inside an open-backed wood box, with boxes atop each other until they form a square.

WINE CHEST

Buy a secondhand, small, front-opening chest, and knock out the back. Push this up against a cool basement wall and load it with wine, and you'll have a stable, cool environment. Any size works (as long as it fits in your home), but one about 3 feet by 4 feet (1 x 1.2 m) will store about fifty bottles of wine. Slide the bottles as far back as possible so they touch or almost touch the wall.

Wine and Spice and Everything Nice

WHEN WINE LOVERS USE THE WORD *spicy* to describe a wine, it can mean everything from "white pepper" to "I can't think of anything to say." If you give it the tone of a question— "Spicy?"—it means, "What the heck is that?"

To understand what you smell and taste, break down the wine into recognizable components or flavors that you would pick out in foods. Is it hot pepper spice or sweet pumpkin pie spice? Fresh or dry? What type of cuisine would use this spice? Thai, Greek, Indian, or other?

In the south of France, a tiny wine region specializes in a Syrah called Côte-Rôtie—"the roasted hill"—whose grapes grow on a steep hill angled acutely toward the sun. The effect is the same as sunning yourself in a beach chair: The Syrah smells like peppery grilled meat with a hint of smoky bacon.

Warm-climate Merlots from California, South America, and Australia often ripen to the point of smelling like cinnamon, nutmeg, clove, and date-nut bread. California Zinfandel brings a hint of black and white pepper.

Raiding the Spice Rack

If you have a stash of cooking spices in your kitchen, line up six wineglasses on the counter and put a spoonful of spice into each one. Swirl, sniff, and smell. Commit to memory the smells of these different spices and the foods they bring to mind. Make notes in your wine journal, and add the spices to your ever-expanding vocabulary. Practicing the art of sniffing and smelling in front of other people can be intimidating, so consider starting with the world of aromas available in the relative privacy of your own kitchen.

Adoring Chardonnay

CHARDONNAY'S ONLY PROBLEM is that it has grown too popular. Because everybody loves it, wine snobs consider it pandering populist trash, the wine equivalent of the art world's immortal *Dogs Playing Poker*. It is well known that novice wine lovers learn to grow beyond white Zinfandel; some feel the same about Chardonnay.

The numbers tell a different story. If wine lovers no longer consume Chardonnay, others must be simultaneously drinking a ton of it. It has been, and continues to be, the number one white grape in California alone in acres planted, tons harvested, money made, gallons produced, you name it.

For a grape that has gone so mainstream, Chardonnay has noble, European roots. It is one of the big four (Sauvignon Blanc, Pinot, and Cabernet constitute the other three) at the core of France's traditional wine identity. Chardonnays in France, known as white Burgundy and famously expensive due to single-vineyard wines, are a far cry from California's modern-day, low-end, daily drinkables.

Other grapes hope to have Chardonnay's same problems: to grow big and popular, beloved and ubiquitous. People go through phases of drinking and not drinking Chardonnay; it falls into and out of favor all the time. In the modern era, most wine grapes work hard to fall into favor once.

Hill full of Chardonnay on the road to Rodney Strong Vineyards in Sonoma, California, United States

Recipe: Lamb Shanks with Leeks and Olives

THE CLASSIC COMBINATION of lamb and dry red wine goes back centuries for good reason: The rich, almost buttery texture of lamb pairs perfectly with red wine's rough and rugged spiciness. In this case, opposites not only attract, but they also make excellent dinner companions.

½ cup (120 ml) dry red wine

¼ cup (60 ml) balsamic vinegar

2 tablespoons (28 ml) olive oil

4 lamb shanks

1 tablespoon (1.7 g fresh or 3.3 g dried) rosemary

1 tablespoon (5 g) cubed bacon

3 medium leeks

½ cup (50 g) pitted mixed olives

1 can (28 oz or 820 g) Italian peeled tomatoes

Combine the wine, vinegar, and 1 tablespoon (15 ml) of the olive oil, and marinate the lamb shanks for 1 to 4 hours. Save ½ cup (120 ml) of the marinade. Preheat the oven to 400°F (200°C).

On the stove, add the remaining 1 tablespoon (15 ml) olive oil and the rosemary to a Dutch oven (or other heavy dish with a lid), and heat until quite hot and the oil begins to smoke. Add the lamb shanks, and brown both sides until well seared. Remove the shanks and reduce the heat to medium. Add the bacon, leeks, and olives, and cook until the leeks just start to brown. Arrange the lamb shanks on top of the vegetable mixture in the Dutch oven, add the can of tomatoes and reserved marinade, and bake for 10 minutes, until bubbling nicely.

Put the dish in the oven and cook at 400°F (200°C) for 1 hour. Reduce to 225°F (110°C), and cook for 4 to 6 hours longer. Serve with risotto or noodles.

YIELD: Serves 4

Wine Pairing: Domaine du Vieux Lazaret Châteauneuf-du-Pape

FRANCE

Châteauneuf, a tiny town in southern France favored by medieval popes—that's what the word *pape* means in the name—is blessed with great soil and beautiful weather. Grenache-based blends such as this Vieux Lazaret occupy the top tier of southern Rhône wine making, but even at the top, the prices barely reach the heights of Bordeaux and Champagne. Though this might be a little pricey for a casual mid-week dinner, for a special-occasion meal, it's a comparatively affordable wine splurge.

New World, Old World

THE PHRASES *New World* and Old World are used throughout the wine industry and in the pages of this book. You may have an intuitive sense of what the geographic and historical differences between the two terms are, but do you know how they affect the wine industry?

Old World refers to regions around the world from Mesopotamia to the Atlantic (including North Africa and all of Europe).

New World is considered South Africa, Australia, South America, North America—in short, places where they only started growing wine within the past 200 to 300 years.

The differences between the two "worlds" can be literal, temporal, geographic, or stylistic. Below is a quick overview for easy reference (note: these are not strict rules).

	OLD WORLD	NEW WORLD
TIME	Centuries to thousands of years of wine-making traditions; winemaking ingrained in culture	Decades of wine-making industry; wine may be more of a commodity than cultural symbol
GRAPES	Blended (Cabernet/Merlot, et al); percentages used to create historically consistent wine flavors	100 percent varietals; individual grapes grown en masse for particular styles
NAME DERIVATION	Geography (Bordeaux, Burgundy, etc.)	Winemaker and/or grape (Carménère, Yellow Tail)
FLAVOR	Earthy	Fruity
MARKETING	Unnecessary	Ubiquitous
EMOTIONAL QUALITY	Traditional, classic, reliable	Inventive, novel, fresh

Mondo Mondavi

ROBERT MONDAVI (1913–2008) WAS a wine god.

After World War II, while the rest of California said, "Let's just sell easy-to-make jug wine," Robert Mondavi believed that California's wines could taste as good as, or better than, the best European wines. This belief made him a prophet. What made him a god? Proving it.

Before Mondavi could conquer Napa Valley, he had to conquer his own family, a group of winemakers decidedly less receptive to his new ideas than anyone else. Mondavi fought with his younger brother, Peter, over the direction of wine making and marketing at the Mondavi family's Charles Krug Winery. (An apocryphal brouhaha over Robert's wife, Madge, and a fur was really about the future of the whole game.) In 1965, Robert was either fired or quit, and he promptly founded his own winery in Oakville.

With the first Fumé Blanc in 1968, made from Sauvignon Blanc grapes fermented in steel and aged in oak, Mondavi reinvented California white wine. At the time, Sauvignon Blanc was unpopular, and dry Sauvignon Blanc countered the conventional wisdom that Americans only liked sweet white wines. Apparently, no one before had aged dry Sauvignon Blanc in oak, and the wine became a huge hit.

Although the famous 1976 "Judgment of Paris" tasting that pitted Napa Cabernet against French Bordeaux did not include Mondavi's wines, just two years later, he partnered with the Baron Philippe de Rothschild to make Opus One. Mondavi's 1979 Cabernet Sauvignon and Opus One's 1979 premier vintage are still legendary California wines.

Like many geniuses, Mondavi was as self-contradictory as he was inspiring. He championed labeling wines with their grape names—rarely done in Europe, where wine names tended to come from the places where the wines were made—yet his greatest successes were Fumé and Opus One, two invented proprietary names. If not the first, Mondavi was certainly the loudest advocate for Napa Valley as the place to look for the United States' wine-making potential. He dragged the Rothschilds into the debate, seemingly for their prestige (which he did not particularly need, even in 1978).

Finally, the man who lived by the motto, "Quality, quality, quality," saw his winery sold to a multinational corporation after the company's focus drifted from premium wines to other inexpensive lines, and the brand lost its luster. This story is long familiar in California wine history (see the story of Inglenook, Day 26), but still, Mondavi could not stop it from happening to his winery.

In 2007, he was inducted into the Vintners Hall of Fame, along with wine legends André Tchelistcheff, Gustave Niebaum, Agoston Haraszthy, Brother Timothy, and others.

21

How to Taste Wine, and Why

ESSENTIALLY TWO TYPES of wine tasting exist: hedonistic wine tasting and technical wine tasting.

Hedonistic wine tasting occurs 99 percent of the time: "I like it," "I don't like it," "I want another glass," or "I want a glass of something else." That's as far as this practical, necessary, and completely legitimate tasting style goes. At dinner with friends and family, wine life is about enjoying wine, not explaining it or defending a thesis. Goal number one is to achieve the best pleasure-taste combo (as it should be). That's what hedonistic means.

Technical wine tasting, on the other hand, happens when wine lovers attend a formal wine tasting. This type of wine tasting intensifies wine's individual aromas and flavors, and creates a more complete sensory profile. It's the wine tasting world's equivalent of getting so close to a painting that you can see its brushstrokes.

How do you complete a technical wine tasting? Here are seven steps:

- **See:** Take in the wine visually, like a new food you have never before tried. It should look fresh, bright, and appetizing.

- **Sniff:** Check to make sure the wine doesn't smell like rotten eggs, burnt rubber, moldy newspaper, or some other unpleasant scent.

- **Swirl:** Spin the wine in the glass and let it climb the inside. Do this for ten or fifteen seconds. Swirling turns up the volume on the wine's aroma, which pays off in the next step.

- **Smell:** Really stick your nose down into the glass and take a deep, slow breath. Intentionally plant in your mind the image of what this wine smells like.

- **Sip:** This is the taste equivalent of the sniff. Wet your lips and let the wine disperse across your palate.

- **Swish:** Take a small sip and swirl it around your mouth gently, as though it were mouthwash. If the flavor intensity gets too strong, ease up on swishing.

- **Spit:** My attorney suggests always tasting wine responsibly. I say, if you spit the wine, you get to taste more wines!

THE "BONUS" EIGHTH S: SLOW DOWN!

Hurry wine lovers, and slow down now. Slowing the tasting process shows respect for everybody in the wine-making chain, and it makes your wine taste better. Putting wine into the middle of a meal automatically slows down the meal a little, making it seem more like an occasion, a reminder to appreciate life.

The Evolution of Taste

THERE'S NO GREATER MOMENT in a bottle of wine's life than the first sip. Tasting is the reason for wine's being. A good wine connoisseur can put on quite a show with swirling, sniffing, slurping, and spitting. For all the grape growing, wine making, and vintage testing, it all comes down to taste: How does the wine taste? And what does it taste like?

Wine drinking is a process of tasting and remembering. Sense memory and sense of taste mature with exposure. That's why for most people, wine is an acquired taste. They start by drinking a single user-friendly wine. Slowly, they branch out into multiple, more complicated wines. It's a natural evolution.

This evolution is not necessarily cerebral. The most succinct observation I've ever heard came from an eight-year-old child, in front of two dozen wine professionals tasting top-drawer white Burgundy. "This wine smells like a cat!" she said. Her candor silenced the crowd, but no one could disagree. The slightly ammonia-like aroma relatively common to Sauvignon Blanc and white Burgundy comes from a compound called urea, a natural fermentation by-product and one that, in small quantities, smells funky or gamey.

Though tastes may evolve, your gut feelings about flavor and preference may be as simple as those of a child.

Petite Sirah: Grapes by Another Name

THE CALIFORNIA PETITE SIRAH is one of this state's mystery grapes (much like Zinfandel, Day 261) with myriad stories about its origins and parentage. Some of the background tales align, some lead to dead-end branches on the evolutionary tree.

Pending DNA mapping, no one will ever really know Petite Sirah's true history. Hugh Johnson, in his *Vintage: The Story of Wine*, references Grosse Syrah, Petite Syrah, Petit Sirah, and Petite Sirah as ancient varietals. In his *Pocket Encyclopedia of Wine*, he identifies Petite Sirah as a "synonym for the obscure French Durif," a little-used European grape essentially ignored and unattended.

Despite its mysterious air, California Petite Sirah has carved out a nice niche as an eccentric, spicy grape that counterbalances the overpowering, super-popular Cabernet Sauvignon. Many Petite Sirahs exhibit all of Zinfandel's spice with all of a powerful Cabernet's tannins. It falls perfectly in the middle of the flavor spectrum. (Check out Day 100 for a complete look at the grape's use in wine today.)

Recipe: Oven-Roasted Tomato Sauce

LIKE FERMENTING JUICE into wine, slow-cooking food produces richer, deeper, more integrated flavors. Fermentation naturally produces heat, and in a 2,640-gallon (10,000 L) tank, fermenting juice gets very warm, almost like a bath that's too hot. Winemakers cool the tanks to slow fermentation, ending with the same result as slow-cooked food.

1 tablespoon (15 ml) olive oil

1 small onion, diced

7 garlic cloves, minced

1 can (12 ounces, or 340 g) artichoke hearts, drained

⅓ cup (33 g) pitted black or green olives

1 can (28 ounces, or 820 g) Italian plum tomatoes

½ teaspoon (3 g) salt

1 tablespoon (13 g) sugar

1 tablespoon (5 g) dried basil or 7 leaves fresh basil

½ cup (120 ml) dry white wine

¼ cup (15 g) chopped fresh parsley, optional

¼ cup (25 g) grated Asiago cheese (or other good hard, dry Italian cheese), optional

Preheat the oven to 400°F (200°C).

Heat the olive oil over medium heat in a large cast-iron skillet or other oven-safe dish. Add the onion and garlic, and cook slowly until the onion softens.

Turn up the heat to medium-high, and add the artichokes and olives. Cook for 2 to 4 minutes, until the artichokes start to brown. Add the tomatoes, salt, sugar, and basil. Bring to a quick simmer, and cook for 5 minutes. Break up the tomatoes by mashing them once or twice with a big fork or potato masher.

Add the wine to the skillet, stir once, then place in the oven to cook for 20 to 30 minutes. Serve over bread, pasta, or risotto. Top with parsley and Asiago cheese.

TIP: Watch your sauce in the oven. If it starts to look too thick, add a little more white wine or a little water. Also, feel free to experiment with the recipe by replacing the artichokes and olives with other favorite ingredients, such as eggplants and caper berries, or cannelloni beans and roasted peppers.

YIELD: Serves 6 to 8

Wine Pairing: Taurino Notarpanaro
ITALY

Italians all over Italy bake pasta, but only those in Puglia, on the heel of the Italian boot, roast tomato sauce. The Taurino Notarpanaro pairs well with this sauce. Notarpanaro, which comes from Puglia, is made from two rustic red grapes, Negroamaro and Malvesia Nero. This wine is full of interesting smoke and wood flavors, with essence of rich, ripe figs and plums. The makers age the wine for a full thirty-six months before releasing it to market.

New Zealand: A New Down Under

NEW ZEALAND'S NORTH AND SOUTH islands are so expansive that the far north experiences tropical climes and the south literally hosts glaciers. These two islands meet at a turbulent ocean stretch that dominates the nearby land with cool winds and fast-moving clouds. Despite the southern hemisphere's hot summer sun, the surrounding southern Pacific Ocean remains cold; once the sun sets, a rush of cold ocean air cools down the land, chills the wine grapes growing on the vineyard hillsides, and slows and alters the grapes' metabolism.

Grapes, left to their own devices, would work day and night purging acid and creating sugar (what we call ripeness). Combine hot days with cold nights—conditions found not only in New Zealand but also Napa Valley, Sonoma Valley, the Rhône, and many other famous wine regions—and the vines essentially shut down at night and preserve their acidity. The grapes make sugar during the day and conserve acidity at night. In the glass, this comes across as balance.

Marlborough, the northern part of New Zealand's south island, is home to wineries that staked out a unique Sauvignon Blanc flavor profile by exploiting the grape's natural acidity and tendency to produce intense perfume.

Wineries such as Cloudy Bay promoted this style, and made it well known and beloved, setting New Zealand apart from California with its Fumé Blanc and white Bordeaux, also made from Sauvignon Blanc.

In New Zealand, Sauvignon Blanc became zippy and wild and intense. New Zealand wines are extremely edgy and high-pitched. The country continues to offer a superb bargain, balancing explosive tropical-fruit flavors—think pineapple and guava—with piercing citrusy zing—think lemon-lime.

On the Wine List

New Zealand may be known for Sauvignon Blanc, but its best wines are actually red. Look for Oyster Bay Pinot Noir, Huia Pinot Noir, and Gimblett Gravels Syrah, to name a few.

Vineyard at Lake Wanaka, South Island, New Zealand

Wine Etiquette for Modern Wine Lovers

ON THE FIRST DAY OF A wine tour in France, at my first meal, I had to send back the first bottle of wine I ordered. The wine that arrived at the table was not only the wrong year, but also it had already been opened, and it tasted funny—an etiquette nightmare that unfolded into a clash of cultures in front of a dinner with new colleagues.

The table started to notice something amiss and began squirming. Our waitress scooped up my glass and stormed away. Guillaume, the dining room master, took over. I admit the scene was not a great moment for me personally. Finally, I said politely, but firmly, that we were not drinking this wine, that some of us had traveled thousands of miles that day, and that we owed it to ourselves to have great wine.

From that moment, Guillaume and I became allies. He joked and teased and brought over special wines and favorites. The meal turned out great after the spat and after we made it clear we were serious about wine. The night ended with kisses.

The moral of this story is to stand your ground, politely, with any wine authority figure the world over and demand a great wine experience. Everyone has a story about a wine served at a restaurant that tasted putrid, but was consumed anyway, so unpleasant was the prospect of returning or complaining about a bottle of wine.

The best approach? Don't let something go wrong in the first place. Check and double-check your order before you open the wine. Tell the waiter what you like and what you typically drink, and get some assurance that the wine you order is what you think it is. Ask questions. And then, ask them again.

If something goes wrong and you hate what you ordered, for whatever reason, think about it the same way you would a food issue, even one that's your fault. Here's a restaurant service secret: if you blame yourself when something goes wrong, restaurants will do everything they can to prove it's not your fault. Imagine you'd ordered steak tartare, not knowing it was raw chopped beef with egg, capers, and onions. You would return the dish to the kitchen, saying it was your fault for not asking, that you feel awful, but that you cannot eat this dish. The same standards apply to wine.

It's your food, and your body—and you are not obligated to eat or drink anything.

Wine Party Themes, Part I

A WINE-TASTING PARTY is a great way to explore your changing tastes and habits. Try these themes and next thing you know, you'll have your own wine club.

WINE NIGHT CHEZ NOUS

As the host, you pick the wine type and ask your guests to bring one or two bottles of that type. This sends your friends out into the wine world and, wherever they shop, salespeople will likely get excited about the theme and offer energetic and good advice. Some starter suggestions: affordable Bordeaux, undiscovered Rhône Valley, Argentine Malbec, Sicilians, Aussie Shiraz. Almost anything works.

FOOD PAIRING SCAVENGER HUNT

Prepare a wine-friendly dish and send your guests out for one white and one red to match. Some great main courses include lamb osso buco (a slow-cooked Italian dish traditionally made with veal), herb-roasted chicken, or bouillabaisse (a classic French fish stew). Anything savory will inspire interesting wine.

MY FAVORITE WINE

To get to know your friends' tastes, nothing compares with this theme. Ask your guests to bring their favorite white and their favorite red. Any guest that protests about not having a favorite wine can bring *your* favorite wine!

Tips and Hints for Hosting a Wine Party

Hosting a wine party isn't difficult, but here are some tips to make it even easier:

- Rent the wineglasses. It's the same price as breaking three nice glasses, which is likely to happen.

- Rent cocktail plates, too.

- Display the wine. Use a mantle above a fireplace or a long table.

- Sequence the wine, lining them up from youngest to oldest, cheapest to most expensive, lightest to darkest, white to red, whatever comes naturally.

QPR: Quality/Price Ratio

AT LEAST A THOUSAND different factors and conditions go into making a really compelling, memorable bottle of wine. Of course, there's the soil, sun, and rain. But think about the angle of the terrain to the sun, wild versus store-bought yeast, the winemaker's art, those heavy oak barrels, the list just keeps growing.

Sometimes, a bottle of wine has too much going on to highlight one aspect that makes it great. This explains why, when challenged with the question, "What makes this wine so good?" wine lovers often cannot articulate it—much like trying to explain why you're in love with someone great!

At the end of the wine-making process, a great bottle of wine must pass two tests: quality and price. Quality drives how much the wine should cost; price is how much it actually does. Reduce these variables to a formula and you get the Quality/Price Ratio, or QPR.

If a bottle costs 10 dollars and tastes like 25 dollars to you, its QPR equals 2.5. A 10-dollar bottle that should have cost 7 dollars in your opinion has a 0.7 QPR. Any wine you wish you'd never bought, regardless of price, gets a zero. Whether you shop in the single-, double-, or triple-digit range, you always want the highest possible QPR. The marvel of this ratio is that it's entirely subjective. One person's 0.3 is another's 4.5.

Sparkle Plenty

COME THE COLD, clear nights of winter, you can walk outside under a cloudless sky and enjoy your sparkling wine by starlight.

According to a now-discredited legend, Champagne's inventor, blind monk Dom Perignon, shouted, "I am tasting stars!" the first time he sipped Champagne. (See Day 89 for more about Dom Perignon himself.) The drink's carbonation, which tastes bright and illuminated, made this legend believable for so long. Plus, after a couple of glasses, pinpoint bubbles refract light into pinpoint stars. Below, some tasty drinks that sparkle.

Saint-Hilaire Brut, France
This sparkler hails from Limoux in southwest France where France, Spain, and the Mediterranean Sea come together.

Saint-Hilaire claims to have been making sparkling wine for more than a century before Dom Perignon, Champagne's purported inventor, used this method. This drink has light carbonation, and is soft and easy to drink.

J & G Musso Crémant de Bourgogne Brut, France
This is another French non-Champagne sparkler from Burgundy, made from Chardonnay. It has light carbonation, bright acidity, and good wine flavor behind the bubbles. This pairs well with roasted chicken or stuffed pork roast.

Hardys Sparkling Shiraz, Australia
Untraditional but tasty, this sparkling Shiraz challenges your ideas about sparkling wines.

Dom Perignon statue in Champagne, France

Recipe: Meat Stew with Garlic Sauce

THIS DISH, WHICH uses six garlic heads, brings out a delicious garlicky flavor. Do not stir this stew. After it finishes cooking, remove the meat and make the sauce from the remaining garlic and juices. If the sauce needs thickening, use a pinch of fine cornmeal.

1 pound (455 g) beef stew meat

1 pound (455 g) boneless pork rib, cut into 2-inch (5-cm) pieces

1 pound (455 g) lamb arm steak, cut into 2-inch (5-cm) pieces

1 cup (235 ml) dry red wine, divided

¼ cup (60 ml) balsamic vinegar

3 tablespoons (45 ml) olive oil, divided

⅓ cup (11 g) herbes de Provence (assorted dried herbs typically used in southern France that can be found in the supermarket spice section)

4 to 6 heads garlic, peeled

1 bouquet garni (herbs traditionally composed of a bay leaf, thyme, and parsley, tied together or bundled in cheesecloth)

1 cup (235 ml) veal or chicken stock

1 cup (235 ml) cool water, or as needed

2 big pinches coarse sea salt

Marinate the beef, pork, and lamb meat in ½ cup (120 ml) of the wine, the vinegar, and 2 table-spoons (28 ml) of the olive oil for 1 to 4 hours.

Preheat the oven to 425°F (220°C). Remove the meat from the marinade and pat dry with paper towels. Save ½ cup (120 ml) of the marinade. Roll the meat in the herbes de Provence, brown in a heavy pot, and set on a plate, outside of pot. You may need to brown the meat in two or three shifts.

Add to the pot the remaining 1 tablespoon (15 ml) olive oil and all of the garlic cloves, and brown lightly. Add the bouquet garni. Return the meat to the pot, covering the garlic in even layers. Add the remaining ½ cup (120 ml) wine, stock, reserved marinade, and water to just cover the meat. Add the salt and simmer for 15 minutes. Do not stir.

Cover and cook in the oven for 45 minutes. Reduce the heat to 225°F (110°C), and cook for 4 to 6 hours. Check every now and then, and add water, if needed, to keep the food in the pot just covered. Do not stir.

Fifteen minutes before serving, remove the meat from the oven and place on a serving dish carefully with a slotted spoon. Cover with foil and keep warm in the oven. Mash the garlic in the pot with a potato masher. Pour the contents of the pot into a blender, and blend slowly until smooth. Return the sauce to a saucepan and simmer for 10 minutes, until smooth and not too thick. Pour the aillade (sauce) over the meat, and serve with arborio rice or orzo.

YIELD: Serves 6 to 8

Wine Pairing: René Barbier Mediterranean Red
SPAIN

Winemaking along the southern European coast starts in Italy and runs throughout France, all the way to the Spanish Mediterranean in the west. The Barbier family came to Spain a century ago from the Rhône Valley and fit right in. The grapes are Spanish—Tempranillo, Garnacha, and others—but the idea remains the same, to blend red wine into a bargain.

Traveling to the Veneto

THE VENETO, in northeast Italy, and its main city, Venice, represent major historic arrival paths into Western Europe from the east. (The word *veni* in Latin derives from the verb "to come.") Here, the water meets a gentle plain that climbs quickly into rolling hills, and farther north and west of Venice, into Alpine territory.

People tend to know about Venice, but know little about the Veneto's best wines. We recognize Soave (the name means exactly what it sounds like it should: suave, smooth, charming, and easy to get along with), but the white grape that makes Soave, called Garganega, never appears on the label, and rarely do the finer *riserva* and *classica* designations show up outside of the region.

Because Venice has its own travel appeal, tourists rarely think about the great vineyards and wineries that practically encircle the city. Venture beyond the waterlogged city and head northwest, into the Colli Berici (the "hills of Berici"), outside the inland city of Vicenza. In certain weather, fog pools in the valleys and clings to the hillsides, giving way to sun.

A good first stop is a winery called Cavazza in the tiny hill town of Montebello. The tasting room still displays the original wine press, handmade in the early 1800s. Upstairs, under a sloped roof, strings of grapes hang from the ceiling, drying nearly into raisins that then become Vin Santo and Recioto, sweet, delicious dessert wines.

In the tasting room, with its floor of Venetian marble, start with the Cavazza La Bocara Gambellara Classica—100 percent Garganega —a wine almost silver in color, that smells of fresh green apples and pears, and will likely be the best Soave you will ever taste.

If you go: Cavazza Vineyards and Winery, 22 Via Selva, Montebello (near Vicenza, northwest of Venice), 011.39.0444.649166 (phone), 011.39.0444.440038 (fax), www.cavazzawine.com.

Francis Ford Coppola and Inglenook

FILMMAKER FRANCIS COPPOLA, already famous for genius works including *The Godfather* and *Apocalypse Now*, performed a work of wine genius by buying and reconstituting the original properties of California's Inglenook winery. Niebaum-Coppola is how the winery is known today, and it's important for several reasons.

First, Inglenook is among the oldest original properties still in production, and now it's back in one piece again. From a wine-making perspective, the land has demonstrated that it can deliver outstanding, world-class quality wine. From 1939 until 1964, Inglenook's cask-numbered Cabernets played a central role in equating California Cabernet with French Bordeaux.

At the height of its success, Inglenook fell into the hands of a string of large multinational booze corporations that had no sense of what to do with the winery, and that drove the place literally into the ground for more than a decade. By the time the corporations finished, the Inglenook name evoked little more than cheap white wine.

In a way, Inglenook's resurrection as Niebaum-Coppola shows how people can survive bad corporate management, turn away from misguided marketing, and return to doing what they had done correctly all along. Now, by saving Inglenook and delivering it safely into the twenty-first century, Coppola has a place in that history.

The Psychology of Buying the Case

You have made the ultimate commitment: to buy an entire case of wine. At first, you are in love, cooing over your stash and marveling at the joy of having so much of what you love—and so handy, too. You drink three or four bottles immediately. After a polite two- or three-week pause, you open bottle number five to nothing but disappointment.

You can't believe you bought so much of this, you think to yourself. Seven bottles yet to go. You curse yourself and the wine, and lapse into a funk, craving diversity and new flavors. The honeymoon is over. Bottles six through eight leave the house as housewarming gifts and impromptu birthday gestures, and you feel you are making progress.

Much time passes. The last four bottles creep to the bottom of the rack in a vinous replay of continental drift. Finally, months later, you hit upon bottle number nine. Pop the cork, and—Eureka! The best bottle of wine in the whole case. In fact, it's your new favorite wine.

"Hey," you think fondly, caressing the glass, "I remember this wine. There was a whole case once. What's wrong with me? I should have purchased two cases." Then you drink the last four bottles with a combination of nostalgia and regret.

It happens every time. So before you commit to a case, think hard, very hard, about the following:

EXPERIENCE

Have you previously had this or wines significantly like it? Be hard and cold about what you know and what you like. A bottle or two is fine, but a whole case means spending money on wine you may like tomorrow instead of wine you know you like today.

VALUE

Are you getting a good deal? You should receive at least 20 percent off for a whole case of wine. Go to www.wine-searcher.com to get an idea about average retail prices around the world.

PERSONALITY

Do you crave variety? Then you're probably not a candidate for twelve-bottle purchases. Are you unashamed that you drink the same wine over and over again, no matter how much people tease you about being a creature of habit? Then you're the kind of person who should buy in bulk.

Keep Wine Talk Relevant

THERE'S A LINGUISTICS RULE that says that everything should be relevant. Much of the time, relevance is exactly what wine talk seems to lack.

For example, if I said, "Do you want some peanut butter?" and you responded, "Stanley Kubrick directed *Dr. Strangelove*," the two statements aren't relevant, and we feel like we're in the realm of Babel. But if I stood by a convertible and said, "Do you want to go for a ride?" and a woman with a bouffant hairdo answered, "I just did my hair," something that makes little sense on paper instead has tremendous meaning. We understand the relevance. Best of all, we take a shortcut to get there, which makes us all a little more clever.

People who are not wine lovers ask reasonable questions such as, "What's this wine like?" or "How's this wine taste?" Because of the linguistic shortcuts we take, the answers sound exactly like, "I just did my hair."

Language is a fun, freewheeling aspect of wine, if only it can relate more relevantly to what most people actually know. Think about how we discuss food. "How were those ribs?" elicits the unequivocal response, "So good I ate them with my hands and then licked the plate," something anyone, anywhere would understand completely. How can we make wine talk more relevant? Check out the chart below.

WINE-SPERANTO (INSTEAD OF SAYING...)	CORE ENGLISH (...SAY THIS)
It's malolactically fermented.	This is delicious.
Aged in oak.	This is also delicious.
Forest floor.	Something's a little gamey.
Rustic.	This doesn't taste very good.
Zippy.	I hope you're a fan of grapefruit.
It's a rosé, but it's a *dry* rosé.	Even the most insecure man could drink this pink wine.

Pinot Gris grapes at the Karma Vista Vineyards
in Coloma, Michigan, United States

Gris with Envy

PINOT IS ONE OF TWO royal wine families (Sauvignon is the other) that give structure and definition to how we understand wine. Pinot Noir is the principal grape of red Burgundy. World-favorite Chardonnay, known as Pinot Chardonnay until after World War II, is white Burgundy. They stake out the middle of the wine spectrum.

Pinot Blanc, a super-light white version with nearly transparent skin, and Pinot Gris, a gray but not black grape that makes white wine, orbit this mutating nuclear family. Let's focus on Pinot Gris. This wine (called Pinot Grigio by Italians) tastes tremendously different depending on where its grapes grow.

In the United States, Oregon has achieved success, fame, and its wine identity through Pinot Noir in the last quarter of the twentieth century. It's no surprise that Pinot Gris flourishes there too; the state's winemakers have embraced it recently. (Bordeaux's Lurton family grows and exports delicious and affordable Pinot Gris from Argentina as well.)

Given the fact that Oregon Pinot Gris didn't exist for the first 8,000 years of wine history, these twenty-first-century experiments are great works of wine:

Firesteed Pinot Gris, United States (Oregon)

Lean, edgy, crisp, clean, and affordable, this wine is a good buy for the house wine of summer.

Bethel Heights Pinot Gris, United States (Oregon)

Big, rich, and a little viscous, this wine seems touched by an oak and butter angel. It has a very pleasing personality.

Adelsheim Pinot Gris, United States (Oregon)

Taste this wine with melon or pineapple wrapped in prosciutto. It has bright, crisp flavors and a floral smell.

Recipe: Tiny Bosc Pears Poached with Wine Glaze

THIS DESSERT IS ESPECIALLY fine served with cheeses and dried nuts. It's not too important which red wine you use because you cook it down, reduce it, and spice it. However, it should be a wine you are willing to drink. Choose an affordable favorite.

8 tiny Bosc pears (slightly less than 2 pounds, or 900 g)

1 bottle dry red wine (such as a Merlot)

½ cup (75 g) brown sugar

1 cinnamon stick (2 inches [5 cm])

1 strip orange or lemon rind (2 inches [5 cm])

1 teaspoon (5 ml) vanilla extract

6 whole black peppercorns

Powdered sugar, optional (for dusting)

To make the pears: Wash and dry the pears. With a small paring knife, cut crossways across the bottom to make a flat base so the pear can stand up straight. Dig out the seeds and core from the bottom, about 1 inch (2.5 cm) into the pear.

Combine the wine, brown sugar, cinnamon, orange rind, vanilla, and peppercorns in a large saucepan on top of the stove, and stir until the sugar dissolves. Add the pears so they stand in the wine-spice mixture up to their necks. Heat the mixture over low heat until the wine starts to bubble, but never let it boil. Turn the heat down very low, cover, and cook for 45 minutes. Turn off the heat and let the pears and liquid cool. When lukewarm, gently transfer the pears to a plate, cover with plastic wrap, and cool in the refrigerator.

To make the glaze: Strain the wine mixture through cheesecloth into a small saucepan. Boil gently on top of the stove until it reduces by two-thirds. When the glaze appears the viscosity of hot maple syrup, remove from the heat and pour into a small creamer or measuring cup with a spout.

To serve, arrange two pears on each plate and drizzle with the glaze. Add a dusting of powdered sugar, if desired.

YIELD: Serves 4

Wine Pairing: Quady Essensia Orange Muscat
UNITED STATES (CALIFORNIA)

In Italy, this grape is called *fior d'arancio*, or orange blossom, and the aroma is so accurately suggestive that there can be no question from where the name derives. Quady specializes in dessert wines from California's hot central region—a place perfect for growing ripe, sweet, syrupy wines.

Buying Up Beaujolais

IMAGINE THE BEAUJOLAIS region of France in the shape of a wine bottle, with the top pointing north and the bottom sitting on the city of Lyon. The bottle's big, southern end represents generic Beaujolais; most classic, inexpensive, bistro Beaujolais comes from this region. It's big and expansive (in European vineyard terms), is relatively flat and accessible, and produces large quantities of easy-to-drink wine at bargain prices.

As you move north toward the bottle's top, the region tapers, with ten tiny wine towns filling up its neck. These towns are called Crus Beaujolais, and although *cru* doesn't literally mean "crew" (idiomatically, it means "carafe" or "flask"), it is pronounced the same and could essentially represent those ten towns. They hang together in the top tier, committed to high-quality, region-specific Beaujolais.

These ten towns—Brouilly, Côte de Brouilly, Régnié, Morgon, Chiroubles, Fleurie, Moulin à Vent, Chénas, Saint-Amour, and Julienas—account for many of the region's best wines. Their soils and geographies drastically differ from place to place, but because each town grows the same Beaujolais grape and makes wine in essentially the same way, it's fascinating to experience the flavors of each landscape in the wineglass.

The winemakers there say the Beaujolais grape has a unique ability to duplicate the soil and render unique flavor profiles based on geologic composition. After a couple of millennia, the ground has evolved as the key variable element in the whole system. Next time you consider a Beaujolais, sample one from the crus.

Wine grower house entrance in Saint-Amour, part of Crus Beaujolais in France

Veni Vidi Monini

ONE OF THE KEYS to understanding wine is realizing that the place it comes from makes a gigantic contribution to how the wine tastes. In the parallel world of artisanal and extra-virgin olive oils, the same thing applies. Wine grapes and olive trees thrive in the same soils and the same Mediterranean climes: Italy, Spain, and France are the top three world producers for both wine and olive oil, in about that order.

Italian olive oil makers are increasingly territory-driven in both production and marketing, much the same way wine has been for centuries. Not too surprisingly, many aspects of the giant Monini olive oil plant located outside of Spoleto in Umbria, central Italy, look identical to what you see in many vineyards and wineries.

On the work floor, the physical similarities begin: giant steel tanks, temperature-controlled by refrigerated cores and icyjackets, hoses running along the floor, low-velocity pumps whirring and pushing liquid from tank to tank or barrel to barrel, bottles of precious juice trundling down the bottling and labeling line into shippers' waiting hands.

Everything appears so similar to a winery that it seems as if you could, in theory, convert the whole place into a wine-making space overnight. Except, of course, for the smells—ground nuts, dusty spices, and olives—and the dress code of white lab coats, surgeons' caps, and booties over shoes.

Founded in 1920, Monini is today run by Zefferino Monini, the third generation of the family. Monini is attempting to position itself as an artisan olive oil producer rather than an industrial olive oil company. But its 6.6-million gallon (25-million liter) annual production makes that a hard sell.

A restored building not far from the headquarters, called *Frantoio del Poggiolo,* or "Mill on the Hill," now acts as Monini's educational center and wine lab. It produces extremely small quantities of olive oil from 5,500 old trees and 1,500 young trees located on the property. "We compete, not with other industrial producers," Monini said, "but with small artisans."

Monini produces a series of oils called DOP: *Denominazione Originata Protezzione*, or Protected Original Domain, a fancy way of certifying that DOP Puglia really comes from Italy's heel, that DOP Sicily comes from Sicily, and so on. Wine does the same with appellation controls around the world. Of course, the laws vary from nation to nation and region to region, but the idea remains the same across borders: enunciate, express a valuable style, and protect a good name with rigid quality standards.

It would be simultaneously easier, cheaper, and more profitable to blend all of these oils together to make one big, easy-to-sell batch of oil. That the Monini family chooses not to signifies its faith in the value of appellation-identified olive oils from Italy.

Green Guide to Wine

ORGANIC, BIODYNAMIC, "made with organically grown grapes," carbon neutral—they all mean that someone, somewhere really cares about and is taking care of the wine-making process. Most wine lovers, however, don't understand or pay too much attention to the technical differences of these governmental categories of greenness. Here's what they mean:

ORGANIC WINE

This wine is made with organic grapes, through a wine-making process that uses no petrochemicals (e.g., fertilizers, pesticides, herbicides, synthetic additives, etc.) and no added sulfites, as well as naturally occurring sulfites of no more than one hundred parts per million (the maximum for any U.S. wine is 350 parts per million).

BIODYNAMIC

This follows the same standards as organic status, but with the guidelines of biodynamics, derived from the late-nineteenth-century social philosophy of Rudolph Steiner. Biodynamics preaches the unity of the farm as a self-contained, self-sustaining entity—in essence, the wine farm as it used to be. (It also preaches some relatively far-fetched hippie-dippy bullhorn and moon rituals.)

MADE FROM ORGANICALLY GROWN GRAPES

Translation: This winery's not fully organic—yet. It has taken a step in the right direction in that it grows its grapes organically, but the winery has not invested fully in organic agricultural practices.

Organic Wine Guide by Monty Waldin lists a few hundred vineyards and wineries that are organic by one standard or another. It's a pleasant surprise to find out that your favorite wineries are organic by tradition, not as result of corporate marketing:

Eugene Meyer, France (Alsace)
Great-tasting, classic white wines such as Gewürztraminer, Pinot Blanc, and Pinot Gris come from vineyards certified organic since 1969.

Mas de Gourgonnier, France (Provence)
The vineyards have been organic since the mid-70s. The winery is organic thanks to its traditional agricultural methods, not for marketing or philosophical purposes.

Château de Beaucastel, France (southern Rhône)
These wines aren't cheap; the vineyard's Châteauneuf-du-Pape is quite expensive, and even its entry-level reds and whites are pricey. Plus, the vineyard's organic bona fides are under dispute. Rumors abound that the owners have developed dung-powered vehicles for use there.

Lolonis, United States (California)
Instead of pesticides, the Lolonis family controls insects with other insects, specifically ladybugs. The Chardonnay and Zinfandel are both favorites.

Frog's Leap, United States (California)
The owners claim organic management keeps the grapes alive, especially with the recent rise of phylloxera, a nasty root louse. Frog's Leap Sauvignon Blanc is the vineyard's most famous wine, full of delicious, ripe fruit and fresh, zippy acidity.

Required Reading:
Napa: The Story of an American Eden

WRITTEN IN 1990, James Conaway's *Napa: The Story of an American Eden* is one of the best books about the trials and tribulations of modern wine making. Conaway paints a vivid picture of struggling yet entrepreneurial wine farmers who persist, compelled to turn out wines within a tiny window of opportunity that they hope will propel them into the wine world's forefront and affections.

He traces the complex familial and tribal relationships (particularly the Italians in California), as well as the unspoken rivalries that continue to churn up the Napa Valley. Hanging over the entire wine-making enterprise, however, is the farmers' fear of natural disasters (often in the form of driving wind and rain), or some other unforeseen, man-made pestilence such as real estate development.

Conaway spends several pages writing about the Wine Train, a touristy trip up an old railroad line with tasting stops along the way, as a cautionary tale against turning an art into a carnival ride. Napa's Wine Train turned out to be utterly harmless compared with real estate expansion and car traffic in the area, but Conaway makes his point: It is human nature to find some way to spoil an Eden.

What happens once the wave crests? Do the farmers dim the lights and drop the curtain? Hardly, but Napa winemakers remember how different it was before success, discovery, and stardom. The lucky descendents of California wine risk takers don't have to take the same chances. Napa is wine royalty forever.

Hillside vineyards overlooking Napa Valley

"M" is for Mourvedre

STOP PEOPLE ON THE STREET and ask them to name every wine they know, and most will say Chardonnay, Merlot—and after a long pause and some encouragement—Shiraz. Sometimes, even the most enthusiastic wine lovers don't absorb new information. Despite that fact, wine lovers claim to love the "new"—new vintages, new regions, new grapes—so winemakers oblige with experiments.

Mourvedre (pronounced moor-VED-rah) is a rustic, southern French country grape that produces a delicious wine of which few have heard. Other than on 600 acres (243 ha) in California, Mourvedre grows almost exclusively in Mediterranean France and Spain (called Mataro there), and is the main grape in the rich, red, concentrated Bandol wines.

Cline Cellars in Sonoma controls almost 20 percent of Mourvedre in California today, producing a wine blended from the oldest blocks available.

Its intense fruit, stunning concentration, and beautiful flavor focus make it taste expensive despite its low price point. A good dose of oak—it is a New World wine, after all—gives it soft, silky tannins, with hints of black and white pepper.

How Ancient is Ancient?

The word *ancient* changes meaning depending on who it references. Ancient Greeks made wine in southern France almost 3,000 years ago. But old plots of California Mourvedre (originally called Mataro after the Spanish city of the same name) are aged in decades, not millennia. In California, one hundred years earns a vineyard the unofficial "ancient" designation.

44

Old Mourvedre vine in Châteauneuf-du-Pape, Rhône, France

Recipe: Easy Cinnamon Lamb Stew

IF THE MONTH OF FEBRUARY were a bottle of wine—cold, cruel, austere, indifferent, and filled with 7 percent less wine than other bottles—you'd never buy it. In nature, the month symbolizes a deal with Mother Nature: If you want July, you have to make it through February (and March, too, for that matter).

February is a month for small illusions, as if lopping a few days off of the calendar actually makes a difference. Wine lovers try to counteract the short, cold days with big, warm red wines and slow-cooked, hearty foods. To ensure flavor alignment, try cooking with the wine you're serving with dinner. A fruity, spicy wine pairs superbly with this lamb stew.

1 pound (455 g) lamb stew meat

1 cup (125 g) flour

2 tablespoons (28 ml) olive oil

1 can (14 ounces, or 400 g) artichoke hearts, drained

1 medium onion, chopped

2 garlic cloves, minced

1 cinnamon stick

1 can (28 ounces, or 820 g) Italian plum tomatoes

¾ cup (175 ml) good red wine

Salt and ground black pepper, to taste

½ cup (50 g) olives, pitted, optional

Dredge the lamb in the flour. Heat the olive oil in a deep skillet until it just starts to smoke. Add the lamb and brown thoroughly, for 8 minutes. Remove the lamb, add the artichoke hearts, and brown thoroughly, for 5 minutes.

Remove the artichoke hearts and add the onion, garlic, and cinnamon stick to the skillet. Cook for 3 minutes, stirring frequently, until the onion becomes translucent.

Add the tomatoes, breaking them up gently with a big spoon. Add the wine, return the lamb and artichokes to the skillet, add salt and pepper to taste, and stir thoroughly. Cover and simmer for at least 90 minutes.

Five minutes before serving, remove the cinnamon stick and add the olives. This is best served over polenta, risotto, or pastas such as orzo or orecchiette.

YIELD: Serves 4

Wine Pairing: Buena Vista Carneros Pinot Noir

UNITED STATES (CALIFORNIA)

This wine is full of ripe, lovely fruit and soft, lush tannins. It smells like an exotic, aromatic wood box. With interesting food, this wine's flavor gets even more interesting.

Sicily: No Wine Is an Island

SICILY HAS BEEN A MAJOR SOUTHERN Mediterranean shipping crossroads for thousands of years. In ancient Roman times, wine and food traveled to and from Rome via Sicily, then went off to the rest of the seafaring world. About 5,000 years ago, ancient Greeks planted wine grapes in southern Italy—the first region to have wine grapes. Some grape names—Greco and Aglianico, for example—hint at these roots. Some people even theorize that Syrah is named for Syracuse.

To date, Sicily's only famous wine is Marsala, a sweet dessert wine much like port or sweet sherry fortified with a little brandy, which brings its alcohol volume to about 20 percent. Today, the brandy addition continues because of tradition, but originally, it kept the wine fresh during shipping.

Twenty-first-century winemakers have begun using different indigenous Sicilian grape varieties and styles that are proving popular.

Nero d'Avola, a Shiraz-like black grape, loves the hot Mediterranean sun and creates wines that will remind you of Shiraz. That's exactly what the producers want: Nero d'Avola is to Sicily what Shiraz is to Australia.

Grillo and Catarratto are two white grapes indigenous to Sicily. *Grillo* means "grasshopper," and when you try wine made from this grape, it tastes green, citrusy, almost chirpy—in other words, true to its name. Catarratto is the second most widely planted single variety of grape in Italy, thanks to its use in Marsala wines.

Ajello Majus Grillo/Catarratto uses these two grapes. In theory, the Grillo contributes a citrusy, tropical fruit zip and zing; the Catarratto grounds it in mellow, ripe fruit flavors of melon and pear. The combination in the Majus performs a little alchemy, starting out explosive, acidic, and tangerine, then quickly mellowing into deep, ripe, woodsy flavors.

Sicilian wines are New World–style wines grown in an Old World place—in some ways, the best of both worlds.

The Speck Family, Henry of Pelham

THIS WORLD THIRSTS FOR new wines from new regions, but they are few and far between. Recently, Australia and South Africa have pleased, and now, Canada is coming on as an improbable wine region making exceptional wines.

North America's eastern shore struggles, in general, to create good red wines, so it's rewarding to find a monster red from this region—the Henry of Pelham Baco Noir from Ontario. Reminiscent of California Petite Sirah in its inky blackness, this wine shows what can happen when winemakers start respecting the hybrid grapes that grow well and yield bountifully in this climate.

Paul Speck, president of Henry of Pelham, says the turning point came when this vineyard committed itself to Baco Noir, limited its yield to increase its concentration, and stopped thinking like much of the wine-making world, which generally disparages this grape. Henry of Pelham's Baco Noir is dense and strong, one of the most intense Atlantic Northeast reds, with hard, prickly, pervasive tannins. The fruit is full-bodied and ripe, proof that even in seemingly forbidding climes, a great wine can occur.

Choosing a Corkscrew

As ANYONE WHO HAS EVER skinned a cat will tell you, there may be more than one way to accomplish the feat, but there are only a couple of ways to do it right. Those methods become much easier with the right tools. How to successfully open a wine bottle remains a mystery to many people; their problems are typically half technological, half physics-based.

First the technology problem. There's essentially one kind of wine bottle opening and one kind of cork, but literally hundreds of different kinds of corkscrews exist. Just when you've mastered the long titanium model that drives the screw through a grip mount into the cork, along comes a wine needle that injects gas beneath the cork and pushes it out using air pressure. When all else fails, fall back on the original: a piece of wood or steel with a screw attached that you wrench into the cork and yank out with all your might, spraying wine everywhere.

Then there's the physics problem. Many corkscrews just don't work, especially the more elaborate ones. The kind with two silver wings that splay upward as you drive the screw into the cork may look beautiful, but once the screw completely destroys the cork, the wings point almost straight up, and you grab the wings and push down, you often pull out the cork in a few crumbly pieces, some of which undoubtedly fall into the wine.

My favorite corkscrew is generically called the waiter's variety, and it combines in one tool the most useful elements of other devices. On one end lives a tiny flip-out blade for use in cutting off the foil capsule, removing a price sticker, or carving your initials into a wine cask.

On the other end, a lever that doubles as a bottle opener (for when the world runs out of wine and we must drink something else) acts as a brace to rest on the bottle's edge to give you leverage when extracting the cork. The simple perfection of the waiter's corkscrew makes it easy to open a bottle of wine without even setting it down on a tabletop.

How to Read a Wine Bottle's Numbers

WINEMAKERS ARE TRYING to tell you something by all of the numbers they put on a wine label. But what?

- **Vintage year:** This important number is always prominent on the label, at the top or in the middle, close to the name. But it always appears without context. Unless it says, "2003 (the hottest, ripest, best growing season since the 1890s)," the year could be any year.

- **Bottle volume:** The bottle volume almost always appears in milliliters or liters. A standard bottle is 750 milliliters or 0.75 liters. A double bottle—also called a magnum bottle—is 1.5 liters, and a half bottle is 375 milliliters.

- **Alcohol percentage by volume:** There are beverages called "wine" with anywhere from 5 percent to 20 percent alcohol. A 12.5 alcohol percentage is typical for both reds and whites. Anything in the single digits is low alcohol; anything higher than 15 percent approaches irresponsible.

- **The number 100:** It can appear on a label many times and have many meanings: 100 percent of wine type, grape, malolactic fermentation, barrel fermentation, oak aged. Ultimately, an abundance of everything, all the time, is too much. A label rich in 100-percent pronouncements usually shows up on a wine trying too hard.

- **Blend percentages:** Wines blended from a number of grapes often offer the precise numerical makeup of the wine (e.g., 55 percent Cabernet, 37 percent Merlot, 6 percent Petite Verdot, 1 percent Petite Meunier, 1 percent Bourbelenc).

Grape percentage numbers conveniently advertise the major grapes in the wine. But from outside of the bottle, there's no real way to imagine whether 2 percent Bourbelenc would have made any difference.

- **Government warnings:** The law requires some wine numbers, including (1) don't drink if you're pregnant, and (2) don't drink and drive (these account for forty-one additional words on each bottle).

- **Vineyard and vine age:** Wine marketers love to tout mythic 500-year-old vines growing on 7-million-year-old soil. In general, vines produce much less wine as they age, but the wine they do produce is typically better tasting, concentrated, and full of interesting flavors.

- **Other numbers:** Brix is a technical measure of grape ripeness at harvest, and riper is normally better. Two or three wines give the actual longitude and latitude coordinates of the winery. Grape tons harvested per acre (or hectare) tells you how aggressive the winery pursues a less-is-more philosophy.

To which numbers should you pay attention? Imagine a common situation for every wine lover: You're trying to decide between wines you don't know, and all you have are the numbers on the label. In the absence of any additional information, you can almost always select based on three numbers: age, year, and alcohol percentage by volume. Pick the oldest vines or the oldest winery, then the most recent year available, and finally, the wine closest to 12.5 percent alcohol.

Australian Wine Grapes

THE AUSTRALIAN CONTINENT survived for thousands of millennia without any indigenous grapes. But since the first large importation of European vines in 1817 (thank you, John Macarthur, also known as the Father of the Australian Sheep Industry, who performed for wine the same service) to the dominance of the world market at the turn of the twenty-first century by Aussie Shiraz and Shiraz-style wines, it's hard to picture the landscape without them. The country grows hundreds of different varietals. A lineup of Australia's most successful grapes includes the usual suspects, plus a surprise or two.

CABERNET SAUVIGNON

Australia saw acres of this classic red Bordeaux grape planted in the 1800s, but Shiraz's immense success forced much of it out. By 1960, only 10 acres (4 ha) grew in all of Coonawarra, and not even 1 acre (0.4 ha) persisted in Padthaway, both in southern Australia. Decades of replanting and relearning later, Cabernet here is now beautifully tannic and full of chocolate and raspberry flavors. Cabernet, a newcomer that has a way to go to rival Australian Shiraz, is being eclipsed by more popular warm-climate grapes.

CHARDONNAY

The most commercially popular grape on the planet is, by far, the most widely planted in Australia. Like most Aussie whites, it meets plenty of oak in the wine-making process, and its tremendous ripeness yields a rich, buttery wine that often tastes honeyed and golden. Every region has excellent examples and producers.

GRENACHE AND MOURVEDRE

These two grapes, the principal red grapes of the Rhône Valley, flourish in Australia. Juicy, affordable blends of Shiraz, Grenache, and Mourvedre abound. Also, some of the grapes go toward making affordable vintage and tawny port.

MARSANNE

Another Rhône transplant, this one a white wine, responds beautifully to the Australian climate and ripens like a round, rich, golden pear, especially at Tahbilk. Mitchelton makes an excellent Marsanne that tastes like honeysuckle.

SEMILLON

Outside of Australia, this white grape grows primarily in France's Sauternes region, where it produces the world's most expensive sweet wines. In Australia, one treatment of this grape makes a super-sweet dessert wine strongly affected by a desirable mold called Noble Rot. However, most Semillon goes into high-quality, dry, white table wines. Semillon reaches a ripeness that gives it great body and a rich, almost oily texture.

SHIRAZ

Everyone else calls this red grape Syrah, but the Australians call it Shiraz. Just as it originally flourished in the hot sun of southern France's Rhône Valley, Shiraz has found a happy home in the Australian summers. It produces wine full of pepper and spice and deep, dark fruit. Shiraz has two personalities. In general, its wines are smooth and velvety, but strong and high in flavor and alcohol. But Shiraz from the Barossa, near Adelaide, is dense, rich, and concentrated.

Recipe: Chicken Baked with Mustard and Parsley

JEAN ANTHELME BRILLAT-SAVARIN, generally hailed as the first food writer, wrote about food in a familiar, semi-modern way. Before him, food writing focused on agriculture. But he said, "Tell me what you eat and I will tell you who you are," guiding food writers to interpret us through our food ever since.

Brillat-Savarin called chicken a canvas, a food medium upon which the chef could perform with spice and technique. In this recipe, the flavors, transformative for the chicken, are quintessentially Burgundy, strengthened by the Dijon mustard from the same city in the heart of French wine country.

2 small chickens, 3 to 4 pounds (1.3 to 1.8 kg) each

3 tablespoons (33 g) Dijon mustard

12 large sprigs parsley

10 garlic cloves

½ cup (120 ml) white wine

½ cup (120 ml) chicken or vegetable broth

3 tablespoons (45 ml) red wine vinegar

²/₃ cup (160 ml) cream

Salt and ground black pepper, to taste

Chopped parsley or tarragon, for garnish

Preheat the oven to 375°F (190°C).

Cut the chicken into serving pieces, and dry with a paper towel. In a large bowl, combine the chicken and mustard, turning the pieces until well-coated. Chop the parsley and garlic together until fine, either by hand or in a food processor.

Pour the wine, chicken broth, and vinegar into the bottom of a deep baking pan. (Note: I often use a large Calphalon-style saucepan or a deep cast-iron skillet.) Sprinkle in half of the garlic-parsley mixture and stir. Place the chicken in the pan, and sprinkle on the rest of the garlic-parsley mixture. On top of the stove over medium heat, bring the liquid in the pan to a simmer. Transfer the pan to the oven, and bake for 40 to 45 minutes, turning the chicken once or twice.

Once the chicken is cooked through, transfer it to a serving dish, and place back in the off-but-cooling oven to keep it warm. Place the pan on the stove, add the cream to the pan, and simmer for 10 minutes over medium heat until it reduces by one-quarter. Add salt and pepper to taste.

Pour a little sauce over the chicken and the rest around it. Sprinkle with some fresh chopped parsley or tarragon, and serve.

YIELD: Serves 6 to 8

Wine Pairing: Domaine de Pouilly Saint-Véran
FRANCE

The Domaine de Pouilly Saint-Véran is a Burgundy paired with Burgundy. Somewhat comically, the mustard of the town strides arm-in-arm with the wine of the countryside. Saint-Veran is almost all Chardonnay, not overly fruity, but deep and almost earthy for a white wine. It's a bargain compared with Pouilly-Fuissé just down the road.

South Africa

SOUTH AFRICA'S WINES have been around for centuries already; according to legend, Napoleon's favorite was a sweet dessert wine from Klein Constantia Estate that saw him through his unhappy years in exile on Elba.

However, because of South Africa's governmental pursuit of racial and political apartheid, the country's wines were banned for years in the United States, and highly restricted in Europe. Today, these wines have finally started to penetrate the U.S. market.

Pinotage, the main red grape of South African wine, crosses Pinot Noir and Cinsault, a relatively unknown, hardy, high-yielding French grape.

This grape grows around the world and produces plenty of juice for winemakers. These are two nice Pinotage options.

Fairview Pinotage, South Africa

This wine's tannins are huge and soft and everywhere. It has a hint of menthol and fruit flavors such as baked apple or roasted pear, with a bit of pumpkin pie spice.

Andrew's Hope Pinotage, South Africa

Stunning, this Pinotage tastes rich and buttery. It has soft, subtle tannins, a quality that makes the wine very drinkable. It's similar in emotional quality to an Aussie Shiraz.

A South African woman carrying a basket of grapes

Edouard de Pomiane
and the Ten-Minute Test

EDOUARD DE POMIANE, in his indispensable book *French Cooking in Ten Minutes: Adapting to the Rhythm of Modern Life* (published by North Point Press), concedes that times have changed, and as such, have changed life in such profound ways that to survive, we must alter how we cook and eat.

As the modern technological world whips by, Pomiane works hard to find a ten-minute window of cooking opportunity. Once you have carved out the time, he advocates creating something spectacular, divided into numerous small courses, the more the better. To Pomiane, a tiny pear, a thin slice of blue cheese, and a piece of crusty bread equal a course, and anybody can prepare that in thirty seconds.

The punch line, of course, is that the book was originally published in 1930, a time when life moved much more slowly. It contains two dangerous ideas: the realization that we're losing control of our time as if it's a commercially tradable commodity, and that French cooking of any value could take place in only ten minutes.

Pomiane masks these insights with relentless good cheer and recipes that are really just adornments of a few lines about cooking, followed by encouragement. In the introduction, "Some Indispensible Concepts for Understanding This Beautiful Book," he says he knows that this book will be beautiful, mainly because he hasn't yet written a word. What else could it be but beautiful?

Pomiane's statement could just as easily refer to a meal not yet cooked or a wine still unopened. Part of what makes cooking great is that it takes time to accomplish. When you store wine for a special occasion, even if it's only for a month, the wine tastes better when you open and enjoy it.

Taste Your Way from A to Z

DON'T GET STUCK in a variety rut. Break out of the cycle of always buying Merlot or habitually ordering Pinot Noir at restaurants. There is a world of grapes out there, and we guide you through dozens of different varieties in this book. This is a mere introduction to the vast population of *vitis vinifera*, true, European wine grapes.

In excess of 10,000 different types of wine grapes exist, though the wine-drinking public focuses on only a handful, with approximately 230 prominent grapes in the world of wine.

So challenge yourself to work through the alphabet of grapes. Choose one new grape for each letter of the alphabet. You have plenty of options.

Reference Tuesday entries for popular grapes you can easily access. Or look to the valuable resource of Jancis Robinson's *Guide to Wine Grapes* from Oxford University Press. Keep a journal to document your grape tour, and invite a fellow wine enthusiast to join you. After all, wine always tastes better when shared with good company.

Court Orders and Aftershocks

WHEN THE BERLIN WALL came down in 1989, a number of far-seeing pundits observed that the event represented the real end of the eight-decade Russian Revolution. The United States Supreme Court's ruling in May 2005 to wipe away all direct-to-consumer interstate wine shipping regulations represented the beginning of the end of Prohibition, also a long time coming.

By 1920, the Eighteenth Amendment to the U.S. Constitution, which banned alcoholic beverages, had led to the Volstead Act, intended to enforce the ban across the land. Thirteen strange and disastrous years later, in the midst of the Great Depression, the government repealed Prohibition, and U.S. wine culture and industry—everywhere around the country—have been shuddering, insecure, and unsteady ever since.

Before Prohibition, Ohio's wine industry was widespread and important, but those vineyard lands, suddenly turned over to other crops, never went back to grapes. New York wine production, still huge today, is nothing like it was before the 1920s. Imagine where it could be if it hadn't been interrupted for more than half a century, first by Prohibition, then by World War II. Parts of California are synonymous with wine territory today, but as late as 1975 the idea of this state competing with Europe was considered absurd.

It just goes to show that in the world of food, wine, and the legislation of culture, the ripple effects of legal decisions run far beyond the courtroom or the halls of government.

Nearly (Native) American Grapes

THE UNITED STATES admires iconoclastic, independent personalities, in people and in wine. Many U.S. wine drinkers quake in awe over ancient French wines and struggle to pronounce Italian place-names, but they beam when a winemaker somewhere in the United States breaks the rules and strikes out in a new direction.

What's good about this cultural trait is how much it pushes U.S. winemakers to take new "American" chances with wine, even when coasting may be easier. The tragedy in this situation is that the U.S. possesses no indigenous grape, no native flavor profile to mine and expand.

All wine created in the United States gets measured against the famous wines of Europe. Only two grapes—Zinfandel and Petite Sirah—have "native" U.S. status, but only because these grapes somehow managed to lose their

pedigrees during the long nineteenth-century journey to California. (Today, genetic testing is starting to teach us about grape origins, but not much progress has been made.)

In 1900, Petite Sirah topped the list of most widely planted grapes in California, but not until 1961 did Concannon Vineyard in Livermore produce the first 100 percent Petite Sirah varietal. Sadly, no white Petite Sirah came along to preserve the old vines through profitability, and only about 3,000 acres (1,215 ha) remain.

According to the *Oxford Companion to Wine*, Petite Sirah has been called many different European grapes (see Day 100). Regardless of what it is or what we call it, Petite Sirah makes great wine that's typically black, almost inky in color, and extremely tannic.

Recipe: Chocolate Bruschetta

START AN EVENING DATE with your favorite wine lover with this sweet-and-salty bruschetta.

1 crusty baguette

Olive oil, to taste

Sea salt, to taste

1 bar chocolate (8 ounces, or 225 g), chopped (either milk or dark chocolate)

Preheat the oven to 400°F (200°C).

Slice the baguette into 12 ½-inch (1.25-cm) thick ovals. Arrange the bread on a baking sheet, drizzle with olive oil, and sprinkle with sea salt. Put a decent serving of chocolate on each piece of bread. Bake in the oven for 5 to 10 minutes, until the bread's edges brown and the chocolate melts. Serve immediately.

YIELD: Serves 6

Wine Pairing:
NV Zonin Primo Amore Juliet &
NV Zonin Primo Amore Romeo
ITALY

These two semi-sparkling wines are just right with only 7.5 percent alcohol in the white Juliet, and 8.5 percent in the red Romeo, about half the alcohol of some of today's biggest reds.

NV stands for nonvintage, which means a wine has no vintage year designation. Part of the Champagne method includes topping the bottle at the end of the process, called the final fill. This happens so long after the original wine productions, and it happens with newer vintages, that consequently the wine has to be called nonvintage.

Oak and Ancient Grapes in California

OF ALL OF THE FACTORS that make California wines so great—from the incredible ripeness of the fruit to the uninhibited use (or overuse, depending on your taste) of oak fermenting and aging—the winemakers' eternal and unabashed pursuit of innovation tops the list.

While other parts of the planet spend centuries exploring and perfecting the specific local traditions with which they're blessed, California embraces what works and what sells, even—or sometimes especially—if it's nontraditional.

Around 1985, California vineyards began to plant European grape varieties other than the standard Chardonnay, Cabernet, Merlot, Pinot Noir, and Sauvignon Blanc. European grapes previously used only for blending began to appear At first, French country grapes such as Mourvedre, Viognier, and even Syrah remained a mystery, having been subsumed in blends or simply named not after the grape but for the European home region. Today, California winemakers dabble in Sangiovese (the core Chianti grape), Tempranillo (a major grape of Spanish Rioja wine), and many others.

Raimund Pruem: Standing the Test of Time

ANYONE WHO THINKS that terroir—the notion that the earth (*terra*) influences the flavor of wine in the bottle—does not exist should visit the Mosel River Valley in Germany.

At the mouth of the river where the Mosel meets the Rhine, the earth is like topsoil, rich and verdant, famous for producing big, fruit-driven Rieslings of ripeness, depth, and power. Not 75 miles (120 km) west on the flood plain of the Mosel Valley, the soils differ entirely, dominated by slate laid down over millennia of flooding and receding. Sugar is secondary here; Mosel Riesling is generally dry and mineral-focused, perfumed and aromatic.

It's the same sun, the same grapes, and essentially the same people with access to the same wine-making techniques. Soil and the near-absence of residual sugar in the wine— dry, especially when referring to a white wine— make these unique among German wines. When the sugar recedes, it exposes a world of flavors difficult to discern when overlaid by sugar. It's natural to imagine that the soil makes the difference between these neighboring wine regions, and it certainly does, but it's also much more.

Raimund Pruem wants to develop another important difference, one he hopes will carry his family's winery S.A. Pruem for generations and beyond: Pruem has embarked on an aggressive modern style of Riesling, and is pushing it out to the world, with a thoroughly modern design that he hopes can compete on a world stage.

Just a few years away from the winery's hundredth birthday, Pruem is focused on a new line of "branded" Rieslings: Essence and Solitaire. "To work S.A. Pruem as a brand, this is the finale of my life," he said, looking not a day older than fifty-something. "I try to put my signature on every wine I make."

"Modern" in Pruem's context has a number of meanings: limited production, contract growers, stainless steel tanks, modern labeling, screw cap closure. But more than anything else, it means dry, sugar-free, and loving it.

Raimund is one of many Pruem winemakers in the Mosel, whose family came here more than eight centuries ago from the town of Pruem in the Eiffel region just north of Wehlen, their home now. One of his ancestors, Jodocus Pruem, was a tireless innovator. In 1842, he built two giant Sonnenuhren, or sundials, one in Wehlen and another in Zeltingen, so the people could improve themselves simply by using the sun to know the time.

The sundials gave the surrounding vineyards their names—branded them, if you will—and over time, unsurprisingly, they've produced relentlessly excellent wines. It makes sense; sun is the first ingredient you need for a functional sundial and great wine.

Oak wine barrels coming and going outside the subterranean cellar and tasting room of Field Stone Winery in Sonoma, California, United States

Cell Phone Wine List: Digital Grabs

IF YOU'VE EVER TAKEN A creative writing class, you'll know they teach you to show, not tell, with your writing. This is great advice for wine lovers, too. It's easy to get bogged down in wine-speak, where rich and fruity to someone may be tannic and undrinkable to you.

Here's an idea: Use your cell phone camera—practically every mobile device comes with one—to snap shots of your favorite wines. This way, you build a personal visual wine list to use as a shopping tool. Best of all, the label, with art and content, contains the wine's name and a visual mnemonic device in the form of the graphic design.

In a wine store or a restaurant, casually open your cell phone and flash a few snapshots of some of your favorite labels. It's a great way to communicate with waiters, sommeliers, and salespeople without the distortion of memory and description. Here are a few tips for taking these information-filled photos:

SHOOT THE LABEL, NOT THE BOTTLE

Remember, you're trying to capture label info, so don't bother showing the whole bottle. Get nice and close to the label. If you have a macro-focus option, use it.

KEEP IT SIMPLE

When showing photos, don't feel obliged to go into much detail. Instead, clicking through, make comments such as, "Loved it," "Really loved it," "She loved it more than I did," and so on. This is deceptively simple, but good information for anyone sincerely trying to help you.

PHOTO A FEW ANTI-FAVORITES

There's no need to carry around a bunch of snapshots of wines you sincerely dislike, but one or two can provide helpful information. If you taste a wine that embodies everything about your least-favorite style or type of wine, take a picture. That way, you'll remember never to purchase it again.

USE LIGHT OVER YOUR SHOULDER

To make sure your label photos turn out bright and legible, have your light source over your shoulder, above and behind you, with the bottle in your free hand. That way, as you line up your shot, you can tilt the bottle to remove any glare.

LOOK AT YOUR WINE LIST

If the restaurant's wine list is too long, complex, hard to understand, or just doesn't contain wines with which you're familiar, fall back on your own wine list. Don't be shy about using and sharing it. It's acceptable to say, "Let's look at my wine list," then start the show-and-tell.

The History of Wine Scores

ROBERT PARKER, American author and publisher of the *Wine Advocate*, was the world's most popular and powerful wine critic. His breakthrough came in 1978 when he applied the familiar scholastic grading scale—90 to 100 is an A, 80 to 90 a B, and so on—to wine, apparently for the first time ever. Parker was such a force in the wine world that many people believe and report that his taste and opinion have altered the wine-making practices of even the world's most famous wineries.

It's not too far-fetched to say that in the first half of the twenty-first century, the world makes and drinks Parker's favorite wine style: big, flavorful, fruit-forward, concentrated reds. The phrase, "Parker gave it a 90," generally indicates the last word on a wine's quality.

The public responded overwhelmingly positively to Parker's easy-to-understand system, and other critics and magazines adopted it widely. *Wine Spectator* magazine, founded in 1979, took the 100-point scale to fantastic commercial levels. Wine shop owners in many markets understand that if a wine earns "only" an 88, they can't sell it; if it scores a 92, they have a hard time purchasing any from their suppliers because of demand. That all this commerce occurs over a four-point differential demonstrates how seriously consumers take wine scores. (A cynic suspects a wine can score a 92 if its manufacturer buys 92 percent more advertising for it in the magazine of choice.)

After the *Wine Advocate* and *Wine Spectator*, a passel of publications crunch similar numbers, but none with nearly as much clout as the leaders. Between all of them, plenty of 90+ scores go around, but that also leads to inevitable grade inflation. The first time a wine earned a perfect score was mind-blowing. Now, it has happened more than a hundred times, making the effect far less dramatic.

Champagne, Sparkling Wine, Fizzy Grape Drink

How do Champagne, sparkling wine, and fizzy wine in glass bottles truly differ?

Champagne, made only in the Champagne region in France, accounts for one of every twelve bottles of sparkling wine worldwide. The French protect the name without fail. On New Year's Eve, Champagne gets a boost, becoming the top twelfth of the market in price, quality, and desirability.

Any wine region worldwide can produce sparkling wine, from Australia and California to Italy and Germany, even some of the less-famous areas in France.

Except for the top brands, most fine sparkling wines remain unknown and undervalued. If you're willing to forget about Champagne for a minute, you can get a delicious Crémant from France's Loire Valley or two bottles of a top semisweet Italian Prosecco for half the price.

Fizzy wine comes from winemakers who carbonate great vats of white wine with CO_2 pumped in through a hose, then bottle, cork, and secure it with a wire closure. Don't pay more than what you'd pay for an equivalent amount (e.g., three or four cans) of soda.

Recipe: Omelette with Smoked Porcini Mushrooms

PORCINI MEANS "the little piglet" in Italian, and these gnarled brown mushrooms taste almost like meat, with much the same tone and texture. Here, the smoked mushrooms get paired with a smoky red from South Africa called Pinotage (see Day 46).

Unlike a typical omelette, which gets folded once or twice, this omelette looks like a big pancake. Slipping it out onto a big plate and flipping it deftly back into the omelette pan is much easier the second time, so do a dry run some breakfast morning with eggs and milk. Look for dried mushrooms at your local gourmet food shops. (Some wine shops have upscale food sections.) I prefer the smoked Chilean porcini, but try any variety that appeals to you.

2 tablespoons (8 g) dried smoked porcini mushrooms

1 cup (235 ml) water, boiling

4 eggs

¼ cup (60 ml) milk

4 tablespoons (8 g) chopped fresh parsley (or 2 teaspoons [0.6 g] dried), divided

1 tablespoon (14 g) butter

2 tablespoons (28 ml) olive oil

Salt and ground black pepper, to taste

Combine the mushrooms and boiling water in a small, heavy bowl and cover. Let it sit for 20 minutes. Remove the mushrooms (discard the juice), dry them gently on a paper towel, and then chop roughly.

In a large heavy bowl, beat the eggs and milk with a fork, and add half of the parsley.

Heat the butter in a 12- to 18-inch (30- to 45-cm) omelette pan until it starts to smoke. Add the mushrooms and sauté for 2 to 3 minutes, turning and jostling frequently, until they soften. Remove the mushrooms from the pan, combine with the egg mixture, and mix thoroughly.

Heat the olive oil in the omelette pan until it starts to smoke, and add the egg-mushroom mixture. Stir once in the pan, and then cook over medium-high heat.

Once the omelette firms up and appears almost dry on top, ease it out onto a plate, then flip it gently back into the pan to cook for 2 minutes. Slide the finished omelette onto a fresh plate. Sprinkle with the remaining chopped parsley, add salt and pepper to taste, and serve hot.

YIELD: Serves 4

Wine Pairing: Zonnebloem Pinotage
SOUTH AFRICA

This Pinotage from Zonnebloem (Afrikaans—the South African language—for "sunflower") is full of smoke, wood, and leaves, with a fruit component juicy like blood orange and concentrated like cola.

The University of Wine

THERE'S NO QUESTION the French take their wines seriously. The government protects wine economically and culturally, like one might a historic artifact. By law, those responsible for recommending wine in France—waiters, sommeliers, wine shop salespeople—must possess an education certificate backed up by verified training in the art and science of wine. The higher up the wine ladder you climb, the steeper the requirements for wine education and training, just as in science, medicine, and business.

In France, the University of Wine (*Université du Vin*) is in the town of Suze la Rousse in the southern Rhône Valley outside Avignon, located in the heart of one of France's largest wine-growing regions.

The Université and other institutions like it play a vital role by accrediting and licensing people for positions at every step in the wine industry food chain. The curriculum includes courses such as "A day of sensibilization to wine tasting," which obviously won't be an easy A.

In North America, the University of California, Davis, has the country's most famous and important oenology program. Cornell offers a degree, and the University of Toronto recently launched its own oenology program.

If you go: Université du Vin, Le Château, 26790 Suze La Rousse (France), 011.33.04.75.97.21.30 (phone), 011.33.04.75.98.24.20 (fax), universite. du.vin@wanadoo.fr, www.universite-du-vin.com.

People Who Don't Like Wine

PEOPLE ASK ME all the time, what's the best wine to serve someone who doesn't know wine or has never before tasted wine. It's always desirable to recruit more wine lovers to the cause, so the pressure is on to recommend something overtly, intentionally delicious. Try these crowd-pleasers:

• Pinot Grigio: Keep it cheap and get the most current vintage possible.

• Red Zinfandel: It's amazing how many people think Zinfandel comes only in pink. Not too surprisingly, however, people enjoy the red version equally as much.

• Semidry Riesling: Semidry means a little sweet, a good idea for a group of people whose tastes you don't necessarily know. Wine lovers always ask for dry white wine, but most people enjoy a touch of sugar; if it keeps their blood sugar up, they stay in a good mood.

• Sauvignon Blanc (sometimes called Fumé Blanc in California): For the more adventurous, this crisp white grape brings good, bright fruit acidity.

Muscadet, the main white grape from the mouth of the Loire River, pictured in the tasting room at winemaker Guilbaud Frères in the town of Clisson, France

Beyond Champagne

EVERY BOTTLE OF CHAMPAGNE is its own little factory. The second fermentation, which gives the wine its bubbles, occurs inside each bottle after the last dollop of yeast goes in, and the cap goes back on to lock in the CO_2.

No two bottles of this wine are ever exactly the same. In fact, with such a profound biochemistry at work in the Champagne method, it's amazing to think that any two bottles (much less thousands at a time) come out tasting at all alike. According to winemakers, Champagne is the hardest wine to make. It's labor-intensive, expensive and slow, and requires multiple fermentations. On top of that, Pinot Noir—a main grape in many sparkling wines—is a notoriously difficult grape to grow, with its thin skin, fragility, and ability to spoil easily.

This is the double challenge of Champagne: challenging wine making and unpredictable grape growing. This explains why sparkling wine typically costs more than other wines. Thanks to the big price tag, it's natural to hold off on the bubbly until New Year's, graduation, or some other special occasion.

To get good value in sparkling wine, break out of the top-tier Champagne and cast a wider net. The farther away you get from the throne, the lower the prices and the higher the Quality/Price Ratio, or QPR (see Day 22).

Sparkling Outposts beyond Champagne

Clairette de Die, France
Tucked away in an otherwise wine-free region between the southern and northern Rhône, the town of Die makes its sparklers in anonymity from white Muscat and another grape called Clairette, hence the name. It's famous for its soft, creamy carbonation.

Sparkling Vouvray, France
Vouvray, in the Loire Valley of northern France, grows Chenin Blanc and makes semidry white wines, turning a small amount into a bargain sparkler.

Cava, Spain
Eastern Spain, approaching the French border, is home to most of Spain's sparkling wine production called Cava, named for the caves used to cool and age the wine. Single-digit, tasty Cava has been around for decades and probably will be for years to come, in the form of Freixenet (the one in the black bottle) and Segura Viudas, two ultra-dependable brands.

Notes on Vegetal Wine

ALTHOUGH THE WORD *vegetal* is not in and of itself negative, when you use it to describe wine, it's rarely positive. It captures a hint of under-ripeness. A vegetal wine doesn't smell like the ripe fruit you wish it did. It's still growing—vegetating—and that's what you taste: nearly fruit flavors that are green, stemmy, and unripe.

There's an exception to this rule: New Zealand Sauvignon Blanc has a distinct style based on razor-sharp acidity and tart, intense fruit. Sauvignon Blanc is naturally zippy, and New Zealand manages the ripeness in the vineyard to get the exact acidity to carry the style.

If you're a winemaker, you likely don't want to hear that your wine tastes vegetal, but the New Zealand way makes vegetal beautiful.

History of Shiraz

ARCHEOLOGISTS HAVE DISCOVERED sites of large-scale wine making going back eons, the oldest from about 8,000 years ago, near the southern Iranian city of Shiraz. This place gave birth to an ancient red grape that the French call Syrah, though traditionally never named after the grape on a wine label.

If you desire the very best Syrah, scout around the Rhône Valley in the south of France for pricey items such as Hermitage, Côte-Rôtie, Cornas, or St. Joseph that top out as sheer luxury purchases. For delicious bargain Syrah, however, look to Australia, where winemakers call their version Shiraz after the old, Old World grape.

Just as it originally flourished in the hot southern European sun, Shiraz has found a happy home baking through even hotter Australian summers. The wine it produces is a worldwide favorite, full of pepper and spice and deep, dark fruit. Shiraz has a couple of different personalities. In general, it is smooth and velvety, but strong and high in flavor and alcohol.

Shiraz from the Barossa Valley, near Adelaide, is dense and rich with great intensity and concentration. At the top of the Shiraz world rests the stellar Grange, formerly known as Grange Hermitage, with a price tag that rivals real Hermitage.

Wine Suggestion:
Rosemount Shiraz
AUSTRALIA

A real tribute to what Syrah has become in its adopted home: dark, rich, chocolaty, and cheap, although Rosemount sells a yummy Shiraz at practically every price point. Serve it with every kind of red meat, from lamb and steak to salmon and tuna.

Recipe: Sautéed Olives

THIS RECIPE IS DECEPTIVELY EASY, but the effect of sautéing olives for even a few minutes is profound. Don't be afraid to embellish the dish with artichoke hearts or a little chopped bacon.

¼ cup (60 ml) olive oil

4 whole garlic cloves

1 pound (200 g) mixed olives

4 canned Italian plum tomatoes, chunked

1 big pinch rosemary

1 big pinch chopped parsley (fresh is preferable, though dried also works)

¼ cup (60 ml) white wine

Heat the olive oil in a skillet over medium heat. Add the garlic and brown lightly. Add the olives, sauté for 3 to 5 minutes, then add the tomato and the herbs and cook for 1 minute more. Stir once, add the wine, lower the heat, and cook slowly for 15 minutes. Serve immediately with thinly sliced, toasted Italian bread.

YIELD: Makes 2 cups (200 g)

Wine Pairing:
Ninety + Cellars Malbec Lot 7
ARGENTINA

By the time you read this, we'll almost certainly be drinking Lot 8 or higher, but don't worry, the concept remains the same: small lots of wine earning 90 points or higher, rebranded with a discount price. This Malbec is dark, dense, and looking for intense flavors to complement, such as these sautéed olives.

Rhône Valley

THE RHÔNE RIVER STARTS life high in the western Alps and flows from Switzerland through central France until the river takes a hard left turn at Lyon. From there, it's straight south to the Mediterranean. The fast-moving Rhône has been carving out the land for millions of years, forming hillsides that curve down to the now deep river basin. From the air, the river's mouth looks like a triangle: Avignon marks the north point, Marseille, the bottom right, and Montpellier, the bottom left, with the Mediterranean Sea at the bottom. More than half of all of the French wine exported overseas comes from somewhere inside this triangle.

Seafaring Greeks planted the first grapes on Marseille's coast in about 600 BCE, and the ancient Romans took firm control by 200 BCE. They recognized the lay of the land as perfect for growing grapes, olives, and other fruit, because the sun hits at a direct angle.

From the Mediterranean Sea to the north, the landscape rises up and up, and faces south toward the sun. Because this has been the case for thousands and thousands of years, you can taste the bright sunny juice in even the Rhône's most intense wines.

Land and light are unique and distinct in this part of southern France, called Provence. It was the ancient Romans' first conquest outside of their peninsula, and they called it simply "The Province."

Rhône wines are almost always red and blended from three dominant grapes: Syrah, Grenache, and Mourvedre. This blending is Old World to the extreme, where wines were known primarily by their place-name—where the grapes grow—not by winemaker first, grape second, as in the New World.

Dick Arrowood Starts Over

WINEMAKER DICK ARROWOOD is quoted as saying in his youth that he made wines so great they would never be drinkable—exactly the sort of statement a brash, proud, young winemaker would make.

Arrowood grew famous fast, first as the founding winemaker at Château St. Jean in Sonoma Valley, California. His wine-making style and skill made the wines (especially the whites) taste like rare boutique wines, except that they were available and affordable. He founded his own winery, then in 2000, at the top of the dot-com bubble, sold it to a drink conglomerate that promptly drove it out of business and into bankruptcy court.

Arrowood's story has a happy ending. A sympathetic and successful new owner bought the winery out of bankruptcy and promptly hired Arrowood as wine master without administrative duties, freeing him up to pursue a new winery venture called Amapola Creek, after a family of flamboyant poppies that grow near the vineyard.

What makes a person start a new winery at the age of sixty? "Complete mental illness," Arrowood said, and no one who's been in the wine business would disagree. His new winery has a permit for 3,000 cases a year (16,000 cases is considered the cutoff point between tiny boutique wineries and small wineries), which guarantees to some degree that the workdays will stay under twelve hours.

If you go: Arrowood Vineyards & Winery, 14347 Sonoma Highway, Glen Ellen, California, 707.935.2600, www.arrowoodvineyards.com. Amapola Creek is not open to the public.

Grape harvesting machinery at a vineyard

Plan a Wine Picnic

WHEN ENJOYING WINE, setting, ambiance, and the company you keep play an important role. Of all of the inexpensive wines you have loved to drink, most have likely been consumed with friends, family, or the love of your life on a picnic blanket somewhere in the great outdoors, possibly even in a vineyard.

Simply putting wine together with a summery picnic improves the wine *and* the picnic. Choosing a good picnic wine doesn't involve matching wine and food, but rather selecting a few hearty wines that can stand being chilled too cold, then jostled overland via pack animal, canoe, or bicycle to their final destination.

Don't pick your favorite aged Bordeaux, which needs time to settle and have its sediment properly decanted. A delicate white Burgundy that demands just the right temperature also is out of the question. And forget about those big, buttery California Chardonnays. Once warm, they taste like an oil slick.

Choose for a picnic wines both potable and portable (but mostly portable). Once you get the wine to the picnic, the rest takes care of itself—as long as you remembered your traveling cork screw, that is.

Perfect Picnic Wines

Vinho Verde

In general, Vinho Verde is low in alcohol (about 6 percent) and has a little fizz to it, so it's easy to drink and nicely refreshing in the heat. Look for the most recent vintage available.

Vernaccia di San Gimignano

In some ways, Vernaccia is the perfect summer-weather wine. It has serious acidity, which makes it a tasty match with all kinds of salads and sandwiches. And it doesn't possess myriad fragile flavors that can jostle in transit.

Pinot Gris

Pinot Gris has an unusual tannic bite that makes it taste great with food. All in all, it's a nice grape to add to the repertoire, picnic or no picnic.

Côtes du Rhône

Many grapes from this region are blended together to make smooth but sturdy wines, muscular and tannic, and perfect with a strong cheese.

Zinfandel

Zinfandel seems to flourish when it's too warm and all shook up—making it the perfect picnic wine.

Cork Versus Corked

As SOON AS YOU yank the cork on that big, beautiful bottle of red wine, you smell it and it doesn't smell good. You've met your nemesis, the corked cork.

This happens when TCA (the chemical compound trichloroanisole) gets into the cork sometime before bottling and eventually infects the wine. The result, years later and thousands of miles away, is an unhappy surprise that smells like wet, moldy newspaper.

In a restaurant, you can send back a bottle if it smells of the three Ms: mildew, musty, and medicinal. If you open a corked bottle at home, it's fair to return it to the shop where you purchased it and get another. The shop receives credit from the wholesaler, and so on up the food chain. In addition, it's good information for the shop and wine producer to have.

Wine-industry estimates run the gamut for how much wine is actually corked. Current thinking says that 10 to 15 percent of all wine contains some TCA, but only 5 to 7 percent of wine contains it at a level you can taste. The bad news is twofold: At least one out of ten bottles is corked, and half of the time, you can't tell. Regardless of actual numbers, experience suggests that the vast majority of corked bottles go unreported.

Wine is a rotten business—literally—and the challenge of keeping fermented fruit juice tasting fresh for years is immense. Synthetics and recycled cork materials represent a natural evolution, but winemakers employ them the same way they do the current failing corks. Screw caps, still considered "down market," unfortunately have a little ways to go before they achieve their inevitable full-market acceptance. There isn't yet a perfect solution, but remember, always feel empowered to return a corked bottle of wine.

Surrender to the Pink

AS WINE DRINKERS GROW more confident and adventurous, they discover a whole new spectrum of food-friendly dry pink wines that possess the bright sunny fruit of a white wine, with a little more oomph like a red.

In theory, you could make pink wine by coloring white wine with a tiny bit of red wine in the blend. But in reality, rosé, blush, pink wine, whatever you call it, is essentially red grapes made in the white wine style.

Normally, red grapes are fermented with their skins, giving the wine its color and drying tannic bite. White wine is solely the juice of white grapes with little or no skin contact. Red grapes treated this way results in pink juice, because they pick up a little color during juice pressing and separation of the red skins.

You can make rosé from any red grape; what we call white Zinfandel is actually a rosé made from red Zinfandel. The method that uses pink juice from black grapes is still the only officially sanctioned technique for making rosé.

Shopping List

• Sonoma's SoloRosa, as the name implies, produces only gutsy rosé from Syrah, Sangiovese, even Pinot Noir.

• Southern France is famous for rosé, especially from Provence, but Spanish producers Muga Winery and Marqués de Cacéres both export dry pink Riojas called rosado.

• Even Chianti is getting into the act, with the Castello di Ama Rosato.

Recipe: Daube of Beef

FEW FOODS TASTE MORE delicious than the first hearty autumn stew. This daube is rich and thick, full of intense flavors and aromas. Don't be afraid to cook it for the entire eight hours. Serve with a big loaf of crusty French bread.

4 pounds (1.6 kg) cross-cut center shin of beef (about 6 pieces)

1 bottle good red wine (preferably, the same wine you will serve with the dish)

3 tablespoons (45 ml) olive oil

2 tablespoons (28 g) butter

3 strips bacon

½ cup (60 g) flour

¼ cup (7 g) rosemary

6 whole garlic cloves

2 large onions, chopped

2 large carrots, chopped

2 large potatoes, chopped

4 stalks celery, chopped

1 teaspoon (6 g) salt

1 teaspoon (2 g) ground black pepper

1 cup (235 ml) water

Marinate the beef in the red wine and olive oil for at least 1 hour. Remove the beef and pat it dry with paper towels. Save the marinade.

Preheat the oven to 375°F (190°C). In a heavy pot on top of the stove, melt the butter and add the bacon, cooking over medium heat until the bacon browns slightly.

Combine the flour and rosemary in a large, shallow bowl. Dust the beef in this mixture, and brown in the butter and bacon. Once the beef browns, remove it from the pot and keep covered, but leave the bacon and butter.

Turn the heat up and add the garlic, onions, carrots, potatoes, and celery. Cook for 15 minutes, stirring occasionally. When the vegetables release some of their moisture, add the salt and pepper, and stir.

Return the beef to the pot, add the marinade and water, and heat until the stew simmers nicely. Stir once, cover, and cook in the oven for 4 hours. Turn the heat down to 300°F (150°C), and cook for another 4 hours.

YIELD: Serves 6 to 8

Wine Pairing: Mas de Gourgonnier, Les Baux de Provence

FRANCE

Bauxite is unrefined aluminum ore, named for Les Baux (pronounced lay-BOE) de Provence, the town where the first large deposit was discovered and mined, a sunny, south-facing place that makes wine the old-fashioned way. Mas de Gourgonnier is technically but unintentionally organic, and the only place you'll see it recognized is on the back label as a tiny logo. The flavors are big and raspberry juicy with a grippy dry texture you really feel. This wine tastes like a miniature Châteauneuf-du-Pape, at a miniature price.

How the Italians Saved Wine

IF YOU LOVE WINE, thank the deity of your choice for the Italian people. Because of them, modern wine as we know it exists.

In Roman times, Italians built the entire European wine infrastructure, and by extension, wine in the world that we understand today. Ancient Romans first planted grapes all over France and Spain, and finally in Germany. The sites that they chose more than two millennia ago still produce some of the greatest classical French wines today.

Draw a line on a map of France from Marseille in the south to Bordeaux in the west, and you can almost see the travel routes the Romans must have taken to this prime vineyard land. A dotted line of tiny wine neighborhoods along the way must be where grapes fell off of the back of the truck, or where someone called it quits and planted vines in the breakdown lane, so to speak.

Either way, Romans laid out a model of how wine works to which we still react today. Even in the Pacific Northwest of the United States, a very new wine region, all roads lead to Seattle, showing that the Roman vision of a calm, pristine countryside feeding a dynamic, percolating city is still in play.

Survival of the Fittest

At the beginning of the twentieth century in the United States, during Prohibition, wine-loving Italian families kept wine alive, especially in California. In contrast, Ohio's wine industry was immense and vigorous before Prohibition, as big as the twenty-first century's California wine industry, but predominately German, very Protestant, and stereotypically practical. Nearly a century later, Ohio vineyards number few and far between, but California has big wine families such as Mondavi, Pedroncelli, Foppiano, Parducci, Andretti, and Signorello. Much of the California wine industry that survived Prohibition did so by producing sacramental wine it supplied to the Catholic Church.

Insurance for Wine

IF A PROFESSIONAL ATHLETE can buy insurance for something as valuable and personal as an ACL (anterior crusiate ligament), it only makes sense that wine lovers with even simple cellars need some way to insure their wine equity.

Many insurance companies offer wine insurance policies (e.g., Thomson & Pratt in the U.S., La Playa in the United Kingdom, and Chubb internationally). Policies typically start with a basic Vintner Package (coverage against theft, fire, breakage, and vandalism), and progress upwards in value and coverage to the deluxe Sommelier Package (everything in the Vintner Package, plus coverage against temperature, humidity, vibration, and light damage).

The insurance plans don't cost much (about the value of half of a case of good Champagne a year for most, paid in cash). But are they enough? When you consider the number of moving parts in a modern, temperature-controlled wine cellar, perhaps the wine world needs day-to-day insurance plans for other, common risks:

THE BAD-JUDGMENT PACKAGE

Protection from ever saying, "Who bought THIS?!" when it was you who bought it. This comes with an optional rider to cover other family members who purchase wine.

THE NUMERICAL-SUBJECTIVISM PACKAGE

The perfect insurance for people who can't stop buying wines other people have given irrationally high numerical scores. Rebates available with evidence of canceled subscriptions to the *Wine Spectator*.

THE ADVICE-IS-FREE PACKAGE

Protect yourself against having to explain to friends and loved ones that a stranger in your local wine shop recommended to you this inexplicably atrocious bottle of wine. A perfect gift for the friend who gives notoriously bad advice.

THE WINE-LIST PACKAGE

Essential insurance for those who eat and drink out often. Coverage includes damage from bad guidance by waitstaff, glasses of wine from bottles left open way too long, and sinful price markups. Toll-free number service for restaurant emergencies.

Vineyard in the central coast of California, United States

Exploring Local Vineyards and Wineries

FOR THE TRUE WINE LOVER, nothing compares with tasting wine right where it's made, at the winery, followed by a picnic in the vineyard, and a nap under a shady tree. Granted, the whole world isn't like Europe, dotted with vineyards and wineries, but you don't have to live near Napa or Sonoma to have a little access to viniculture.

Getting to know small, local wineries near where you live is a good first step toward plugging in to your local wine culture.

BEFORE YOU GO

Although almost all vineyards offer tours and tastings during the summer, their hours vary from day to day and season to season. Call first to confirm hours and get directions. Some wine farms live well off the beaten path, making them sometimes tricky to find. Feel free to pack a picnic lunch to bring to most spots.

Many have picnic areas and outside seating available. If you ask nicely and show that you understand the importance of respecting the vines, they may let you picnic out in the vineyard. But be sure to ask permission first.

THE ART OF SPITTING

Wineries don't stage free wine samplings so people can drink wine and drive from one winery to the next. Tasting and spitting with real discipline is not rude. In fact, it shows respect for the process and the product.

EXPECTATIONS

Small, local wineries are often family-run, mom-and-pop operations that have only been making wine for a few years. It's not realistic to have the same expectations as you would when visiting a winery from a 1,000-year-old wine culture. Be prepared for an adventure, and let however that turns out be good enough.

Remember When

VINTAGE YEARS ARE wonderful tools for staking time to mark and celebrate our personal histories. When buying wine as gifts, try selecting bottles that represent milestones or turning points in the recipient's life: one from the year a happy couple met, one from the year of the couple's wedding, and one from the year their first child was born, for example. Celebrate college graduations, new jobs, any significant (or playful) life event with a vintage year.

If you have a cool, dark place to store a little wine, I recommend keeping your eyes out for at least your wedding anniversary year as you shop, and buying it on sight. If you have children, get the years they were born, and the grandkids, too, and other people's kids while you're at it.

It's an utter cliché to say that wine is "time in a bottle," but in a lot of ways, it is. And it's wine's connection with time that gives wine much of its sentimental weight and value. Vintage years, which appear on even the most modest bottles, are automatic triggers for memories and meaning, and they're wonderful tools for staking time to mark and celebrate our interpersonal histories. The beautiful bittersweetness of marking milestones with wine is that the wine—like the year it commemorates—is gone and irreplaceable in no time as well.

Gewürztraminer

GEWÜRZTRAMINER IS A white grape similar to Riesling. It grows in many of the same regions as Riesling, on both the German and the French sides of the Rhine, but it has an off-center flavor, slightly like wet wool, but in an earthy way.

Gewürztraminer comes mostly from Alsace, the most Germanic part of France. *Gewurz* is German for "spice," and this grape definitely lives up to that name; it's famous for being fruity, fresh, and highly perfumed, smelling like wildflowers, rose water, and lilacs all at once. The fruit is usually light, sometimes tropical, sometimes like pear and melon, often with a strong acidity. Gewürztraminer's rub is its funky, earthy, slightly animal flavors. It's only one layer, but it's a crucial one beyond which many wine lovers cannot move.

Once you've fallen for Gewürztraminer, however, you may find yourself begging your friends to give it a chance. Gewürztraminer is like modern art or an obscure band: Give it ten or fifteen tries, and you will fall in love.

Wine Suggestions: Gewürztraminers

From Canada

Vineland: This is the best North American example, which comes from near Niagara Falls.

Pelee Island: This is the second-best North American example, from the same area as Vineland.

From France

Pierre Sparr: A nicely bracing acidity, this wine has much fruit flavor.

Rene Schmidt: Light, bright, and refreshing, this is a great summer wine served as cold as beer.

Sipp Mack: Extreme concentrations of tropical fruit flavors make this wine memorable.

Trimbach: A classic from a classic winemaking family, this has it all. Great fruit concentration, rich spicy aromas, and persistent flavors make it the top of the class.

Willm: Creamy and smooth, this wine smells like rose water and ripe pears.

Ziegler: This wine is floral, fresh tasting, and a little sweet.

From New Zealand

Huia: An exciting find with tremendous tropical fruit and soaring perfume, this is my favorite.

Recipe: Rosemary-and-Mushroom-Stuffed Leg of Lamb

1 cup (235 ml) red wine

⅓ cup (80 ml) balsamic vinegar

3 pounds (1.2 kg) whole, boneless leg of lamb, butterflied (if you ask your butcher to butterfly and trim for you, which is recommended, ask for pieces approximately 2 inches [5 cm] thick)

1 medium bunch green chard

1 medium bunch red chard

1 medium onion, finely chopped

4 to 6 garlic cloves, minced

3 tablespoons (45 ml) olive oil

1 pound (450 g) assorted mushrooms (cremini, portobello, shiitake, or whatever is available), finely chopped

1 cup (115 g) fresh bread crumbs

½ cup (120 ml) milk

Salt and ground black pepper, to taste

3 tablespoons (5 g) fresh rosemary

1 tablespoon (2 g) herbes de Provence

Combine the wine and balsamic vinegar in a bowl, add the lamb, cover, and marinate for 1 to 3 hours.

Once the lamb has marinated for long enough, cook the chard leaves in boiling water for 5 minutes, drain and chop, and transfer to a large bowl. In a medium frying pan, sauté the onion and garlic in olive oil until translucent. Add the chopped mushrooms and cook for 10 minutes.

Combine the mushrooms, chard, and bread crumbs in a large bowl. Mix well, adding milk as necessary to keep the stuffing smooth. Season with salt and pepper to taste.

Preheat the oven to 425°F (220°C). Remove the lamb from the marinade, and dry thoroughly with a paper towel. Place the butterflied lamb on a cutting board, with the interior, butterflied surface up. Sprinkle with fresh rosemary in an even layer. Spread the stuffing and smooth it into a layer approximately as thick as the meat below. Roll the lamb up tightly around the stuffing and tie off with string (or with several strategically placed bamboo skewers).

Sprinkle the top of the lamb with herbes de Provence, salt, and pepper, and cook in a heavy roasting pan for 30 minutes. Reduce the temperature to 325°F (170°C), and cook for another 45 minutes for medium-rare (cook longer for a warmer center). Remove from the oven, let stand for 15 minutes, slice, and serve.

YIELD: Serves 6

Wine Pairing: Hawk Crest Cabernet Sauvignon
UNITED STATES (CALIFORNIA)

Stag's Leap made California Cabernet Sauvignon famous by essentially winning the red wine category in the famous 1976 France versus California tasting, "The Judgment of Paris," reintroduced to audiences and wine lovers in the 2008 major motion picture *Bottle Shock*. Hawk Crest is this wine's second label, a delightfully more affordable version of dignified, well-made California Cabernet.

Greek Revival

THANKS TO AN UNFORTUNATE domination by the Ottoman Empire from the middle of the fifteenth century until 1821, Greece's wine industry was heavily suppressed. Although the nation has a rich pre-Ottoman history, modern wine making began anew about the same time as the California wine industry, in the mid-1800s.

Military rule kept Greece at arm's length from the rest of the world until 1974, and the country didn't enter the European Union until 1981. But since the early 1980s, Greek wine has gained in investment and quality, although a bad reputation from years of exporting Retsina still lingers.

Retsina, like the English word *resin*, refers to the pine tar pitch ancient Greeks used to seal their barrels. The flavor and aroma naturally seeped into the wine, and winemakers eventually started manipulating resin levels in Retsina to express different styles. This acquired flavor profile is one that few actually acquire and the reason many people think that all Greek wine tastes like pine tar.

Happily, this is starting to change. Cambas Mantinia is a beautiful white wine whose aromas smell of 100 percent Muscat grape with white flowers, melons, and rose water. On the tongue, the flavors taste round and ripe, with peach, pear, and honeydew.

It's easy to suspect that the Greek countryside hid great wines that simply never made it beyond the country's borders, but the Cambas Mantinia far exceeds anything imaginable. Its fellow labels from Cambas—Arkadia (an entry-level Soave-style white), Savatiano (a zesty, tropical white), and Nemea Reserve (a rich, oaky red)—also are worth seeking out.

Cork and Memory

I WAS EATING DINNER at the bar of a small, neighborhood Italian restaurant. A woman came in and sat down beside me, and the bartender asked whether he could get her something to drink. "Yes, a glass of wine," she replied. He asked what kind. The woman reached into her purse, pulled out a wine cork, and said, "I'll have a glass of this," and without an ounce of self-consciousness, handed it to him.

He read it, and the two had a short conversation about where she tasted this wine and what about it she liked. Then he handed it back and said, "Try this." He poured her a little taste, and she said it was perfect. "We're an Italian restaurant," the bartender said, "so I don't have any Australian wine, but if you liked that, you'll like this." Sure enough, she did.

> Remembering which wines you like is key to reproducing a great wine experience. Find a medium-sized eye hook (with a screw post) and key ring. Screw the hook into the cork of your current favorite, and loop the eye around a key ring. As your tastes change and you fall in love with new wines, change the cork.

Starting a Wine-Tasting Club

SOMETIMES WINE LOVERS simply have to take matters into their own hands. If you really want to learn about wine, outside of class—organized tastings, restaurant wine dinners, wine classes, and so on—do what college students do: Start your own study group. This offers a great excuse to learn about wine with friends and family all within the structure of a wine-tasting club.

Once you have the people, lay out a monthly meeting schedule, each with a theme. Begin with meetings that focus on different grapes.

Some clubs organize meetings such as individual scavenger hunts, for which each member brings one or two bottles of the theme wine. Rotate wine, food, and hosting responsibilities among group members.

There's no right or wrong way to host these tastings, but be sure to include the core element of documentation. Buy a big, blank book or scrapbook to record your club's tastings—something forgiving and roomy that will hold clippings, labels, photos, and other ephemera—and write down everything you taste. Bring it to each tasting, and review the tasting notes from time to time.

Wine for the Fun of It

YOU LIKELY KNOW MORE about wine than you think you do. How do you uncover this hidden wisdom? By thinking and talking about wine like a food, not a mystical potion.

When you're out to dinner and someone asks you how your steak tastes, you have much to say: It's juicy, dry, overdone, underdone, perfectly done, tender, tough, crispy, spicy, fatty, lean, and so on.

But when asked how the wine drinks, you'll likely say something like, "I'm no wine expert, but it's red and wet and that's the best I can do."

Even if you don't have a PhD in wine, you (like every wine lover) have years of experience understanding what tastes good and what doesn't. You may not be a meat expert, but you react to its taste. You're entitled to the same when it comes to wine.

Sauvingnon Blanc: Wild Vines

AT THE END OF A long wine trip in France, my sleep is disrupted, my palate blasted from tasting literally hundreds of wines, and my metabolism altered from an influx of rich French dining. I—and my taste buds—get sleepy. It's a professional talent to act awake and alert when necessary.

Our plan on one such wine tour included tasting wines throughout the Loire Valley, starting at the Atlantic Ocean and traveling relentlessly east. We would eventually end up in central France, the far eastern edge of the Loire River, only 75 miles (120 km) from Paris.

Sauvignon Blanc dominates these regions, and the wines possess explosive acidity, citrus, and flavor. The name tells you much of what you need to know about these wines. Sauvignon is a conjunction of two French words, *sauvage*, which means "savage," and *vigne*, or "vine." *Blanc* signifies a white grape. The name suits this grape perfectly. It grows wild and lush, and wine growers spend much of their time trying to slow down and tame it. Grapes that grow like weeds taste like weeds too, green and stemmy, like spinach or celery. That's not always considered good.

However, unknown Loire towns such as Quincy (pronounced con-SEE), Menetou-Salon, and Rouilly produce compelling Sauvignon Blanc that deserves a higher profile.

Wine Suggestions: Sauvignon Blanc

Domaine Mardon Quincy, France
Super balanced between fruit and acid, with an exciting, zippy bite, this is almost viscous.

Domaine de Chevilly Quincy, France
It has mind-bending vibrant green aromas, and is grassy, oily, and juicy lemon-lime.

Silice de Quincy, France
Another flavor of Quincy, this golden-colored wine has low acid and high oaky flavors. Vanilla comes through more than anything else. This is unusual for a Sauvignon Blanc, except for those from California.

Domaine de Reuilly, France
This wine possesses soft, round aromas, with a little bright grassiness, and flavors of mineral water and herbal notes on the tongue. It has a great bite, and tastes of round, ripe, intense fruit.

Jean-Michel Sortie "La Commanderie," France
Tremendous perfume, herbal aromatics, and soaring acidity characterize this wine. It's wonderful in the high end, but with a deep base of concentrated juice.

Flinty, stony soils, typical of the eastern Loire, approach the wine cellars of Sauvignon Blanc producer André Dezat in Sancerre, France

Recipe: Potato Gratin

IN HIS EXCELLENT BOOK, *Wine-Taster's Logic*, Pat Simon explores the biochemical reactions that occur between a forkful of steaming food, a cool glass of wine, and this crazy thing called life. For the scientific, it all boils down to a clash of pH levels between food and wine, which are typically acidic, and the human mouth, which is just the opposite, or basic.

For the romantic, of course, that's not good enough. What about all the parts of food that don't lend themselves to easy categorization? Where, for instance, do those delicious half-burnt peaks and edges of potato gratin fit? These crispy bits form an edible frame around the gratin's creamy, cheesy middle, and they provide the crunchiness that prevents the dish from becoming baked potato goo.

2 tablespoons (28 g) butter

8 large potatoes, sliced the long way, about a coin's thickness

1 large onion, thinly sliced into rings

1 cup (235 ml) milk

1 cup (235 ml) chicken or vegetable broth

Salt and ground black pepper, to taste

½ pound (112 g) shredded Swiss cheese

½ pound (112 g) grated smoked Gouda (or plain Gouda)

Preheat the oven to 375°F (190°C).

Melt the butter in a large baking dish or cast-iron skillet on top of the stove. Arrange in alternating layers potatoes, then onions, then back to potatoes, and so on, ending with a layer of potatoes on top.

Add the milk and broth to the dish and increase the heat until the mixture bubbles. Cook for 15 minutes.

Turn off the heat, add salt and pepper to taste, and top with a mixture of the two cheeses. Bake in the oven for 45 minutes, or until the top of the gratin turns a nice brown.

YIELD: Serves 8

Wine Pairing: Willm Gewürztraminer
FRANCE

This is a bargain Gewürztraminer from Alsace, right on the France-Germany border, full of ripe pear and melon flavors, much soft acidity, and that unique rose water aroma for which Gewürztraminer is famous. A little less expensive and also delicious is Willm "Gentil," a white blend that goes a long way toward explaining why France and Germany have fought over this turf for the past millennium.

The Oregon Wine Trail

WHEN YOU TALK ABOUT wine in Oregon, you talk almost exclusively about Pinot Noir. Yes, Oregon produces some extremely good Pinot Gris, which you'd expect as a cousin of Pinot Noir, as well as Chardonnays and Rieslings. The rest of Oregon's grapes combined do not amount to the Pinot Noir the state grows.

Oregon's most successful vineyards lie in the west, close to the Pacific, where the ocean keeps the clouds and rain away from the coast. The vineyards sit miles south of Burgundy in latitude, so Oregon's Pinot Noir gets a bit more solar radiation and more complete ripening than Burgundy does, but it's nothing like California 700 miles (1,125 km) to the south.

Oregon wine making began in the 1840s, halted in the early twentieth century during Prohibition, and resumed in earnest in 1965, with the first plantings of Pinot Noir, Chardonnay, and Riesling. The initial criticism of Oregon as a wine-growing region was its weather: too cold, too wet, too cloudy. Wisely, winemakers there focused on Pinot Noir, a grape that thrives in precisely this environment.

In the 1960s, as the vines matured, the wines started to exhibit real character. Vineyard practices and wine making improved steadily, and a decade and a half later, the wine world began to take notice, especially of the Pinot Noir. Eyrie Vineyards won the 1979 Wine Olympics Pinot Noir competition staged by French wine and food magazine *Gault Millau*. Oregon Pinot Noir joined the ranks of high-quality international wine.

The Legend of Dom Perignon

ACCORDING TO LEGEND, blind French monk Dom Perignon accidentally "invented" the first Champagne. A batch of his white wine started a spontaneous second fermentation in the bottle, and when he tasted it, he is said to have exclaimed, "Come quick, I am tasting stars!" (See Day 23 for Champagne and sparkling wine recommendations.)

Winemakers in northern Italy produced sparkling wine a thousand years before Dom Perignon's time, but by a much different process. They made ancient sparkling wine in winter, and allowed it to freeze in the middle of the fermentation process, trapping carbon dioxide bubbles in the frozen wine. Come spring, when the wine thawed (after

being transferred into much smaller barrels), the result was a gentle, bubbly wine with easy fruit and low alcohol. Today's Prosecco, Moscato d'Asti, and Spumante descend from these original sparkling wines.

Like so many great stories that have long lives, the charming and compelling details of the legend of Dom Perignon come apart with prodding. Saint-Hilaire, a monastery in southwest France famous for its sparkling wine, claims to have record of a visit by Dom Perignon years before he allegedly made the first Champagne. Brief research shows that Dom Perignon didn't go blind until the end of his life, long after the star-tasting story.

Your Wine Journal

As you experience new tastes, visit wineries near and far, share a new bottle with friends, or discover a bit of history about wine that intrigues you, write down these thoughts so you can keep a vibrant record of your wine life. Use your journal to jot down varieties that surprised you and the wines you used to toast a special occasion. By journaling your adventure, you can revisit exciting experiences with wine.

You don't need a special book to document your thoughts, but creating a personalized journal will make your writing time more special. Why not decorate the front of a composition book or plain journal with favorite wine labels? Inside, your journal can contain much more than words. Save labels and maps of wine countries. Include photographs. You can even choose a theme for your journal: a tour of grapes as you try each one in the alphabet, wine-related travel, favorite wines and when you drank them, and so on.

So many have written so much about wine—yet there's so much more for you to write! Here are some journal prompts to get you started:

• What winery would you like to visit someday and why? How would you plan your day there?

• When did your interest in wine begin? Why? Was it a variety you tried, an event you attended, a trip you took, a person who influenced you?

• What is your favorite wine ritual?

• Do you remember which wines you drank at important celebrations in your life? What were they and what about them do you remember?

• What is the most surprising wine you tasted and why? Did you ever buy it again? Why or why not?

• What was your biggest wine splurge?

Vines at Bodega Otazu in Navarra, Spain

Never Judge a Wine by Its Bottle

FROM THE OUTSIDE, the bulbous, inelegant, bottom-heavy liter jug screams cheapness and makes no real promise of quality. Even if a wine salesman convinces you to buy it, your expectations can't really fall any lower. The wine inside—in this case, Three Thieves Zinfandel—actually tastes much better than the squat little moonshine bottle and its screw cap imply, but who dares taste it seriously?

In many markets, any wine container other than a standard 750—three-quarters of a liter—is the kiss of death. Even classy, double-bottle magnums have a hard time selling. There's something about the nonstandard format that hurts a wine's value in consumers' eyes.

New forms and ideas—artistic, scientific, philosophical—always meet resistance. With wine bottles, the form is literal, but its message can be misunderstood. Just as people resisted screw-cap closures initially because the message of this cap once indicated "low-quality wine inside," and then slowly but surely came to accept them, they will eventually accept new bottling forms.

Bocksbeutel

jug

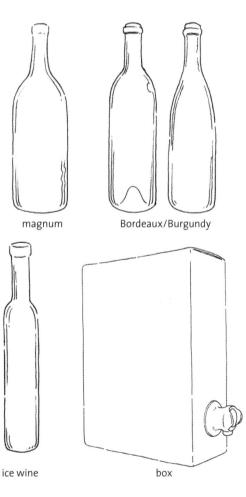

magnum

Bordeaux/Burgundy

Champagne

Riesling

ice wine

box

The Perfect (International) Host Gifts

WINE WAS, IS, and always will be the perfect all-around, internationally appropriate gift. However, you must gift wine appropriately, especially when gifting it across cultures.

Don't, for example, bring a California Cabernet to Bordeaux, a French red Burgundy to Oregon Pinot Noir country, or a Virginia Sangiovese to Italy. You risk saying something with your wine gift that gets lost in translation.

You may mean to say, "This is one of my favorites and I thought you would find it interesting," but instead, you end up saying, "Now this is what this grape should be." The sentiment can come out wrong in spite of itself.

Here's what to do instead: Bring your region's local specialty, and present it as such. What's native to one wine lover but unknown and not grown in another's region will almost always be appreciated.

Wine, Food, and Science

IT'S ONE THING TO accept wine and food into your life as an enjoyable, sensual experience. But learning about the biochemical connection of pH between the acidic wine and the alkaline tongue may squelch the magic.

The true gourmet knows exactly what's in a dish and can still love it. This explains tripe (cow stomach), haggis (sheep innards), and raw oysters. "Fleshy," "briny," and "gritty" sound tasty in reference to a chilled oyster, but they may be grounds for sending a different dish back to the kitchen.

Science and chemistry lie at the root of what makes many traditional wine and food matches so great. Take the old adage, "Red wine with meat." Scientifically, you could rephrase that as, "Tannin with protein."

Tannin is a family of compounds found in grapes' skins and seeds. If you grind a grape seed between your teeth, you get a bitter drying sensation caused by tannin. Red wines turn their red color from being fermented with their red skins; therefore, they have a high concentration of tannins. Biochemically, tannin binds with protein—something that's in abundance in red meat.

Burgundy Versus Bordeaux

DIVIDING THE WINE WORLD into tidy, easy-to-comprehend categories is a shortcut to understanding and remembering wine. You can divide by grape (e.g., Zinfandel versus Cabernet versus Syrah), by geography (e.g., California versus New Zealand Pinot Noir), or even by style (e.g., oaked versus unoaked Chardonnay).

One classic wine distinction is between red Bordeaux and red Burgundy. These are the two most famous French wine regions. Bordeaux is in western France bordering the Atlantic Ocean; Burgundy lies inland, in east-central France. Their climates differ greatly, and they map pretty directly to specific grapes.

Red Bordeaux produces Cabernet Sauvignon and Merlot; red Burgundy produces Pinot Noir. They sit at two ends of the red-wine spectrum: dark-red Cabernet versus light-red Pinot, wood versus fruit, earth versus sky. Red Bordeaux fans applaud the hugeness of their wines, while red Burgundy fans extol finesse. The rivalry, disturbingly similar to the "tastes great/less filling" beer debate, has been going on for centuries.

To be taken seriously on the world stage, New World winemakers must make either a world-class Pinot Noir, Cabernet, or Cab-Merlot blend. Anything else is lovely, but one of these red Bordeaux or red Burgundys is the master's thesis presented and defended—simultaneously a test and a tribute to what wine classicists tell us about great wine.

Wine Lover, Teach Thyself

WHEN PEOPLE SAY they don't like Bordeaux or Burgundy or Riesling, the best advice is usually, "You need to drink more Bordeaux or Burgundy or Riesling." If you are not crazy about Italian wine—is there such a person?—the first step toward changing that is intentional tasting. Think of it as a wine immersion program.

Deliberately drink more Italian wine by buying from the Tuscany section of your favorite wine shop until you do find something you like. It's also about finding a frame of reference for the wine, so you know its characteristics, the flavor spectrum, and so on.

Nervous to try this alone? Befriend someone in your favorite wine shop who can help you arrange your own wine-tasting program. Pick one grape or wine region a month, and buy only from that section of the store. Next month, select a different grape or region. Keep detailed notes of all of your wine tasting, so that by the end of the "curriculum," you've assembled a great many personal observations.

Red wine being poured into a glass at MoS Café in Sydney, Australia

Stock Your Bar on a Budget

Maybe you're hosting guests this weekend or just building up reinforcements at your home. Splurging on a special bottle is fine from time to time, but you shouldn't have so many pricey bottles that you feel guilty opening one to enjoy with pizza or burgers. When hosting a large crowd, economical wine purchases are a must.

Many people collect value bottles these days. Finding a fabulous wine at a value is like nabbing designer jeans at half price. It's exciting to un-earth a great one that doesn't strip your budget. And it's freeing to uncork a wine that doesn't need special permission to be consumed.

But how do you know whether a value wine is solid or swill? Let a few geography lessons guide you toward the good stuff:

GO SOUTH AMERICAN

Argentina and Chile put some great, affordable wines on the shelf that taste richer than their price tags let on. Why? These countries have readily available, cost-effective land and labor.

Essentially, winemakers can make more for less and then charge less for more. Look for more Argentinean Malbec, already an international favorite, plus the still undiscovered Torrontes, which tastes like a G'vertz meets Sauvignon Blanc flavor mash up. Chile grows Carmenere, a minor French Bordeaux variety that has flourished in South America. It reminds people of a spicy, rustic Merlot.

SPEAK SPANISH

Spanish winemakers are experimenting an awful lot these days, especially those in the foothills of the Pyrenees Mountains (in Navarra) where French grapes grow on Spanish soil. They churn out crisp, clear, unoaked Chardonnays that are affordable and memorable.

LOOK FOR CALIFORNIA DEALS

The wine regions in California today turn out value wines that match the quality of more expensive competitors. Labels to watch include Round Hill Merlot and Four Vines Naked Chardonnay.

Chardonnay's Butter and Oak

A delicious glass of Chardonnay wine has at least two components present: malo and oak.

Malo (short for malolactic fermentation), a process induced during wine making, converts malic acid—think Granny Smith apples—into lactic acid, the same acid in milk, butter, yogurt, ice cream, and the like. Malo adds flavor compounds to wine that translate into buttery, creamy flavors. It imparts oiliness to a wine's mouthfeel that makes even a white wine feel big and not thin.

Oak, literally oak in wine transmitted by fermentation and aging in two sets of oak barrels before

bottling, gives wine flavors such as toast or a toasted marshmallow. There's a whole science to oak aging, from issues surrounding grain in the wood to ratios of gallons to square feet of wood exposed to juice.

Malo and oak typically serve wine well, especially Chardonnay. When Australian vintners started making unoaked Chardonnay, the wine market responded, "What? But we like oak!"

Next time you sample a new Chardonnay or even an old favorite, tune your taste buds to the malo and oak flavor profiles for a rich wine experience.

Petite Sirah

CALIFORNIA HAS A WAY OF taking unknowns and elevating them to celebrity status. Southern California's entertainment industry does it with flesh and bone and good production values. Wine country does it with earth and wood and grapes: unique places, juice you've never heard of, different techniques.

Zinfandel is the most famous grape California has "discovered" so far. Sweet, slightly disrespected white Zinfandel kept many wineries alive for years before wine drinkers fell in love with red Zinfandel. Red Zinfandel's rise in popularity almost rivals the emergence of Aussie Shiraz, though it wasn't quite as immense. Both grapes succeed thanks to novelty, personality, and overt deliciousness, not tradition or pedigree.

Other unknown wine grapes always fall in line to be the next big star: Grignolino (still best in the pink), Cabernet Franc, Mourvedre, Cannonau, Nero d'Avola, and remember you heard it here first, Bourboulenc.

Next in line is Petite Sirah. Neither petite nor Syrah, it is the California name for a southern French red grape called Durif. It flourished in California's heat and sun from the late 1800s on, and the grape ultimately became more popular there than in France.

Old wine families such as Foppiano, Parducci, and Pedroncelli kept heritage vines alive through Prohibition, and today, they lead Petite Sirah in quality and character. New expressions of the grape naturally tend toward the modern: ripeness and concentration are everything, and luckily the juice contains loads of bristly tannins to prop up that art form.

Best of all, plenty of great choices are bargain prices, and although you can spend much more, you generally don't have to. (In fact, many of these wines are generally underpriced, but that's something the sales and marketing folks are working overtime to change.)

Wine Suggestions: Best Bargain Petite Sirah

- Concannon Petite Sirah
- Foppiano Petite Sirah
- Guenoc Petite Sirah
- Parducci Petite Sirah
- Pedroncelli Petite Sirah

If you've never tasted Petite Sirah before, some combination of these five wines will offer you a good, affordable look at the state of this grape today. At one end of the scale falls Parducci, with its rich, ripe, fruitful, approachable style. At the other, Pedroncelli Petite Sirah focuses on structure over fruit, and as a result, tastes like traditional French Syrah. Guenoc and Concannon play the finesse game with wine, resulting in deliciously aromatic, herbal, delicate tastes. Foppiano makes a big, rugged, bodybuilder of a wine, with a broad flavor profile and prices well within shouting range of my budget.

Cooking with Wine

A FRIEND ONCE WENT shopping for "cooking wine," and when a salesperson at the wine shop directed him to a low-price Balkan red, he naturally felt hesitant.

"Won't that taste . . . terrible?" he asked. "Sure," said the salesperson, "but you're just going to cook with it, right?"

"Maybe," he replied, "but mostly, I'm going to drink it while I cook."

Recipes call for anything from a small amount to several cups of wine. You don't have to use an entire bottle of your favorite Pinot Noir for cooking a beef Burgundy, but it is a good rule of thumb to cook only with wine you would be willing to drink, even if it wouldn't necessarily be your first choice.

North Fork of Long Island

ON LONG ISLAND'S North Fork, about a two-hour drive from New York City, there's a cluster of established, excellent vineyards.

If you follow the Long Island Expressway east from New York City, it ends at Riverhead. The island forks and extends into the Atlantic many miles. To the south are the Hamptons, well known for their mansions, summer parties, and celebrities. On the North Fork, more than fifty vineyards and wineries flourish in old potato fields now thick with grapes.

A Long Island wine tour offers a great combination of landscape and weather. The land tilts gently up and to the south, so the sun hits the soil at a direct angle. The ocean effect often holds back inland clouds and rain. This makes the North Fork the state's sunniest part, a condition necessary for great wine and great day-tripping.

Wine touring at its best involves a little serendipity. Once you start wandering from winery to winery, you can just follow your nose. However, there are a few wineries on the North Fork you should not miss.

Bedell Cellars (www.bedellcellars.com): A real pioneer on the North Fork, Kip Bedell makes great wine. Go for the Alsace-style Gewürztraminer and the ripe, chocolaty Merlot.

The Lenz Winery (www.lenzwine.com): Eric Frey is another long-toiling winemaker who has much to show for his efforts. From sparkling wines to Gewürztraminer and Chardonnay, Lenz wines represent variety and quality.

Pellegrini Vineyards (www.pellegrinivineyards. com): This is probably the most modern, photogenic winery on the North Fork, and the wine's tasty, too! Be sure to tour its picture-perfect wine cellar when you visit.

Pindar Vineyards (www.pindar.net): If you are lucky, entrepreneur/owner Herodotus Damianos will be in the house and giving tours. Plan to spend at least an hour standing in this vineyard's vast sunflower field soaking up the rays.

Wine: The New Health Food

IN JANUARY OF 2002, Antonio Todde of Sardinia died at age 112. He was not only the world's oldest documented living man at the time but also the oldest living self-proclaimed wine lover.

Todde consistently credited his tremendous longevity to wine, especially red wine. One obituary quoted him as saying, "Just love your brother and drink a good glass of red wine every day." With this kind of advice, I frankly find it hard to argue. It's the sort of statement proclaimed by wine lovers—especially after they've had more than one glass of red wine.

More than a mountain of medical evidence exists to prove pretty much anything when it comes to wine and longevity. When I look at the numbers without the burden of needing to draw a respectable scientific conclusion, I see that people who can maintain a strictly moderate wine diet for many years live almost a decade longer than people who drink with abandon, or those who don't drink wine at all.

In the end, it's the moderation that's essential, not the wine. That said, ciao Antonio Todde! We remember you as the Italian shepherd you were, drinking red wine in the Mediterranean sun and living long in the process, without paradox.

Wine Mixology

STRETCH THE BOTTLE by using wine as a main ingredient in a mixed drink, and surprise guests by serving signature beverages that feature combinations of wine and liquor, wine and soda, and wine and juice.

At your next party, serve up some of these memorable, easy-to-prepare drinks. Each combines just two ingredients, with equal parts of each, and requires no fruit chopping or additional sugar or flavors.

Mimosa = Sparkling wine (Champagne) + orange juice

Bellini = Sparkling wine (Prosecco) + peach purée

Icetini = Ice wine + vodka

Bloodbath = Chambord (raspberry) + cranberry juice

Bambus = Red wine + cola

Only as Old as It Tastes

THE BEST WINES PERSIST and survive into old age. Like all of us, they don't always do it gracefully. Two persuasive metaphors describe the aging cycle of wines, one romantic, the other cynical.

The romantic metaphor equates wine to a lake, full and smooth. As the lake of wine ages, the water level drops, and the fruit falls away, slowly but surely. Eventually, it reveals rocks and contours of the lake bed that the water kept hidden in its youth. With age, the lake of wine presents a deeper understanding of itself, an understanding with more texture and complexity than in its youth.

The cynical metaphor equates wine with a skeleton, one from a body so long dead the flesh has fallen off its bones, leaving nothing but the bleached shadow of some former self.

Some wine lovers sip the skeletal remains and marvel at what the wine once must have been. Others will gaze at the carcass of a fallen monster of a wine and say, "My, what a tiny, delicate head it actually had," entirely in retrospect.

Extensively aged wines are only so thrilling, though they can have attached sentimentality (when a wine shares your birth year, for example). So few wines actually improve with age that vintage awareness is almost pointless. Most wine lovers buy and drink what's current, regardless of vintage designation. Every now and then, while scouring the close-out bins for something really interesting, vintage information comes in handy. However, most people like their wines fresh and forward.

Bottles of champagne

Germany Beyond Riesling

I COME TO PRAISE German Riesling, not to point out its image problem, being perceived as predominately sweet, and as sweet wine, often misclassified as cheap wine. Sometimes sweetly delicious wines come under suspicion for tasting too good, as if good wine should in some ways taste less delicious, and that's not fair.

German winemakers work overwhelmingly with Riesling grapes, and they do an amazing job of making distinctly different wines from essentially the same starting point. This is their genius, but they do grow other grapes—Scheurebe, Gewürztraminer, Huxelrebe—white like Riesling, and with very different personalities.

Wine Suggestions: Beyond Riesling

Weingut Gysler Weinheimer Holle Silvaner Halbtrocken, Germany

Silvaner—named for the forest—is funky and a little earthy tasting behind the white juicy fruit. It's inexpensive and good with cheese and pork sausages.

Machmer Bechtheimer Stein Gewürztraminer Spätlese, Germany

This superbly rich wine with notes of guava and rose water pairs perfectly with smoked fish.

Weingut Wittmann Scheurebe Trocken, Germany

Thanks to Dr. Georg Scheu, who created the Scheurebe grape in the greenhouse, we have a great white wine that's flowery and herbal.

Weingut Kurt Darting Forster Schnepfenflug Huxelrebe Auslese, Germany

Don't worry about saying the whole name out loud. For your information, "Weingut Kurt Darling" is the winery, "Forster Schnepfenflug," the type of wine, and "Huxelrebe Auslese," the grape. Just remember the grape—Huxelrebe—and enjoy this affordable Sauternes-like dessert wine.

Recipe: Baked Fish with Bouillabaisse Sauce

BOUILLABAISSE IS A seafood stew from Marseille. What I love about this recipe, which evolved from Simone Beck's recipe in *Simca's Cuisine*, is that it simplifies the hard-to-make bouillabaisse component, and concentrates its flavors in a sauce.

For the wine, go for the vinous counterpart: something local yet unique, like one of the famous pink wines from the south of France that brings real body to the glass (like a red), but maintains zip and zing (like a white).

2 tablespoons (28 ml) olive oil

2 large onions, diced

1 large leek, diced

1 can (28 ounces, or 820 g) Italian plum tomatoes

3 garlic cloves, crushed

2 cups (475 ml) chicken or vegetable broth

2 cups (475 ml) dry white wine

2 teaspoons (10 ml) Tabasco sauce (or to taste)

1 bouquet garni (herbs traditionally composed of a bay leaf, thyme, and parsley, tied together or bundled in cheesecloth)

3 pounds (1.4 kg) fillet of halibut, flounder, cod, or other firm white fish

½ teaspoon (3 g) salt

1 teaspoon (6 g) ground black pepper

Heat the olive oil in a large, heavy skillet. Add the onions and leek, and cook slowly for 15 minutes, until they soften.

Add the tomatoes and garlic, bring to a simmer, and cook for another 15 minutes, stirring occasionally.

Purée the tomato-vegetable mixture in a food processor or blender, and return to the skillet. Add the broth, wine, Tabasco sauce, and garni, and simmer for 35 to 45 minutes, until reduced to the consistency of typical tomato sauce.

Preheat the oven to 375°F (190°C). Season the fish with salt and pepper. Pour half of the bouillabaisse sauce into a shallow baking dish. Layer the fish fillets in the dish, and cover with the remaining sauce.

Bring the baking dish to a slow simmer on top of the stove, then bake in the preheated oven for 15 to 20 minutes, until the fish is cooked through. Serve over buttered rice, risotto, or orzo.

YIELD: Serves 6

Wine Pairing:
Domaine du Poujol Rosé
FRANCE

This wine, from the hills of Languedoc along the French Mediterranean, is so dense and ruby colored, you almost have to ask yourself whether it's a very light red or a supremely dark rosé. Very viscous, almost oily on the tongue, it perfectly matches the richness of the fish and sauce.

Yecla, Southern Spain

LOOK AT A MAP OF EUROPE, and you'll see that southern France and southeast Spain form a giant south-facing arc that opens onto the Mediterranean Sea. Regardless of political or geographic boundaries, wine culture along this arc is relatively continuous.

Delicious Grenache and Mourvedre from the south of France grow beautifully even as the names change to Garnacha and Monastrell in Spain. Thanks to decades of bad postwar politics, international trade in Spanish wine remained weak in the twentieth century. The planet is just now seeing great Spanish whites and reds from places other than than Rioja. Superb wine regions, including Valdepeñas, Jumilla, and Yecla, will one day be as familiar.

Monastrell (Mourvedre) is Yecla's principal grape, but the region is newly focused on growing and blending modern Cabernet Sauvignon and Syrah. Blending these, just about the three biggest, most intensely flavorful red grapes, captures the best parts of each: the Monastrell is bright and full of fruit; the Syrah is smoky, full of roasting meat; and the big tannins of the Cabernet contribute an almost architectural structure.

As an aside, in addition to wine making, the other main industry of Yecla, a remote town accessible only by car, is furniture making.

Walter Clore

THE SON OF TEETOTALERS, Walter Clore was also the Father of the Washington State Wine Industry, an official title the Washington legislature awarded to the passionate horticulturalist, viticulturalist, and researcher. Clore (1911–2003) moved to Washington in 1934 after landing a scholarship with what is now Washington State University (WSU) for $500, as the fourth faculty member to staff the WSU Irrigated Agriculture Research Extension Center in Prosser. He stayed for forty years, cultivating a passion for growing fine European grapes and proving to locals that their soil would welcome fine wine-making vinifera grapes.

Clore tested vines to figure out which would grow best where. He performed meticulous research to determine how grapes could successfully grow in Washington.

This he compiled into a book called *Ten Years of Grape Variety Responses and Wine-Making Trials in Central Washington*, which he published in 1976 after retiring from WSU. He also co-authored *The Wine Project: Washington State's Winemaking History* with Ron Irvine.

To Clore's credit, Washington's viticulture expanded exponentially, and today the state is the second largest premium wine producer in the United States, supporting nearly 20,000 jobs. Clore worked as a wine-industry consultant for notable wineries such as Château Ste. Michelle Vineyards, and dedicated his life's work to promoting viticulture in Washington.

To honor Clore, a center in his name, The Walter Clore Wine & Culinary Center in Prosser, Washington, is in the works and will showcase the state's viticulture, oenology, and culinary practices.

Exploring Urban Wineries

YOU DON'T HAVE TO DRIVE to the countryside to experience a winery.

Taking up space in old warehouses and modern retail storefronts are urban wineries—a growing trend that gives city dwellers easy access to an authentic wine-making experience. You won't get a vineyard tour or the escape of traveling on rolling, rural roads, but you will get to taste, see fermenting tanks, learn the process, and in some places, make and bottle your own wine.

Essentially, urban wineries include everything but the vineyard. Instead, they partner with vineyards and commercial wineries that sell grapes. Once the urban wineries receive the grapes, which have been carefully shipped, they process

the fruit into wine by crushing, fermenting, barreling, bottling, and storing right on site.

Urban wineries host tastings and tours, bottle their own varieties, and, on occasion, sell to nearby restaurants. Due to the sheer proximity, an urban location can be advantageous for cultivating relationships with restaurant wine directors. Some urban wineries also act as teaching facilities where professionals teach enthusiasts how to make wine. They process the grapes, turn them into wine, and frequently leave with bottles, even cases, bearing personalized labels. (Talk about a great gift!)

Cork as Medium and Message

AS CORK SLOWLY BUT SURELY disappears from wine bottles—only 5 percent of New Zealand wines still get sealed with cork, and Australian wines aren't far behind—a hint of nostalgia hangs in the air, a yearning for an aspect of a bottle of wine most of us ignored much of the time. Someone unscrews a wine bottle at dinner, and people look at each other sheepishly, as if to ask, "Is that it?" For a moment, everybody feels the palpable absence of occasion, especially compared with the corkscrew ritual, with its physicality and sound effects. In concrete terms, we lose the memento, the wine keepsake you hold in your hand when you leave a restaurant, as well as what's written on it.

Although we think of cork as traditional, it's actually a recent blip on wine's 8,000-year timeline. Cork didn't seal individual bottles until we had individual bottles, which didn't arrive until we could mass-produce them during the Industrial Revolution. Bottle and cork didn't become widespread until the early 1800s.

Often the cork represents the winery's last chance to communicate with its consumers before those very same people taste its wine. Many corks, especially synthetic corks, start off as blank, unmarked canvasses, then get emblazoned with vintage year, winery name, and famous wine regions. Some corks feature elaborate website addresses, toll-free numbers, marketing messages, and provenance. Some offer tasting guides, such as "Think of chocolate."

In most cases, wineries take the high road, sticking to information they think consumers need should the label get washed away or made somehow illegible. Without corks, placing this information firmly in consumers' hands will be harder and harder to achieve.

Malbec

UNKNOWN, UNLOVED, unappreciated, ignored. Those four words sum up the attitude of most winemakers toward a red grape from western France called Malbec. During the past twenty-five years or so, however, this hardy grape has lived the ultimate immigrant success story, flourishing in South America while simultaneously declining in importance and respect at home in Europe. Today, Malbec has found a new home in Argentina (and Chile, to a lesser degree), where it is slowly but surely getting the love it deserves—and kicking some serious bung in the marketplace.

Nomenclature contributes to this grape's decline in the Old World; Malbec has so many different names in France that they mean almost nothing there. The *Oxford Companion to Wine* cites nearly 400 synonyms for the grape (*cot* being the most popular), pointing to how widespread Malbec must once have been.

Growing side by side with the rightly famous Cabernet Sauvignon and Merlot, however, Malbec doesn't stand a chance. These days, it is a minor blending grape in some red Bordeaux wines, and grows in the Cahors region south of Bordeaux. Malbec's real future sits half a hemosphere away, in Argentina.

In South America, Malbec achieves a ripeness and richness completely unlike its old self. It comes out deep and dark in color, almost inky, with ripe plum and berry flavors. The tannins are plenty but velvety.

More than 25,000 acres (10,000 ha) are in production now, mostly new plantings just coming of age. Malbec's New World persona is reminiscent of California Merlot: strong on fruit and structure, amenable to barrel-fermenting and oak-aging, enough tannin to let drinkers know they've tasted something real, but also smooth and user-friendly. The skeleton of South American Malbec may seem red Bordeaux in style, but with chocolate and raspberry dominating flavors, instead of earth and autumn leaves.

Ironically, Argentina gave up on Malbec in the 1980s, going so far as initiating a vine-pull program until only 10,000 acres (4,000 ha) of the grape remained. Just as Argentineans finished the job, wine exports from South America started to grow, illuminating Malbec's potential. Winemakers were left pining for every acre of Malbec they yanked up and planted with the still-immature grapes of the moment.

103

Cheese, Please

WINE IS THE GREAT EXTENDER of grape harvests. Vineyards easily produce tons of grapes per acre, and in the millennia before refrigeration, wine preserved the rapidly rotting fruit load. Cheese serves the same preservative function for milk, with the same delicious results. So it's no surprise that the two go together so beautifully. They have answered the same need—on many levels—for thousands of years already.

France is the undisputed world leader when it comes to cheese. Estimates vary on exact numbers, but the French government has sanctioned at least 400 different French cheeses. Perhaps the same number of unsanctioned cheeses exists as well, so it is impossible to keep them all straight.

Here are some examples of cheese from each place on the spectrum:

Ricotta fresca: Perhaps the lightest of all cheeses. Even farmer's cheese is heavier in density and stronger in flavor. It's made by cooking and cooling the liquid whey (*ricotta*, "to recook").

Chevre: *Chevre* means simply "cheese made from goat's milk." Goat cheese can taste wild and gamey. The goat milk's herbaceous flavor comes through in the cheese as a tangy bite that contrasts beautifully with the fruit flavors of wine.

Fougerus: Named for the local fern that adorns the top of the cheese, fougerus is a member of the Brie family, soft and rich and delicious with white wine. It can stand up to big reds, too.

Parmigiano-Reggiano: This cheese is named for Parma, where the style originated. With age, sugar crystals reform, giving the cheese its trademark crunch.

Fourme d'Ambert: This is France's oldest continuously made cheese, introduced more than 2,000 years ago by the ancient Romans. While it looks extremely blue, it tastes surprisingly mild and buttery.

> To visualize the world of cheese, imagine a spectrum, much like the spectrum of wine color. All the way to the left sits ricotta, then light, flaky goat's milk cheese. Creamy brie is in the middle, with Parmigiano-Reggiano and blue cheese to the right. If you overlay the spectrum of cheese onto the spectrum of wine, the two lined up side-by-side would give you a good sense of which wines go with which cheeses.

Wines of Australia

Wines of Australia, from the long-established vineyards of Victoria and New South Wales to the new wave of cold-climate grapes from Tasmania, are, as Australians like to say, brilliant. Not "brainy" or "over-intellectual" brilliant, but brilliant like a gem or a radiant painting.

Great ripeness, fullness of fruit, intensity of varietal character, and an aggressive pioneer style characterize the continent's grapes. "Pioneer style" implies wines that speak for themselves, true to their own characters rather than a winemaker's or some current world trend.

For example, California winemakers work hard to enunciate individual styles of Zinfandel, from powerful to finessed. But comparable Australian reds resist being tamed. More than one Aussie winemaker has said, in essence, that there's no

point in trying to "engineer" Shiraz this way or that; instead, pick the grapes at the best time, impart a little wood aging, and stand out of the way. These winemakers are content with the fate that a big wine can almost make itself.

You'd never call an Australian wine subtle or sublime. The white wines tend to taste big and rich and round, full of fruit and freshness. The reds taste muscular and direct, with high alcohol content, tannins, and rich color. Best of all, Australian wines work well for beginners and longtime wine lovers alike. The Australian continent, rich in wine with interesting varieties of style and flavor, is currently number nine on the top-ten list of wine-producing nations, ahead of both Portugal and Chile.

Didier Dagueneau

Didier Dagueneau is a vine fanatic, perfectionist, and micro-manager of his vineyard in Saint-Andelain, France, in the Loire Valley, a diverse place best known for its crisp, white wines. Dagueneau, arguably the best producer of Pouilly-Fumé made from Sauvignon Blanc grapes and characterized by its smoky flavors and minerality, was a risktaker, a dedicated vintner who became an international celebrity because of his intense practices and the manner in which he went about the art and science of making wine. He openly criticized neighbors who overproduced, and to prove to the media his tireless commitment to preserving the integrity of Pouilly-Fumé and his vines, he took journalists on tours of his property. He took appellation regulations to the extreme: He pruned, debudded, deleafed, thinned clusters, and maintained low yields.

Dagueneau was less interested in pleasing the masses or following rules than producing the finest wine. He didn't advocate *biodynamie* (biodynamics)—essentially, a supercharged system of organic farming and processing. He used some sulfur, disliked natural yeast fermentations, and focused on making the very best wine by allowing his grapes to guide the process.

Dagueneau died in a small plane crash in September 2008. Joe Dressner of Louis/Dressner selections wrote this about the wine crusader:

What many of us take away from Didier is his total dedication to his vines. Didier started with nothing and became an international celebrity because he brought an insane level of rigor, love, and attention to his vineyard. He was intense and extreme in everything he did, but nothing matched his fantastic devotion to his vines.

Navigate the Wine Menu with Confidence

YOU'RE DINING IN an elegant restaurant: white tablecloth, candlelight, sconces, the works. A piano player tickles the ivories while demure guests carry on quiet conversation. The sommelier, dressed in a tuxedo, stops at your table to present you with a wine menu and answer inquiries about the selections.

Wine *book* is a better term—reading *Ulysses* would probably be less intimidating. But you act smooth, thank him kindly, and return to the list. You study it, looking for a sign, a clue of how to figure out which bottle to order from what seems like a roll call of every wine made in the entire world since the first winemaker harvested the first grape.

Never fear. All you need are a few hints to help you confidently make a selection from a heady wine list that you'll enjoy. (And next time you bring a guest to the restaurant, you can suggest the wine you chose and knowingly rave about its superb quality.) The list is organized one of several ways, and knowing how to navigate each type will help you find the wine you have in mind.

BY COUNTRY

Some wine menus list varieties by country. This is especially helpful in ethnic restaurants when you want to choose a wine that complements your meal. Narrow down your wine selection by country, decide whether you want red or white, then ask your server to recommend a selection. This filters out a great deal of the wine list, and allows you to ask a more specific question as opposed to, "I'm looking for a white." Well . . . from where? (There's nothing wrong with that question; just prepare for some follow-up inquiries from your server to help refine the search.)

BY VARIETY

Lists arranged by variety lump together Merlots, Cabernet Sauvignons, Chardonnays, Sauvignon Blancs, and so on. If you know what type of wine you like, these lists allow you to hone in on the section that most appeals to your palate—and you can simply ignore the rest. (See, that wine list isn't so daunting after all!) From there, consider what you may eat and ask the server to make a varietal suggestion based on your order. Again, you're asking for advice, but narrowing down the options first.

BY BODY

Progressive lists organize wine by body type (e.g., light-bodied, medium-bodied, full-bodied, etc). This is a consumer-friendly way to arrange a wine list because it means that choosing a wine doesn't require knowing which country's you want to drink, which variety you prefer, or even whether you want red or white. You choose the bigness of the wine, and coordinate your wine and meal choices. In general, dishes with higher fat quantities call for fuller-bodied wines. When in doubt, scope out the food menu before selecting your wine. Based on the richness of your meal, choose a wine equal in body so it won't dominate your meal or get lost.

Listening to Wine

I LOVE THE INHERENT flexibility and expandability of language. Unless you know exactly what you want to say—"Small coffee with milk and two sugars," for example—there's leeway, an opportunity to try out different words and combinations of words for different meanings. The language of wine takes this concept to the extreme. A simple transcription of an overheard conversation at a wine tasting is its own complete indictment.

Try listening to wine conversation much the same way a dog must listen to human conversation: without much concern for the words themselves, but with an ear to the overall emotional content. If three people use the word "intense" to describe a wine, for example, the person making the happy face means, "I like it," the person grimacing means, "I hate it," and the third person means anything in between.

We will never know unless we continue the conversation.

A bottle of Château d'Yquem in front of a wine list

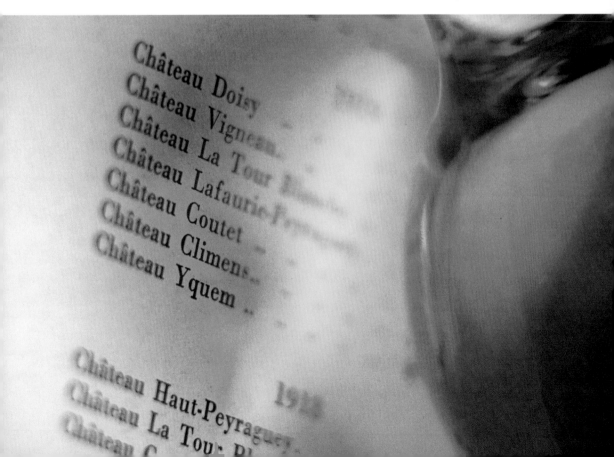

Grüner Veltliner

GRÜNER VELTLINER IS Austria's go-to grape, accounting for about 40 percent of the country's vineyard area, primarily in lower Austria along the Danube River, north of Vienna. The grape has always been a high-production fruit, and because it adapts to many soil types, Austria grows it readily and Austrians drink it plentifully.

Recently, winemakers, in their pursuit to continue raising standards of Austrian wine, have toyed with lower yields and higher ripeness, and they've discovered a grape that can produce intense, concentrated wines that please the palate with exotic tropical fruit, white pepper, lentil, and an appealing vegetable aroma when grown in mineral soil.

Grüner Veltliner acts like a chameleon in some ways, truly soaking in the elements of the soil in which it is grown—a quality it shares with Riesling. Both feature a clear, pure flavor. So in rock soils, Grüner grapes get big; after aging, you can taste the earthy stone. Grapes planted in soils with sandy loam and loess (i.e., glacial dust) produce wine that ages elegantly and becomes more refined with time.

Generally, Grüner Veltliner is a full-bodied, dry wine with up to 14 percent alcohol and a mineral backbone. What all this means to you, dear reader (and drinker), is that you really can't go wrong pairing Grüner Veltliner with most meals. And Austrians always consume this wine with food.

Harvested Grüner Veltliner grapes in Unterloiben, Niederösterreich, Austria

Recipe: Prosciutto and Pineapple

IT IS CLASSIC TO SEE prosciutto lounging atop cantaloupe or honeydew, next to a glass of Pinot Grigio. The contrast between pineapple's tropical citrus and prosciutto's richness gives this dish its personality.

1 whole pineapple, peeled and cored

12 slices Parma prosciutto

Extra-virgin olive oil, to taste

Sea salt, to taste

Halve the peeled, cored pineapple the long way, and cut each half into 6 slices lengthwise. Arrange 2 pineapple slices on each plate.

Arrange 2 slices of prosciutto per plate on top of the pineapple. Drizzle with olive oil and sprinkle with a tiny pinch of sea salt.

YIELD: Serves 6

Hint: Use medium or small salad plates that you've chilled for 1 hour before you prepare this dish. Keep the prosciutto at room temperature. Serve this as an appetizer, with a small piece of thin, toasted bread (crostini). I make the same dish with speck, sort of like prosciutto from northern Italy and southern Germany that's both cured and smoked.

Wine Pairing: Château Ste. Michelle Pinot Gris
UNITED STATES (WASHINGTON STATE)

This Washington State Pinot Gris balances between bright, zippy, citrus flavors and a rich, almost-weighty texture. It's as if you took the crème brûlée character out of Chardonnay, but kept its smooth, slightly viscous texture.

Earth in a Glass

To MAKE GREAT WINE in a place where sunshine is at a premium takes a special kind of grape and a strong commitment to weathering—literally—the winds of change.

Sunny southern Europe and pleasant California make wines from ripeness on which they can almost always rely. They seem blessed. You could almost say that they get their flavors from the sky, in the form of the sun.

Cold northern wine-growing regions such as the Loire Valley depend on a more complex interplay of sun, rain, and soil to produce distinct and marketable flavor profiles. Savennières sits on the north bank, at a bend in the Loire River, a few miles south of Angers and a short drive to Le Mans. This ridge of land faces south, oriented toward the sun, and produces fragrant, perfumed wines that have been famous for centuries.

The white grape here is Chenin Blanc, like in much of the central Loire. There really is no red grape. Chenin Blanc is an ideal cool-climate grape that ripens early and completely. Grown on the complex, ancient soils the river's course reveals, the Chenin Blanc of Savennières represents one of the world's subtlest, most elegant, flavorful white wines.

Wine Suggestions

Château de Chamboureau Cuvée d'Avant Savennières, France
The name *Cuvée d'Avant* translates to "old style," a salute to its classic nature, structure, and balance. It smells mainly of flowers, lavender, lemon, and orange blossom.

Château Soucherie Clos des Perrières, France
Clos means "enclosure" and *perrières* means "stones," so in effect, this wine comes from a rock yard. You can taste this in the wine's focused, resonating minerality.

Domaine aux Moines Roche aux Moines Savennières, France
Now and again, you encounter a wine that smells so good, you almost don't want to drink it, but rather, you want to inhale it. The nose is intense and soaring, herbal and aromatic, smoky and spicy at the same time. That's this wine. Taste it—it's delicious.

Vineyard in Umbria, Italy

Decimus Magnus Ausonius

HISTORIANS WHO STUDY wine making frequently cite Decimus Magnus Ausonius, a figure born in the Bordeaux region in 310, during the days of the Roman Empire. His father was a noted Greek physician, his mother a descendent of aristocratic Gallo-Roman families of southwestern Gaul. In those days, rhetoric—the use of language as a means to persuade—was a popular profession, and Ausonius embraced it as a teacher, opening a school of rhetoric in Bordeaux.

Ausonius eventually earned the highest titles and honors as a tutor to Roman emperor Valentinian before retiring to his estates near Burdigala in Gaul, now the lush wine region of Bordeaux. Allegedly, his estate included land now owned by Château Ausone, a vineyard named for this statesman-poet.

The seventeen-acre vineyard has a variety of 50 percent Cabernet Franc and 50 percent Merlot, and because of its petite size, picking at the optimal moment usually requires just two afternoons. Annual production amounts to little more than 2,000 cases. But despite its small yearly output, this vineyard's wine is one of only two ranked the Premier Grand Cru Classe (A) in the Classification of Saint-Émilion wine. (The other is Château Cheval Blanc.)

The legacy of Ausonius lives on in this fine wine, and historians appreciate his literary works because they give early evidence of large-scale viniculture in the famous Bordeaux wine country. *Very* early evidence. Likely, Ausonius savored the region's grape around the same time the capital of the Roman Empire moved to Constantinople.

Host a Home Tasting

WINE IS BEST SHARED with others, and hosting a tasting party is one way to gather friends and wine lovers, learn more about wine, and expand your horizons beyond the same old bottles. You can approach a party like this several ways, though the prerequisite, of course, includes making a guest list of people interested in trying and talking about wine.

We've all attended parties about drinking and talking masked as tasting parties intended to evaluate wine. If the former sounds like your idea of a party, then hop to it. But to host a true tasting party, ask guests to participate in at least thirty minutes of tasting (and spitting), without noshing before you let the spirits flow.

To set the mood for a formal tasting:

- Print out rating sheets and provide paper and writing utensils for taking notes.

- Set up a wine station on the counter or dining table with each unlabeled wine displayed with number cards. Identify the wines by number until the unveiling at the tasting's end.

- Invite guests to bring a wine. Ask them to cover the label before arriving. Or you can ask a retailer to bag six or eight bottles and remove the capsules from the bottle top. (The bag covers the wine label.) Choose reds and whites.

- Provide a Wine Aroma Wheel (see Day 243) to spark vivid descriptions of each selection.

- Take turns pouring each guest a taste of wine from every bottle, one by one.

- Pass the spit bucket—this portion of the party is for tasting, not drinking. (That will come later.)

- Keep appetizers under wraps until completion of tasting. Food can alter wine's taste, and because you and your guests will not imbibe (at least not until later), it's not necessary to soak up the alcohol with snacks.

Blind tasting at a party always generates interesting results, including a potentially surprising wine of the night. Tasting without seeing the label or knowing a wine's reputation allows you to approach each with a completely open mind. For example, you may discover that the budget white tastes better than the splurge bottle with the fancy label. To really create a blind testing environment, use opaque glasses, pour the wines for guests so they do not see the color, and ask everyone to sip and spit without peeking. People may actually mistake a red for a white.

After dedicated tasting time, reward your guests by enjoying the wines and pairing them with foods. Guaranteed, everyone will learn something new.

Party Prep

What you'll need:

- Plenty of wineglasses—two or three per guest (you may wish to consider renting them)

- Several bottles of wine

- A wine aroma wheel

- A rating sheet for each guest

- A notebook for comments, or notepads for guests to record their thoughts

- A bucket (or two) for spitting out wine (an ample-sized bowl works fine)

- A cheese platter and other goodies for after the tasting

Putting Cork to the Test

IN A STUDY CONDUCTED BY Hogue Cellars in Washington State, during a four-year aging period, screw-cap closure wines outperformed cork or synthetics.

A panel of tasters found a few interesting patterns. First, synthetic cork wines tasted consistently oxidized. In other words, air had gotten into the wine after corking. Synthetic cork, like natural cork, leaks but apparently worse. Second, the panel concluded that for both reds and whites, screw-cap wines maintained fruit and tasted less developed and relatively fresh. In addition, they weren't "corked" (tainted by TCA [2, 4, 6-trichloroanisole]).

The next year following the study, Hogue Cellars planned to bottle 70 percent of its production in screw caps—a ringing endorsement of not only the winery's own research but also an indicator of trends to come. Corking may be a quaint, 300-year-old tradition, but corked and funny-tasting bottles of wine can wear on wine lovers.

Ice Wine

ICE WINE, ONE OF THE great exotic treasures of the wine world, is so novel and extreme that it almost doesn't taste like wine, but more like a rare honey or the sweet, otherworldly nectar of ambrosia.

After harvesting everything else in the vineyard, winemakers leave their ice wine grapes on the vine until the first hard freeze—usually late November or early December in the northern hemisphere, and May or June in the south—and then pick the frozen grapes.

In some ways, this is the ultimate late-harvest wine, because the grapes have to come in before they thaw (after that, they turn to mush), so winemakers often conduct the harvest in the middle of the night.

Once the sun rises to warm up the vines, it's too late. One German winemaker confessed that he made ice wine every year except 1996, when his alarm didn't go off and he overslept.

Because ice wine grapes hang on the vine for a month or so longer than the regular harvest, they're increasingly susceptible to the hazards of vineyard life: hail, birds, mold, clumsy tractor drivers, you name it. Risks are high, labor is intense, and yields are tiny. But it's usually worth it. Even though ice wine can be astronomically expensive, every wine lover should seek it out when possible.

Days of Wine and Chocolate

ALL FERVENT WINE LOVERS need to explore other palate regions on occasion. Humans cannot live by wine alone. Sometimes, your family, friends, and loved ones simply need a break from relentless wine talk. Tasting new foods takes you out of the familiar and into the shoes of novice gourmets. Consider attending a chocolate-tasting class.

At the beginning, you may feel like a philistine in love with obviously delicious chocolate that the experts know tastes too good to actually be any good. Soon you'll read chocolate labels like people used to read album liner notes. You'll aspire to raise your cocoa percentage, where varietal components reside. Talk of terroir, microclimates, and varietals fly fast and furious, making you feel right at home.

Like wine, the market for upscale chocolate has widened, moving the complexity of flavors to the forefront. With that, consumer confusion has increased, too. The answer, as it is so frequently in the similarly complex wine world, is to read the label, both front and back.

Caroline Yeh, owner of Temper Chocolates in Boston, leads a class that begins with the introduction of Toscano Brown, Toscano Black, Madagascar, Trinidad, and the much sought-after "old tree" Chuao. The two Toscano chocolates were blended chocolates for the same reason winemakers blend wines: to achieve balance between different flavor profiles, and to maintain consistency between harvests.

Wine and chocolate are a great match, and what you learn about one can apply to the other. When you go for cocoa, taste with the wine lover's palate, apply the same standards, and look for similar characteristics you seek in wine:

- Texture: Is the chocolate smooth or rough? Oily, buttery, or creamy? What's the feel of the chocolate in your mouth?

- Finish: Does the flavor disappear quickly or does it linger and last? For how long does it linger?

- Complexity: What's the flavor? Is it one note or many? How do the flavors combine?

Being a chocolate connoisseur is a rich pastime that you can enjoy on a reasonable budget and that will only add to your epicurean resume.

Saint-Émilion, Home of Merlot

THE STEEP SLOPES and deep limestone terrain of Saint-Émilion, situated on the right bank of the Dordogne River in southwest France's Bordeaux region, is supple soil for growing Merlot grapes. Timing also has much to do with why Saint-Émilion has embraced Merlot. The area receives frost earlier than its neighbors, and Merlot ripens faster than Cabernet Sauvignon.

During a visit to Saint-Émilion, you'll feel like you've walked back in time, with structural evidence of the city's centuries-old past all around you. The city was named for a Benedictine monk, Émilion, who arrived there in the eighth century to live as a hermit. But his affect on the townspeople prompted them to name the city after him. During those early days, Saint-Émilion was a center of religious life and, eventually, commerce. It is home to Europe's greatest monolith church, which monks created during a 300-year period by carving the structure from a single, enormous piece of limestone.

Much effort went into protecting the city, with walls built around it, a moat dug, gates erected, and a king's tower raised to prevent the wars that marked the region during the thirteenth through sixteenth centuries from reaching Saint-Émilion. None of this worked. The town was looted, then abandoned during the French Revolution in 1879. It remained virtually empty for a hundred years.

But then wine opportunists recognized Saint-Émilion's fortunate location in Bordeaux and traders began to flock there. Residents began to restore the town, and today it is a travel destination with more than 1,200 châteaux in the surrounding countryside. Eleven of the thirteen highest-rated properties are just steps away where the rugged, limestone topography makes an ideal home for Merlot.

Vines near the town walls in Saint-Émilion,
Gironde, Aquitaine, France

Gallo's Comeback Kids

IN FAMILIES, THE OLD saying goes that everything skips a generation, both affliction and genius. After Prohibition in the early 1930s, brothers Ernest and Julio Gallo started a winery that would grow into one of the planet's largest. The Gallo brand's expansion paralleled the arc of the growing appetite for wine in the United States.

In the early days of this winery, the Gallo name became synonymous with cheap, bulk wine, cementing the brand's reputation as a jug winemaker. From 1970 on, the label was never on the radar screen of fine wine lovers. When Gallo launched a pricey (for the winery) Estate line in 1993, people mocked, finding the use of a regular bottle and traditional label incongruous and the notion of paying even moderate prices for a bottle of Gallo unthinkable.

But this marked the beginning of a generational change at Gallo that saw the emergence of the talented grandkids: Gina as third-generation winemaker and Matt in the vineyard. Immediately, the wines improved, and the winery starting saying so—loudly. It began producing bold Chardonnay and powerful, structured Cabernet under the Gallo name that took its rightful place on the shelf.

At the same time, Gallo began to develop other company-owned labels unencumbered by any name association. Rancho Zabaco, for instance, makes outrageously edgy Zinfandel; Frei Brothers produces a traditional Cab-Merlot; and MacMurray Ranch makes superb Pinot Noir and Pinot Gris, both from vineyard land once owned by actor Fred MacMurray. All are Gallo wines, but you would never know it.

This type of relationship between the giant and tiny vineyards benefits the world of wine in that some lessons learned making these boutique wines could find their way into mainstream operation, potentially improving the quality of millions of bottles of wine. In practical terms, the work of a great generation typically falls flat in the eyes of the next generation, but then gets rediscovered by the one after that. Behind the good wine making and excellent marketing of Gina Gallo, the family brand has been redeemed and is refocused for the twenty-first century.

Non-Wine Gifts for Wine Lovers

YOUR WINE-LOVING FRIEND'S birthday is around the corner. It's the holidays and you're shopping for the man who has it all. You heard your boss is a wine connoisseur, but you are afraid to choose a bottle for her. You need a gift to complement wine, something practical but special. The perfect gift means finding something that the recipient would love to have but would not splurge on. (And splurge doesn't necessarily mean spending tons of money. How many times have you spotted something you want and thought, "What a perfect gift!"?)

A bottomless inventory of merchandise exists out there for the wine lover. Anything that is themed with grapes, appears Tuscan in style, involves opening or corking a bottle, or pertains to entertaining enters fair-game territory. There are knickknacks galore. And there's also plenty of junk. Here are some thoughtful gifts you may consider wrapping up for a wine enthusiast:

BOTTLE COASTER

This is a beautiful wine bottle coaster that doubles as table art. Technically, a wine bottle should never touch a tablecloth. When serving wine to guests, an elegant coaster placed under the bottle is a proper, attractive touch.

UPSCALE CORKSCREW

If the recipient of this gift always relies on a trusty wine key, introducing this gadget to the wine-opening ceremony will be a real treat. Models such as the Rabbit have two gripping handles that latch on to the top of the wine bottle, and a handle that drives the corkscrew into the cork, popping it out in seconds.

DECANTER

A simple, sophisticated decanter dresses up the dinner table and always looks better than the bottle. Whether or not the wine needs to breathe, pour it into a decanter and the drinking experience becomes classier. Seek out interesting designs that complement your friend's style.

DRIP CATCHER

These gold or silver metal rings lined with felt slip easily over the top of any wine bottle. Their purpose: to catch drips that slip from the opening as you pour. Now your friend can put away that linen napkin always in use to wipe the bottle of trickling wine.

ICELESS CHILLERS

With an instant chiller close by, your friend will never again have to prepare ahead of time for a party. These chillers bring bottles to perfect temperature in minutes. You select the wine you're about to chill from a database, then the machine does the work of a sommelier.

GRAPE COSMETICS

You can purchase facial products made with grape pips (seeds) bursting with beneficial antioxidants.

GRAPE INGREDIENTS

Vinifera is flour produced from grape skins. Many creative cooking staples use the grape and make interesting gifts for someone who thinks he or she has seen everything wine-related.

SUBSCRIPTIONS

A wine-of-the-month club gives the recipient a gift twelve times each year. The same goes for subscriptions to wine magazines such as *Decanter*, *Wine Spectator*, and *Wines and Vines*.

119

Wine Numerology Phrasebook

THERE ARE ALL TYPES of wine-speak. Here's a quick translation of some of the more common phrases:

"This wine will age for fifteen years."

Translation: This wine is undrinkable today. Wine salespeople tout how well wines will age all the time, but it means nothing to people who plan to drink their purchases this Friday or Saturday night. Any wine that can age for fifteen years is probably at its worst right now.

"They only brought six cases into your state/region/country."

This wine will cost a pretty penny. Hard-core wine lovers go for "boutique" wineries, a concept that, by its nature, means small quantities and high prices.

The limitation alone makes buyers sweat a little and crave a wine in inverse proportion to its availability.

"This winery was founded in 1357."

Old wine, old wineries, old winemakers are all good in the wine business vernacular. On the other hand, young, good-looking winemakers from new wineries photograph better. Go figure.

"They age this wine for two years in wood barrels."

Rarely do those "wood barrels" come from any old wood but are usually Slovenian oak, chestnut, or even old whiskey barrels. The implicit message is that the longer the wine ages in wood barrels, the better the wine and the more robust the flavor.

Cabernet for Carnivores

FOR WINEMAKERS outside of Europe to be taken seriously, they have to produce either Cabernet Sauvignon (the classic red Bordeaux) or Chardonnay (white Burgundy), a preoccupation that dates back to when French wine symbolized the international benchmark of quality. Specializing in a white grape such as Pinot Blanc, Riesling, Gewürztraminer, even a major player such as Sauvignon Blanc is akin to pushing your winery off the edge of the earth.

Here's a classic example. Twenty years ago, Callaway Vineyard and Winery in Temecula, California, just east of Los Angeles, created a line of outstanding heavyweight dessert wines, stupendous Rieslings, and unique, less-aged Chardonnays. Its ad slogan at the time was "White wine: It's all we make." Today, its ads tout red wine—especially Cabernet Sauvignon—for all. It is survival of the fittest, evolution in action.

Two big reds dominate the Cabernet family: Cabernet Franc, grown in northern France, and the more famous Cabernet Sauvignon, grown in southwest France. The two are genetically related; Cabernet Sauvignon is a cross of Cabernet Franc and Sauvignon Blanc.

Once ripened and tamed, Cabernet Sauvignon possesses a unique balance of earth, sky, and wood. It pairs classically with meat, the redder the better, and is famous for its texture, sometimes soft and velvety, sometimes gritty and abrasive, or when at its best, a balance between the two.

Wine Suggestion: Mirassou California Cabernet Sauvignon

UNITED STATES (CALIFORNIA)

Mirassou is California's oldest winemaking family, and the winery produces a full spectrum of dependable, delicious wines. This Cabernet Sauvignon is dark and brooding with date, fig, apricot, and nut flavors.

Recipe: Auguste Escoffier's Favorite Omelette

CONSIDER THE OMELETTE. It's frequently considered a breakfast food, but many European cuisines serve it at the afternoon or evening meal. Auguste Escoffier's tremendous cookbook *Ma Cuisine* lists more than two dozen omelette recipes, yet with only a few of the lighter, simpler offerings intended for a morning meal. Omelette with Beef Marrow, Kidney Omelette, or Truffle Omelette with Foie Gras start a grand meal, not an ordinary day.

An omelette for dinner is more socially acceptable than a glass of wine for breakfast, but the challenge of matching a wine to this dish is still formidable. Because the sautéed macaroni gives this omelette such a smoky, nutty flavor, I automatically think Gewürztraminer (see the pairing suggestion below).

1 ¼ cups (130 g) large macaroni or other Italian pasta (fusili and penne work well)

3 tablespoons (42 g) butter

6 eggs, beaten

Salt and ground black pepper, to taste

Cook the macaroni in boiling water until fairly firm, drain, and let cool.

Heat the butter (or lard such as bacon fat, which tastes delicious but is nutritionally incorrect) in a large frying pan, add the macaroni, and cook slowly until it turns a beautiful golden brown. Add the eggs, season with salt and pepper, and stir well with a fork.

Increase the heat to medium-high and cook until the omelette is just moist on top. Do not fold this omelette, but rather turn and brown it on the other side. To do so, slide the omelette onto a large plate and reverse it back into the pan. When done, serve the omelette on a large round dish. Slice into wedges and serve with steamed asparagus or sautéed greens.

YIELD: Serves 4 to 6

Wine Pairing: Trimbach Gewürztraminer
FRANCE

Don't let the name throw you. This is a French wine from Alsace, a region on the German border near Strasbourg. Rich and viscous, full of pear, peach, and melon flavors, this classic G'vertz comes from a family that has produced wine for centuries. The wine has an aroma of rose water, gardenia, and guava.

Michigan Vineyards

MICHIGAN WINES ARE TOUGH to come by outside of the region, but if you can find them, their quality and character will reinforce your desire to think globally and drink locally.

On paper at least, the midwestern American vineyards around Lake Michigan have everything they need to be successful: a unique and temperate micro-climate moderated by the giant, omnipresent water; a latitude equal to the well-known wine growing region of Bordeaux in France; and people who are committed to high-quality wine making.

The only problem with these delicious Michigan lakeside wines—which is not a real problem but more an image problem—is that they're overwhelmingly white, and they don't get the respect they deserve. It's not fair, unless you can really finesse the issue, that the absence of a strong red wine is a quality problem. Michigan does grow plenty of red grapes, but because the weather is so cold, the white grapes Riesling, Gewürztraminer, Pinot Blanc, Pinot Gris, and others are making some of the midwest's best wines.

Michigan's shore vineyards also boast—if that's the right word—their own quasi-celebrity winery in the form of Ciccone Vineyards, owned by the father of superstar singer Madonna. The wines, I'm relieved to report, are simple Italian-styled whites and reds, un-glitzy and happily Hollywood-free.

Wine Suggestions:
Michigan Favorites
UNITED STATES (MICHIGAN)

Peninsula Cellars Island View Vineyard Pinot Blanc
The Peninsula Cellars produces a tasty Pinot Blanc that's bright and brilliant and smells of pear and apple with a nice zippy, acidic perfume. The color is so light and silvery that the wine's fullness is almost a surprise; it's big, rich, and almost oily, literally mouthwatering from layers of subtle citrus. Island View is a 1 acre (0.5 ha) vineyard that yields only 245 cases of wine—about 3,000 bottles—each year.

Peninsula Cellars Manigold Vineyard Gewürztraminer
Manigold Vineyard represents 2 acres (1 ha) of grapes that yield only 300 cases of wine, but this tiny production is superb. This wine's aromas are rich and interesting, full of rose water, melons, peaches, pears, spice, and cream. It has a great citrus bite at the finish, with a deliciously smooth and viscous texture.

Shady Lane Cellars Sparkling Riesling
This is a wine that makes you wish more wine makers took a chance on making a sparkling Riesling. It's crisp and fruity, kind of snappy like a ripe apple, with good carbonation and a nice flowery perfume. Chardonnay and Pinot Noir make the most expensive sparkling wines on the planet; Riesling just makes the most under-appreciated and delicious.

Young, green Chardonnay on the vine at MacMurray Ranch in
Sonoma, California, United States

Fred MacMurray's Ranch

ACTOR FRED MACMURRAY was in his movie-making prime in the 1940s, acting in three, sometimes four films a year, when he bought what's now known as MacMurray Ranch, site of the Sonoma Showcase Grand Tasting Festival. Film titles with a slightly ominous tone dominate MacMurray's work from this period: *Too Many Husbands* (1940), *Take a Letter, Darling* (1942), *Double Indemnity* (1944). Luckily for wine lovers today, MacMurray invested some of his movie money in a small cottage and some hillside farmland in Sonoma.

He farmed for almost fifty years, and after he died in 1991, his neighbors—the Gallos (see Day 131)—bought it and planted it with grapevines.

Today, MacMurray's daughter Kate lives on the property in a cabin her father built, and she promotes the label's delicious Pinot Noir and Pinot Gris wines.

Each summer, the tidy white house gets dwarfed by the many giant festival tents dotting the property, themselves overshadowed by the oak- and redwood-covered hillsides surrounding the ranch. Walking through the tents, tasting from winery to winery, is like drifting through the best "Sonoma" section of the best wine shop on the planet, but better, live and in person with tastings and gourmet food. Surrounding the tents, the MacMurray Ranch grapes sit patiently, months away from harvest, still hard and green. They represent wine we'll drink in a year or two.

Journal Entries, Part I

By now, your journal (see Days 90 + 91 on getting one started) is filling up with memories and musings about wine. Here are some prompts to help you keep your momentum going:

• Have you visited a new winery? Describe that trip. Who did you meet? What did you see? What varieties did you taste, and what were your impressions of each? What interesting fact or bit of history did you learn about the winery? After the visit, do you feel differently while drinking these wines? How so?

• Is there a wine personality you would like to meet? Who is it and why?

• Have you tried any new recipes that pair well with your favorite wines? Jot those down.

• Have you attended some great wine-themed parties recently? What made these parties special?

• What surprises did you encounter during a blind tasting?

• Have you read any good wine-related books lately? How about a review?

• What restaurants have you visited that boast exceptional wine lists? Describe your experiences at each.

• What's the best value wine you have ever tasted and what makes it a standout? Challenge yourself to try new grapes by making a list of those you will try in the next year. Review this list regularly and check them off as you taste each one.

Required Reading: *Wine and War*

IN THE BOOK *WINE AND WAR*, network television reporter Donald Kladstrup and his wife, Petie, chronicle the uneasy and unsettling coexistence of France's wine industry with the country's Nazi conquerors during World War II. The two forces—wine and war—end up sadly compatible, proving that in some places, war is often economics gone awry.

Wine and War is a tale of vintner heroes, frightened, worried families, and wine saved by fake walls so well built that the Germans never spotted them.

Though it is a challenge to stay focused on wine-cellar politics when you know what's happening on the front lines, the story of the wine industry mirrors the climate of the times.

The Kladstrups repeat the old superstition that a bad vintage portends war and a great vintage rewards the war's end, bracketing their tales of wine woe with the weak (if not downright bad) 1939 vintage and the 1945 vintage, legendary even today for its excellence and endurance.

Let Syrah Be Syrah

OH, HOW THE MIGHTY have fallen to marketing, I thought. A California giant has begun calling its California Syrah by the (very trendy) Australian name Shiraz. But when I read the bottle's fine print, however, I saw that it was, in fact, Australian Shiraz under the Ravenswood label.

Much to the winery's credit, Ravenswood got on the Shiraz bandwagon the old-fashioned way: by actually making, bottling, and selling Aussie Shiraz. Many more have taken the shortcut of simply renaming every Syrah they own. Logic reveals the brilliance of this thinking: We make Syrah, people love Shiraz, we love people to love our wine, therefore we'll call everything we make Shiraz.

It's hard to blame them, of course, until the first time you see a Syrah-Shiraz blend on the shelf. Then it becomes easy to blame them. As one winemaker lamented, "Sometimes you eat the marketing folks, sometimes the marketing folks eat you."

Although plenty of wineries are turning their Syrahs into Shiraz these days, many are resisting the allure of popular nomenclature. This represents the difference between a massive relabeling campaign and the resurgence of truth in advertising. The latter is heartening.

French Meals: Dejeuner, Dîner, Frômage, Dessert

ALEXANDRE DUMAS, in his classic b132-1330ok *Grand Dictionnaire de Cuisine* of 1873, laments the passing of the formal multicourse French meal from two or three dozen courses down to just a dozen in his day. The burden of a protracted meal (i.e., more than four or six courses) was too much for even European sensibilities to bear, prompting Edouard de Pomiane to write *French Cooking in Ten Minutes* in 1930 as a tribute to the rapid pace of modern life (see Day 47).

Even with this paradigm shift, a wine lover's visit to the Loire Valley in northwest France can still include tasting dozens of wines and eating two, sometimes three entire meals a day. And in France "meals" go on for hours, course after course, patiently working their way toward coffee (and a cigarette).

First comes an *amuse-bouche* (translated as "mouth joke"), a one-bite tiny taste of an exotic creation. Next is the French entrée, the first course, a small, organized plate of food, flavorful and rich. A white meat course of fish or chicken comes next, followed by a red meat course, and sometimes a simple green salad. At last the cheese course arrives, typically a selection of four to six varieties. Dessert follows, the lighter the better.

The French cheese course, unique among most wine cultures, is often accompanied by its own wine selection (or a splash of the red left over from the meat course it normally follows).

Wine Suggestion: Domaine Dozon Clos du Saut au Loup Chinon

FRANCE

In the middle of the Loire, bracketed by white wine regions to the east and west, Chinon makes rich red Cabernet Franc that conjures spicy aromas of cinnamon, allspice, and vanilla, with bright citrus fruit and soft, toasted oak from fourteen months in the barrel. It also has very little tannin. Serve this with a light meat such as pork or veal, or save it for the cheese course, where its big flavor and soft tannins match perfectly.

Cooperative Spirit: Cantino Beato Bartolomeo

ALMOST EVERY WINE neighborhood in Europe has its own local wine co-op. Grape farmers who may not have the interest or facilities to make their own wine can easily sell grapes to the co-op, which takes on the responsibility for making them into wine and selling it back to the community.

Cantino Beato Bartolomeo, a co-op in the small town of Breganze, about 50 miles (80 km) northwest of Venice, celebrated its fiftieth anniversary in the year 2000 by producing in excess of 160,000 hectoliters of wine, or about 22 million bottles or almost 2 million cases. The bottling plant at the co-op does 10,000 bottles an hour, and it would have had to operate an average of fifty hours a week, every week, just to fill those millions of bottles.

That was not typical for the co-op. Usually, much of the wine leaves Cantino Beato Bartolomeo not in individual bottles but in jugs, barrels, and giant modern personal amphorae that wine lovers bring in and fill up on their own. The storefront of the co-op presents a long row of what look like miniature gasoline pumps that dispense wine. Different grapes cost different amounts, but in general, the alcohol levels set the price—the higher the alcohol, the more expensive the wine. Simply select from red, white, or rosé, and then pump.

Co-ops throughout Europe represent some of the best bargains in wine, but they are normally a local experience, almost never on the tourist itinerary.

Without a Corkscrew?

YES, WINE EMERGENCIES HAPPEN, SO we wine lovers have to be ready to open the occasional bottle of wine without the proper tools on hand. It can be done!

Essentially, there are two ways to do this. The easiest involves pushing the cork into the bottle of wine. Do this slowly and carefully with a blunt object such as the end of a butter knife or a short screwdriver. Be sure to don an apron or wrap a tablecloth around you in case the wine splashes or sloshes (which it inevitably will). If you don't have an apron or a tablecloth, stand way back.

A more refined technique that actually gets the cork out of the bottle requires a small knife such as a paring or cheese knife. Slowly but surely work the knife's blade into the cork until it's well in, about 1 inch (2.5 cm) or so. Twist the knife gently back and forth until the cork starts to turn. By twisting and pulling simultaneously, you can get the cork extracted far enough to get a hold on it.

Although neither technique is graceful, each gives you and your companions the pleasure of enjoying wine, rather than just admiring an unopened bottle.

Vineyard in Napa Valley covered in mustard blossoms

Journal Entries, Part II

DAYS 90 + 91 EXPLAINED how to get a journal started, and last week, Days 139 +140 offered some prompts to get you writing.

Have you leafed through earlier entries in your wine journal yet? Go ahead and peek! Can you see how much you have learned and experienced? We always think we will remember details about trips or names of wines, even goals we have to broaden our wine horizons. But without writing down these thoughts, we often forget them.

Keep writing. Here are some more prompts to keep the momentum going:

• What is the most unusual taste you have encountered in a wine?

• What drinks have you mixed using wine? Jot down these recipes.

• Have you ever made a wine faux pas at a restaurant, a tasting, with friends, or otherwise? How did you recover?

• Do you remember a toast you gave at a special occasion? Write it down.

• If you could make a toast to someone important in your life, who would it be? How would you honor that person? Which wine would you serve, and why?

• Who do you go to when you have questions about wine? How has this person influenced your interest in wine?

• Which bottles do you hope to collect some day? Why?

• Which bottle are you saving, and on what occasion do you expect to open it?

130

Personal Narrative: Oh, Canada

MY WIFE IS CANADIAN. Because of that, I know much I'd never have learned without her, such as which famous musicians are Canadian (for example, jazz genius Gil Evans), how to sing "O Canada" (in English, at least), and how to say "please," "thank you," and "excuse me" all the time. This is a generalization, of course, but Canadian culture is overwhelmingly polite, soft-spoken, and eager to see everybody get along.

When we first met, I didn't completely understand that last bit, especially the soft-spoken part. When I asked her out to dinner the first time, she said, "That would be fine." I interpreted this to mean "fine" in an ambivalent, tentative, take-it-or-leave-it kind of way. Fine, but not great.

Over time, I realized "that would be fine" actually translates into "my heart soars like an eagle." From that moment, I began consciously turning up the volume and intensity of what she said to me until I began to understand her.

My wife has her own personal wine-scoring scale that goes something like this, from lowest to highest.

No: Will not drink it

It's wine: Will drink at least this glass of it

I'd drink it: Would like another glass

Yummy: My heart soars like an eagle

I thought "yummy" was as high as this scale went, but I'm considering adding "Now *that's* good wine" since her discovery of the grape Viognier. If my wife likes a wine, that's good enough for me, but if she actually says so, that's when I pass that wine along to everybody else.

Outdoor bistro in Old Montreal, Canada

Grapes and Weather

WINE GRAPES ARE FICKLE, fragile things. They like sun, but not just any kind—direct sun can burn them, so dappled sunlight works best, but they need a lot of it. They like it warm but not hot during the day, and cool but not cold at night. Grapes need water, but not necessarily rain. The smallest bit of rain at the wrong time can devastate a vintage; a foot of rain at the right time can be divine.

For that reason, wine lovers were naturally concerned about the 2006 late-winter/early-spring rains and flooding in Napa and Sonoma that left three people dead and water 5 feet (1.5 m) high in some towns. Arnold Schwarzenegger, California's governor at the time, estimated 50 million dollars in damage for the region, and the *New York Times* said that it could cost the state 100 million dollars.

As for the grape vines and the 2006 vintage, the floods have had no effect, because the vines essentially shut down during winter. *Decanter Magazine* quoted wine-making legend Warren Winiarski as saying the following about the long-term effects: "The floods will have been inconsequential for the vineyards."

When rain and flooding came at the exact wrong time in southern France in 2002, however, grape farmers had a disastrous harvest on their hands. While trying to decide the best moment to harvest, the farmers suddenly had no best moment, and they lost many grapes to the violent weather. Vineyards that had harvested before the rain fared fine. The rest made do with what they could salvage or buy from others. With the quality of the grapes so low, many wineries made vast quantities of rosé instead of red wine, unintentionally setting the stage for a resurgence of rosé around the world in the decades to follow.

Recipe: Herb Roasted Chicken

ROASTED CHICKEN is a simple recipe improved by the cumulative effect of a few techniques, tips, and secrets (see the sidebar). That and a great bottle of wine.

1 whole chicken (4 pounds [1.8 kg])

1 medium onion, quartered

Cotton string

2 bacon slices, diced

1 tablespoon (15 ml) olive oil

1 tablespoon (3.3 g) rosemary

1 tablespoon (2 g) sage

1 tablespoon (4.5 g) basil

Preheat the oven to 425°F (220°C).

Discard the giblets. Wash the chicken and cut off the tail and wing tips. Place the quartered onion inside the cavity and tie the ends of the legs together with the string. Slide the diced bacon beneath the chicken skin around the breast and legs.

Place the chicken in a medium roasting pan or cast-iron skillet. Drizzle the olive oil over the chicken and sprinkle the herbs on top so they form a sort of coating. Roast for 45 minutes, then reduce the temperature to 325°F (170°C) and roast for another 30 minutes. Adjust the final cooking time by the weight of the chicken, adding 10 minutes per pound for birds heavier than 4 pounds (18 kg).

YIELD: Serves 4

Roasting Tips

Trimming: Snip off the tail and the wing tips just above the last joint. In a hot oven, the wing tips can get charred and burnt, and at a certain temperature, the tail may impart a nasty aroma. Also, remove the fat from the torso.

Stuffing: Stuffing the cavity of the chicken with onion or celery doesn't add flavor but ensures that the chicken cooks evenly from the outside in. An empty cavity creates a hot center while the chicken roasts, which tends to dry out the bird. Stuff the chicken beneath the skin to add flavor.

Wine Pairing:
Pouilly-Fuisse La Roche
FRANCE

Pouilly-Fuisse (pronounced poo-wee fwee-SAY) is a classic white Burgundy from France that is 100 percent Chardonnay. In the French style, it is light on the oak and fruit and strong on mineral flavors and bright acidity. Swish it around in your mouth with a bite of chicken and herbs, and you'll feel the magic.

Alsace

THOUGH STRONGLY INFLUENCED by its neighbor, Germany, the Alsace region in northeast France produces decidedly different Rieslings known for their elegant, dry character. German whites, on the other hand, are sweeter, with lower alcohol content. In Alsace, you'll nosh on sauerkraut and take in the French-German charm of this unique region of France. There is plenty of crossover, which makes sense because Alsace was actually part of Germany between 1871 and 1919.

When it comes to wines, however, Alsace and Germany speak different languages. It all derives from the processing after harvest. In Alsace, Riesling grapes are fermented to bleed every last bit of sugar. In Germany, a small bit of naturally sweet unfermented grape juice returns to the mixture. Dry, Alsace Rieslings have an alcohol content of 11 or 12 percent; more saccharine German Rieslings are 8 to 9 percent alcohol. Another character-builder for Alsace wines is the old, inert oak barrels in which wines are produced, imparting a richer flavor.

Alsace produces mostly white wine from four key grape varieties: Riesling, Gewürztraminer, Pinot (Klevner), and Tokay (Pinot Gris). Other grapes include Muscat and Silvaner, which is often blended with Riesling to produced Edelzwicker. This red Pinot Noir grape is also used to make rosé such as Clairet d'Alsace, Schillerwein, and a Pinot-Riesling blend called Crémant d'Alsace.

Long, narrow Alsace has diverse terroir and vineyard climates, thanks to the Vosges Mountains that keep the region dry and protected from cold Atlantic weather. There are steep, south-facing vineyards planted in this region's thin, rocky soil. Foothill vineyards have complex, deeper soils with mineral deposits, and also benefit from warmer temperatures. There are fewer vineyards along the Rhine River Valley with its silty, sandy soils. The mountain soils tend to produce elegant wines with lower acidity, and foothill soils lend a floral character to the wines.

Tour the region by the rural Alsatian Vineyard Route, which stretches from Wissembourg in the north to Thann in the south, and east to Mulhouse and is divided into four regions. You'll see medieval wine-producing villages on the slope of the Massif des Vosges.

Émile Peynaud and Modern Wine Making

ÉMILE PEYNAUD'S LIFE as an influential wine expert marked the transition from premodern to modern wine making, first in France, and then in the rest of the world. He spent much of his professional life at the University of Bordeaux, in the Enology department, and after World War II, he began to urge French winemakers toward three changes: riper fruit, softer tannin, and new oak barrels. His French colleagues disregarded him, but generation after generation of New World winemakers from California, South America, Australia, and other places did exactly what he said, and today's fruit-forward, oak-aged wines are legacies of his vision.

Peynaud wrote two important books. *Knowing and Making Wine* is practically scripture in the wine world, though for the average wine lover, it's dense and academic.

The Taste of Wine explores the experience between wine and people much more, and it's less dry. Peynaud's realization that a bottle of wine must taste good only once, on the day it's consumed, gave rise to flavorful, fresh, fruit-forward wine making. He was the first champion of slow, cool, controlled fermentation, a technique that preserves ripeness and juiciness in wine, and cellar hygiene practices that are standard today.

When he died in 2004 at age ninety-two, the French wine world was struggling against challenges from the New World, which, thanks to being more attuned to Peynaud's modern approaches from the beginning, flourished against the European traditionalists he fought.

The aging cellar at Château de Beaucastel, Domaines Perrin Courthézon, Courthezon Vacluse, France

Wine Tours by Bike

ON A BIKE TOUR through wine country, you can truly immerse yourself in the vineyard surroundings for a sensory experience quite different than traveling by car. You'll pedal up and down rolling hills and through vineyard trails. You'll smell the sweet wildflowers and hear nature's voices. On two wheels, you get to *feel* wine country.

Many wine regions have companies that provide bike tours or rentals if you want to go solo. You can take a group tour with a guide, or leave with a map in hand, money for tasting fees, and a backpack with some reinforcements in case you get hungry. Generally, bike tour companies map out routes according to difficulty, so novice bikers can rest assured that the trails they ride will not wear them out after one winery stop.

Here are some tips to consider before booking a bike tour or renting bikes to tour wine country on your own:

ASK A LOCAL

If you're unfamiliar with the wine region, call the visitors bureau and find out about available bike tours. Usually a couple different tour company offer options, so seek recommendations.

MAKE A PLAN

You can rent a bike and design your own itinerary, but make sure you take the time to actually plan. That way, you can enjoy the trails and make plenty of stops. Tours are a solid idea if you want to mentally check out and let someone else do the guiding. (You'll still be doing some work with all the pedaling.)

PACK SNACKS

You'll probably run into country stores that sell cheese, bread, and other snacks. But don't count on it. Pack some reinforcements so you can keep on pedaling. Some bike tour companies offer packages that include a boxed lunch at a particular winery. Also ask about services that pick up purchased bottles. These are readily available.

TAKE YOUR TIME

You chose the scenic route, so savor your time on two wheels. Soak in the environment and write about this in your journal so you can revisit the experience for years to come.

History and Hedonism

REGULAR, SENSIBLE PEOPLE look on agog when wine lovers taste wine, wondering about the ritual's origin and meaning. In fact, the process of technical wine tasting has its roots in history as well as hedonism.

We live in an unusually clean and sanitized era, and our world economies don't ship too much (verifiably) bad wine around the globe. But imagine it's the year 1125, and your medieval host offers you seven-year-old homemade wine stored in the cellar, a hole in the ground. You won't sling that wine (poison) into your mouth heedlessly; you approach with caution.

A skeptical, unconvinced attitude, followed by some ritualistic sniffing and smelling, might keep you from putting any bad wine in your mouth. This is the practical side of technical wine tasting, but ironically enough, it also intensifies the tasting sensation of good wines that pass the test, thus contributing to your hedonism.

Chardonnay with Attitude

CALIFORNIA CHARDONNAY SEEMS to be wandering in the wilderness right now. Wine lovers shun it actively, yet slurp down untold millions of gallons (and liters) each year. California Chardonnay breaks the first rule of serious art: it's just too popular. In spite of being yesterday's wine news, it continues to reign as the United States' favorite white wine.

What's better than drinking Chardonnay is not drinking Chardonnay for a very long time and then coming back to it. After a fast, that first Chardonnay sip tastes like heaven, all sun and sky, apple butter, vanilla, and crème brûlée. For a glass or two, you will understand anew, on a cellular level, why people love Chardonnay.

Wine Suggestion: Napa Valley Vineyards Chardonnay
UNITED STATES (CALIFORNIA)

This is a big and ripe, sunny Chardonnay, round and fruitful, with oak and butter, flowers and vanilla. It is a crowd-pleaser that will surely impress the most embittered Chardonnay-haters with its quality. People who think they don't know anything about wine will be able to tell it tastes good. Those who buy wine by the label already know that only a really good wine could be behind such a bad label.

Consider serving this wine nice and cold with big sea scallops, either sautéed in butter and diced bacon, or grilled as a kebab with fennel and cherry tomatoes.

137

Personal Narrative: Dessert Wine in a Pinch

HAVE YOU EVER FOUND yourself with company for dinner in a tight spot for an after-dinner course? After the onslaught of food and wine, one guest might say offhand, "That was fantastic! I can't wait to see what's for dessert." Dessert?

One evening, that very issue cornered my wife and me. In the kitchen, we hastily pulled together a slab of sweet, creamy French cheese called Brie d'Affinois, a piece of Robiola a tre latti (Italian cheese made from equal parts cow, goat, and sheep's milk), and strawberries drizzled with balsamic vinegar and brown sugar.

We added to the plate a couple of slightly over-ripe pears that would never have made it in a lunch bag. At the last minute, I remembered a bottle of not-too-sweet German Riesling in the refrigerator. A few hours ago, we pondered opening it when our guests arrived. Now it looked a whole lot like a dessert wine.

A simple bottle—or even half-bottle—of sweet, interesting wine can sometimes act as its own dessert course. Most wine wants company in the form of food and conversation. Thanks to the wine, no one knew we had improvised dessert.

Nîmes

LIKE THE APOCRYPHAL ENTERTAINER who becomes an overnight success after twenty years in show business, undiscovered wine regions sometimes wait centuries for the world to discover them. Southern France is rich in these unfamiliar, ignored, or undervalued wine neighborhoods now new to us.

Nîmes (pronounced NEEM) is a small city in southern France on the outskirts of the more famous Côtes du Rhône wine region. On the hills outside the city (the *costieres de Nîmes*), which generally face south, grow typical rustic red grapes: Grenache, Syrah, Carignane, and others.

Thanks to its close geographic proximity to super wines such as Châteauneuf-du-Pape, Gigondas, and Lirac, the *costieres de Nimes* has played second, third, or even fourth fiddle for a long time. Technically part of the Languedoc region, it has much in common with its Rhône neighbors, too: Carignane is no longer a sanctioned varietal, and the modern version blends Syrah and Grenache, just like the Rhône reds do.

138

Wine Suggestions: Nîmes Varietals

Château de Campuget Costieres-de-Nîmes Rouge, France
Syrah dominates this dark, brooding, fruited, intense wine. In the background, fragrant flowers and green forest scents come through, with good tannic grip and real meatiness in the foreground.

Château de Campuget Viognier, France
This Viognier is a rich, round, freshly ripened wine with great body and forward fruit. Its melon, pear, honey, and rose water flavors blend beautifully.

Historic building in the town of Nîmes, southern France

Paul Draper

THE PHILOSOPHER-WINEMAKER Paul Draper is CEO of Monte Bello Estate Vineyards. He's known for crafting fine Cabernets and Chardonnays, and as a pioneer in producing complex Zinfandels. Draper has a philosophy degree from Stanford University and lived in northern Italy for two years before attending the University of Paris and traveling France extensively to gain wine-making experience.

This practical winemaker takes a hands-off approach to wine, intruding minimally in the process, relying more on nature and tradition than technology to produce recognized wines. He joined Monte Bello in 1969 after a venture setting up a small winery in Chile's coast range, where he produced vintage Cabernet Sauvignon. He returned to California and brought with him knowledge of fine wines and traditional wine-making methods.

Monte Bello Winery is situated in the Santa Cruz Mountains in Santa Clara County, California. The estate is built on three levels, terraced slopes with grape-loving soil and varietals that have produced winners such as the Geyserville Zinfandel with its forty consecutive years of vintages.

Draper expanded Monte Bello by acquiring the neighboring Perrone Winery, restoring it, and bringing up its quality to gain international recognition. In 1991, Lytton Springs in Sonoma County became part of the Ridge Estate.

To this day, Draper and Monte Bello maintain a straightforward approach to wine making. This winemaker's mission is to find intense, flavorful grapes, intrude upon the process only when necessary, and draw the fruit's distinctive character and richness into wine.

Monte Bello Vineyard, Ridge, Santa Cruz, California, United States

Pace Yourself on a Winery Tour

YOU'RE SOAKING IN WINE COUNTRY for a day, stopping at more vineyards than you can count on two hands. You plan to start your excursion after breakfast so you can visit a number of wineries before evening. Wine country is a hands-on education. And whether you travel to a place 20 miles (32 km) or 2,000 miles (3,220 km) away from home, the people, hospitality, and vinicultural environment will make you feel worlds away.

You want to savor every moment of your journey—and you want to last the entire tour without taking a nap. Follow these pointers to carry you through the long haul.

SPIT, DON'T SIP

If you drink every tasting at every winery, you will only truly taste one wine; alcohol in your system changes your ability to detect tastes. By lunch, you'll be down for the count. Wineries keep their spit buckets visible for a reason. Use them. And if you feel uncomfortable spitting, sip a drop of the wine sample and leave the rest.

DON'T BE AFRAID TO DUMP WINE

You're in wine country, so there's no shortage of the drink. Pour out a fraction of what's left over in your tasting glass rather than drinking it. It's acceptable to take a tiny sip, then dump the wine. It's even better to sip, taste, and spit.

SAVE YOURSELF FOR THE BEST STOP

You may be anticipating a visit to a particular winery you admire, and you plan to drink the wine at the tasting. Plan this stop for last. That way, you can truly taste wines at your other stops. Remember, once you sip and swallow—and keep swallowing—the tasting is really over.

EXPERIENCE EACH WINERY

Forget about the numbers. Visiting more wineries will not enhance your excursion, but experiencing and learning about each winery's people, vineyards, and history will provide cherished memories. We always remember the conversations we had with winemakers and what we saw during a tour; we may not remember exactly how a wine we sampled there tasted. So savor each stop and don't rush. This will also give your palate recuperation time so you can safely fit in more sipping.

REMEMBER REINFORCEMENTS

Pack snacks in the car, and seek out roadside picnic stops where you can take a break and nosh on some cheese, bread, or cured meats that will complement your day of tasting. With all that running around, you'll need the energy!

DRINK AT DINNER

After a full day of tasting at wineries, make your final destination a winery with dinner service or a restaurant with a regional wine list so you can enjoy a glass of the selections you sampled earlier. Now you can unwind and savor a glass or two of wine while discussing the day's best stops.

The Swirl

You can drink wine from the palm of your hand or from a plastic cup. You can even drink it straight from the bottle. But appropriate glassware with a larger bowl shape will allow you to swirl the wine and fully release its aromas. With wine, most of the experience relates to its smell.

So what is it with the wine swirl, and why do you need a glass that allows you to gracefully slosh the liquid around? You don't enjoy any other beverages in this manner. But there is a reason. The swirling motion actually increases the surface area that molecules travel, and causes alcohol to evaporate, leaving a more intense aroma. The effect acts much like perfume on skin. The skin absorbs the alcohol, leaving behind the scent. You need to swirl the wine to release the aroma, dissipate the alcohol, and truly capture wine's sensory pleasure.

To do the swirl well, you need a glass with some head room. Choose a glass based on the wine you pour. Red wines and bold whites, such as Chardonnay, need to air out in a glass with a globelike shape or at least plenty of height to prevent any rogue sloshing.

Crisp whites such as Sauvignon Blanc work best in glasses with a large bowl to provide surface area so the wine can breathe, releasing its aromas. As a rule, the higher a wine's alcohol content, the fuller the body, and the larger the glass you need to release the aroma.

Going Stemless?

The purpose of a wineglass stem is to provide a place for you to handle the glass and avoid changing the wine's temperature. You always hold a wineglass by its stem so whites stay cool and reds don't warm further than necessary.

But what about the new, trendy, stemless wineglasses? If you use them properly and fill them only one-third full to allow room for swirling the wine, you will still have ample room to handle the glass at the top. This way, your warm hands don't warm the wine.

Personal Narrative:
Think Global, Drink Local

VICTORY FOR ANY KIND of fundamentalism is bad news for wine, and don't most Americans know it.

First came the Pilgrims, with their grim, self-fulfilling worldview transplanted into a pleasure-less new world. Much farther south, the likes of Thomas Jefferson tried to grow European grapes in the Piedmont heat and got nowhere. Settlers and entrepreneurs had to cross the entire North American continent to find suitable grape lands, and they dropped much wine culture along the trail. North American wine making began in California in about 1850, hibernated during Prohibition after World War I, and was reborn in the new prosperity after World War II.

Right in the middle of all of this, my parents were born in a dry but drunken county where the mountains of Kentucky, Virginia, and Tennessee all meet. The county is still dry today, and when I drove through a few years ago, I risked everything (well, a fine) to bring home some Virginia wines.

My mother swears a new winery opened up near her hometown outside Seco, Kentucky, called Seco Wines. As far as I know, it's the only intoxicant sold in the open in that part of the country for decades. I haven't tasted any of the winery's wines because it can only sell by the bottle at the shop or one glass per person at the winery.

A man studies a glass of wine at a vineyard in Galicia in the northwest region of Spain

Low-Fat, High-Wine Diet

THE POPULAR PRESS PRINTS many wine stories, usually alternating between wine's positive and negative health effects and under exactly which circumstances each applies. The best news of late: the discovery that white wine and red wine have equal positive effects on heart disease and blood cholesterol. On the other end of the spectrum, a new study linked moderate wine drinking with an increase in breast cancer incidences. Down the middle of the road is yet another report that wine neutralizes unpleasant microbes in the digestive tract, great news for daredevil eaters.

Like the role of naturally occurring sulfites in wine and asthma events, or the ongoing search for exactly what in wine gives people headaches, we have no final answers, just contradictions.

Careful observation shows that the studies that link wine with positive health factors are careful to promote moderate wine consumption only. Theoretically, people who drink wine moderately probably behave moderately overall, and the health benefits we see actually result from a life lived in moderation. A little wine, a little low-fat cooking, a little high-fat cooking ... eventually, it all balances out.

Heat of the Harvest

WINE GRAPES ARE IRONIC, contradictory creatures. They behave differently under different circumstances.

Wines from young grape vines taste very different than old-vine wines. The same grapes from vineyards only a short distance apart can make entirely different wines with wildly disparate prices. Grapes facing southwest—the sweetest agricultural aspect in the northern hemisphere—produce much-preferred wines to grapes oriented to the northeast.

Just think of all the Danish, Welsh, and Russian wines the planet doesn't produce, and you understand why the French call this phenomenon terroir, meaning that it comes exclusively from the earth and its relationship to sun and sky.

Most grapes like sunny-but-not-hot conditions. This contradiction presents quite a challenge to wine growers given the strength of direct sunlight.

In the sun-splashed Mediterranean, relentless sea breezes cool the land at night and keep the grapes dry and safe from mold and mildew during the day. Hundreds of miles (kilometers) north and west of the Mediterranean, the world's most sought-after and expensive wines grow on France's west coast, cooled by the north Atlantic winds that also push back the clouds. Puglia, the deep southern heel of the Italian peninsula, produces cheap, delicious wines sought after only as ready-to-drink bargains.

In 2003, a European heat wave meant human suffering across the continent. More than 10,000 French citizens—mostly the elderly and infirm—died as temperatures climbed above 100°F (38°C) for weeks at a time. The dark irony of this tragedy was that the 2003 vintage all over Europe tasted fantastic. Some grape harvests occurred a full month ahead of schedule. The year 1893 recorded the previous earliest harvest in France's Beaujolais region; 2003 beat that by a full week.

Thomas Volney Munson

A COLLEGE CHEMISTRY PROFESSOR turned Thomas Volney Munson on to grapes in 1873 by giving him clusters of more than forty grape varieties. The potential to breed varieties exponentially hooked Munson, and his romance with viniculture began.

As the second graduate of the Agricultural and Mechanical College of Kentucky University, Munson developed a passion for nature and a horticultural background that laid the groundwork for a lifelong career in important grape research. He once stated, "The grape was the most beautiful, most wholesome and nutritious, most certain and most profitable fruit that could be grown."

Indeed, Munson's assessment of the grape played out over time. But in the early 1870s, his pioneering ideas about grapes and their potential were unique in the United States. He eventually moved to Denison, Texas, on the Red River in northern Texas Hill Country, today a recognized wine region. There, he conducted the bulk of his research and wrote about grapes, publishing *Foundations of American Grape Culture* in 1909—a work still considered one of the most practical guides to the American grape.

Throughout Munson's career, the wine world regarded him as an authority on grapes and grape growing. He hybridized and perfected more than 300 distinct varieties, which won him a diploma from the French government in 1888 and the decoration of the Legion of Honor. By developing insect- and disease-resistant rootstocks, Munson helped save several French wine varieties from extinction due to an infection of phylloxera.

Munson held appointments in various horticultural, wine, and community organizations, including presidency of the Texas Horticultural Society and vice presidency of the American Pomological Society, the oldest fruit organization in the United States.

Munson passed away on January 21, 1913 at age seventy. Everywhere in the world, and especially in Texas where Munson performed his research, wine lovers celebrate his influence on grape growing. Interestingly, Munson is also known for his innovative spirit and such inventions as a primitive helicopter.

Join the Ice Wine Harvest

A COLD SNAP AND FREEZING WEATHER equal good news for ice wine producers who leave grapes on the vine until they freeze. The cold doesn't affect sugars and other dissolved solids, but it freezes the water. Upon pressing, the frozen water stays behind, leaving a highly concentrated juice. Freezing before fermentation results in a small quantity of very sweet wine.

Canada produces the largest quantities of ice wine, though vineyards in the northern United States and part of Europe also make the saccharine delicacy. Because these wines are so limited, they are generally expensive. But even a sip of ice wine for dessert will satisfy a sweet tooth. (For more about ice wine in general, see Day 128.)

In some communities, you can participate in the ice wine harvest by volunteering to help pick grapes. This job has a couple of caveats: Often the harvest happens late at night while the grapes remain frozen and not warmed by the daylight sun. To be sure, temperatures will be chilling.

However, there's something magical about a still vineyard at night, the thrill of plucking frozen grapes from the vines in a hurry, and the novelty of this annual event. At many vineyards, the ice wine harvest is an event indeed. (Those who prefer a warm bed to an ice-cold harvest can read about it in the paper the next morning.)

An ice wine harvest is so special because cold temperatures and grapes do not guarantee a healthy harvest. It takes a hard freeze and healthy, ripe fruit still hanging on the vine. Temperatures must drop to 9°F (−13°C) to 14°F (−10°C), and pickers must pick grapes by hand.

Contact your local wineries to find out specifics about harvest time and whether they hold events open to the public. Winery websites are always useful tools (but you never know how up-to-date they are, so it's best to call). Call in advance (i.e., summertime); don't wait until late fall, especially if you want to participate. Learn more about ice wine in John Shreiner's book, *Icewine: The Complete Story*, published by Warwick Publishing, Toronto, Ontario.

A worker at Schloss Vollrads, Weisbaden, Germany, empties a shovel of frozen grapes during the ice wine harvest

Goût de Terrior

To UNDERSTAND HOW THE same grape can taste so different from place to place, you have to tap into an esoteric French understanding of *goût de terroir*. Terroir implies a mystical combination of mostly soil, but also sun and weather conditions expressed in a wine's flavor. Of course, like all wine expressions, it's a matter of taste, and that makes it tough to pin down.

Consider Hermitage, a French red grown on the slopes of a massive hill in the Rhône Valley. You may imagine you can taste the time the grapes have spent baking in the hot summer sun. More likely, you're reacting to what you've read about that demon sun of Hermitage and its effect on this famous wine.

True enough, Hermitage often exhibits overt flavors of toasted grain and roasted meats, but it seems far-fetched to think that this comes purely from the grapes' time in the sun. If that were the case, California reds would out-Hermitage the Hermitage (and as a general rule, they don't). The difference is that Hermitage ripens in the hot Mediterranean sun but in a cold climate, much colder than and 600 miles (965 km) north of California wine country, at about the same latitude as Nova Scotia, Canada.

The contrast between hot sun and cold climate makes Hermitage what it is. And that, in a nutshell, is terroir.

The True Marriage of Wines

BLENDING WINE IS both an art (making it taste great) and a science (making it taste the same across thousands of bottles). Modern New World wineries revel in creating single-vineyard 100 percent varietal wines. The wines still taste great, but the wineries no longer have the challenge and labor of mixing many hectoliters of wine.

Traditional European vineyards blend out of ritual and necessity. In Tuscany, winemakers combine a dozen different wine grapes to make traditional Chianti. Doing it this way allows the winemakers to adjust the blend from year to year to take advantage of great harvests or correct for shortcomings. Over time, a wine with a stable, distinct, and reproducible style results.

Not every grape automatically grows everywhere, and the grape farmer sometimes has to plant different vines on different pieces of land to achieve production. Almost by default, to make the land profitable, the winemaker must create a blended wine.

Take Bordeaux wines. They are mostly Cabernet Sauvignon and Merlot, so they have some blending latitude built in. Merlot softens the Cabernet, and Cabernet toughens up the Merlot. Still, Bordeaux is famous for wide vintage fluctuations of both price and quality.

Winemakers who rely on only one grape are open to vulnerability. If they grow only Syrah, for example, and a pest attacks or the vineyards get hit with a Syrah-specific disease, they lose their profit in one hit. By growing other grapes, winemakers give themselves balanced ingredients for making and blending wine each year. A bad year for one grape doesn't mean a bad year for all, and they can adjust the blend accordingly.

Recipe: Steak Balsamico

ONE OF THE EASIEST WAYS to start cooking with wine is to use a simple meat marinade made with wine. Soaking meat in a broth of wine, oil, spices, and, in this recipe, balsamic vinegar, adds flavor and tenderizes the meat before cooking.

The secret to an unforgettable wine and food match is to cook with the wine you plan to serve. This recipe calls for only ¾ cup (175 ml) of red wine—about one glass.

1½ pounds (675 g) rib-eye steak (with the bone is best, but boneless works, too)

3 tablespoons (45 ml) balsamic vinegar

3 tablespoons (45 ml) olive oil

¾ cup (175 ml) red wine

2 tablespoons (28 g) butter

Salt and ground black pepper, to taste

Fresh lemon juice

Slice the meat into very thin cutlets approximately ¼-inch (¾-cm) thick. In all, you should end up with 6 thin cutlets, each the size of an index card. If you buy your meat from a butcher shop, ask the butcher to do this for you. If you do this yourself, try putting the steak in the freezer for 1 hour before starting. This will firm up the meat and make it easier to slice.

In a shallow bowl, combine the balsamic vinegar, olive oil, and red wine, then marinate the steaks for 15 to 30 minutes. Remove and drain on layers of paper towel.

Melt the butter in a large skillet over medium-high. Sprinkle the steaks with a little salt and pepper to taste. Just as the butter starts to brown, put the steaks in the pan to fry.

Cook for 5 minutes, then turn over the steaks, add the lemon juice, turn the heat down to medium, and cook for 4 minutes longer.

Arrange the steaks on a layer of arugula or spinach leaves on a serving platter. Drizzle a bit of the sauce from the skillet over the steaks, and give the whole dish another small squeeze of lemon before serving.

YIELD: Serves 6

Wine Pairing: Erik Banti Morellino di Scansano

Italy

Sangiovese, the well-known red grape of Chianti, is grown all over Italy. In coastal Tuscany, an area called Maremma (mare is Latin for "sea"), Sangiovese goes by the name of Morellino, after the tart brown Morello cherry. Naturally, this local variation plays up the grape's natural delicious tanginess. Some Tuscan reds can be earthy and rugged, but this Morellino is bright, radiant, and fruity, able to stand up in flavor to the depth of the balsamic marinade.

Ripasso Style: Just Passing Through

STYLE IS DIFFICULT TO VERIFY, and one person's style may be another's lapse of taste. Recognizing and applauding someone's style doesn't mean you like it.

When wine lovers say a wine has style, they mean that somebody has made choices they can taste in the glass. For wine, style relates to what's done, but also to what's not done. The exotic Ripasso method from Italy represents an extreme example of wine styling. The idea (and motivation) behind this method involves taking ordinary grapes such as Valpolicella and doing something dramatic to make them into extraordinary wine.

Valpolicella as a plain red wine can taste light and bright, but usually just tastes plain. Late-harvest Valpolicella, on the other hand, frequently produces two expensive and sought-after wines: Recioto (a sweet dessert wine) and Amarone (dry, opaque, and like port).

Ripasso means "to pass through again," and in this method, fresh Valpolicella wine goes into barrels that, at one point, contained Recioto and Amarone. In contact with the unique and flavorful organic residue in the barrels (called the lees), the wine goes through a slight refermentation. It comes out of the barrels higher in alcohol, a little more concentrated, and full of a new, rich spiciness. Next time you're browsing for wines with great style, look for Ripasso wines.

The Birth of California Wine

HIS ESTATE WAS advertised as the largest vineyard in the world—and Agoston Haraszthy lived large in every way. In the wine world, by growing and crushing classic European varietals, called *vitis vinifera*, on a commercial scale as early as 1857, he laid the foundation for wine giants such as Robert Mondavi, Johann-Joseph Krug, Joe Heitz, Jacob Schram, and Gustave Niebaum.

But Haraszthy's legendary status transcends wine. He was the first Hungarian to permanently settle in the United States, and he founded one of the earliest towns in Wisconsin, which became Sauk City on the Wisconsin River. He owned and operated the first steamboat to engage in regularly scheduled traffic on the upper Mississippi River. And after he moved his family west to California (during the days when gold equaled opportunity), he continued to embellish his track record.

He moved to Sonoma Valley just sixteen years after leaving Hungary (after his time in San Francisco). There, he began to build what is now one of the world's most vibrant wine regions. He introduced hundreds of European grape varieties to California and planted more than a thousand acres of vineyards. He wasn't quiet about his work. He made a trip to Europe and returned with clusters of varieties to grow in California, then wrote a notable book about California wine growing. His most successful venture was Buena Vista in Sonoma County, which he eventually sold.

Many laud Haraszthy as the Father of California Wine (though some may argue this). He's been called bold, extravagant, devious, visionary. Above all, Haraszthy was ambitious.

A wine cellar in the Veneto Region, Valpolicella, Italy

Wine and a Movie

WHY NOT MAKE IT A wine-movie weekend and rent some flicks that celebrate your drink of choice? Wine is a recurring theme or the storyline for these movies. Do they inspire you to try new varieties, visit a wine region you've never experienced, or simply uncork a bottle at home while you watch?

THE GODFATHER

Throughout this Italian mafia classic, the characters consume, talk about, and celebrate wine. There's the wedding scene, the Don speaking of his enjoyment of wine, and wine at every social gathering. You can't take the wine out of Italy, after all. Why would you want to?

A WALK IN THE CLOUDS

A vineyard called Las Nubes—which means "the clouds"—sets the bucolic backdrop for this movie, in which a young woman returns home to harvest the grapes in her family's vineyard. There's a grape-stomping scene, prevalent consumption of wine, and most of all, the inspiring setting.

SIDEWAYS

If you want a movie in which wine is the storyline, not just a character or background nuance, this is the film. Two friends, Miles and Jack, go to California wine country for a last hurrah before Jack's nuptials. Miles professes his love for Pinot Noir—causing the wine's popularity to jump after this movie—and his distaste for Merlot. After watching these friends tour and taste their way through California's vineyards, you'll be booking a trip to wine country in no time. The bottles of wine consumed, depth of wine talk, and gorgeous scenery might even convince a beer drinker to pour a glass of Pinot.

BOTTLE SHOCK

The wine-making romance, based on the famous 1976 blind tasting in Paris during which two California wines came out on top (much to the surprise and disappointment of the French wine tasters), tells of the significance of blind tastings and California's coming of age in the wine world.

MONDOVINO

This wine business documentary explores how business and the globalization of the wine industry are changing the way winemakers make wine. It looks at the influence of critics such as Robert Parker and consultants such as Michel Rolland in defining tastes, and tells the story of big wine business and traditional winemakers struggling in today's climate.

In Vino Veritas

WHEN I FIRST STARTED WRITING about wine, my brilliant friend and editor Betsy Neidich presented me with a small silver pin shaped like a grape leaf and inscribed with the words *In Vino Veritas*. This ancient Latin phrase translates literally as "in wine truth." The Romans were a very literal people, and in one sense, the words meant that when you drank wine, you told the truth. At dinner, guests would encourage each other to make drunken, misguided speeches by shouting, "*In vino veritas*!" and letting the wine speak its truth.

How a person behaves when intoxicated often reveals his or her character, and this is another of the phrase's classical meanings. Do you keep your wits about you when the wine flows freely, or are you the person who wants to drive when everybody else knows better?

In vino veritas for the winemaker can mean staying true to a grape's character. You can expose Pinot Noir to oak and radiation and make it taste like anything you want, but staying true to its character means keeping it true in taste to type. *Veritas* means truth to regional wine traditions as well, such as matching food to wine in direct, authentic, and even historic ways.

An *In Vino Veritas* relief in Weingut Milz-Laurentiushof, Trittenheim, Germany, depicting workers picking grapes

The Pink Spectrum of Wine

IT SEEMS OBVIOUS THAT white wine comes from white grapes and red wine from red grapes, but consider this: If you press red grapes gently, you still get white juice. Some of the most famous Champagne—considered a white wine—comes from red grapes and always has.

Here's the difference between white and red wines. After pressing out the juice, red wine gets fermented with its grape skins; white wine does not. All manner of tannins, pigments, and other compounds come from the skin contact. This is what makes red wine a "bigger" glass than white. The juice literally contains more stuff.

If you press red grapes normally, you get pink juice. If you just ferment this juice and don't add the skins back in, you get pink wine. Around the world, it's called rosato, rosado, rosé, gray, gris, pink, and even white, as in white Zinfandel. Pink wines are stereotypically considered weakened, softer versions of real red wine, and some even see rosé as—forgive me—a lady's drink.

In fact, rosé wine is typically something of a guilty pleasure among wine lovers: it's almost always cheaper than its white or red cousins, it tastes great in an unserious way, and you can chill it down for summer as cold as you like.

Wine Suggestions: Pink Wines

Les Baux de Provence Rosé, France
Southern France is famous for delicious rosé. This wine's strawberry-apple-raspberry flavor profile is pumped up a little, making you wonder about the line between red and rosé. Serve it nice and cool.

Guigal Tavel, France
Famous for quality and dependability, this Guigal rosé delivers structure, flavor, and balance. A classic example of great Old World rosé, it's best with fish stew, even bouillabaisse.

Renwood Syrah Rosé, United States (California)
Syrah is an extremely intense black grape, and this pink version has a tremendous amount of body and weight, with rich fruit and red wine acidity. It's enough to make you forget all the bad white Merlot that someone somewhere still makes.

154

Belle Époque rosé enameled bottles in pupitre in the cellar of Champagne Perrier Jouët in Épernay, Marne, France

Recipe: Steak au Poivre

FOR THIS CLASSIC DISH, use an extremely lean piece of meat, London broil or thick shell sirloin, if you like meat rare. If you like it done or well-done, choose a fatter cut, because the marbling cooks up as the meat cooks longer.

2 steaks (about 1 pound [455 g] total and 1-inch [2.5-cm] thick)

½ cup (120 ml) dry red wine

¼ cup (60 ml) balsamic vinegar

2 tablespoons (30 ml) olive oil

⅓ cup (30 g) freshly ground coarse black pepper

⅙ cup (50 g) coarse salt

1 tablespoon (2 g) rosemary, minced

Marinate the steaks in the wine, vinegar, and olive oil for 1 to 4 hours. Remove the steaks and pat them dry with paper towels. Dispose of the marinade.

Preheat a grill or cast-iron skillet until it is very hot. Combine the pepper, salt, and rosemary. Encrust both sides of each steak by pressing them into this mixture. Make certain the steaks are well-covered.

Grill the steaks for 3 to 4 minutes per side until rare or medium-rare. Adjust the cooking time to your taste. Serve with sautéed greens (broccoli rabe or kale) and tiny roasted potatoes.

YIELD: Serves 4

Wine Pairing: Penfolds Bin 407 Cabernet Sauvignon
AUSTRALIA

Penfolds considers Bin 407 the little brother to the very expensive Bin 707, itself second only to the ultra-famous Grange in the Penfolds family. This strong, oaky red has good ripeness and lots of tannin.

Saumur château and vineyard in the Loire Valley of France

Loire River Wines

THE LOIRE RIVER BEGINS IN southern France and flows due north, as if to empty directly into the English Channel. About halfway along its 600-mile (965-km) course, at the city of Orleans, the river takes a hard turn left and flows west until it reaches the north Atlantic Ocean.

Near this bend in the river begin the Loire's acres (hectares) and hundreds of wineries. The region is France's third largest wine producer and third most popular tourist destination (behind Paris and the Riviera).

Loire whites come from Muscadet (a grape unrelated to Muscatel), Chenin Blanc, or Sauvignon Blanc (better known in the form of white Bordeaux). Happily, a few areas grow Cabernet Franc and produce dense reds, deep and black but often strangely light in tannic abrasiveness.

The hard-core wine lover may vaguely recognize the towns and subregions of the Loire: Muscadet de Sevre et Maine, Savennières, Saumur, Chinon, Bourgueil, Vouvray, Sancerre, Quincy, Pouilly-Fumé, and many others.

Wines of the Loire challenge our prejudices and misconceptions about what we think we're supposed to like in white and red wines today. But it's the challenge that makes the wine life worth living.

Wine Suggestion: Château Moncontour Vouvray

FRANCE

With 280 acres (113 ha) of vines, Château Moncontour is the largest vineyard in Vouvray. In the glass, this wine starts out smelling like green herbs and mineral water. Round, ripe flavors of pear, apple, and melon follow. Save it for the cheese course to serve with Brie. This wine is a great way to get introduced to Loire Chenin Blanc.

Charles Shaw

THE TWO-BUCK CHUCK has bucked the typical wine-cult trend of paying lots of money for a popular wine. This wine *is* popular and cheap, explaining its catchy nickname.

So what's the story behind this infamous wine?

Shaw, a dentist from Chicago, started his winery in 1974 and produced quality wines from Valdiguié, Gamay Noir, and Pinot Noir grapes, blended and sold as Gamay Beaujolais or Napa Gamay. At the time, Charles Shaw Gamay Beaujolais was said to be one of the better blends because it contained the true Gamay Noir of Beaujolais.

But business got tough, and Shaw struggled. He divorced in 1991, sold his winery assets and vineyards to Charles Krug, and sold his brand name (Charles Shaw) to Bronco Wine Company in Ceres, California. Eleven years later, Bronco's Fred Franzia decided to revamp the label as a value wine by mixing grapes from Central Valley.

Because the wine is bottled by Bronco in Napa, the label contains the attractive "Napa" name. Pity the wine drinker who thinks that Charles Shaw is a veritable Napa Valley AVA find (i.e., made from grapes grown in that American Viticultural Area). But cheers to the drinker who can appreciate a truly drinkable bargain wine.

Charles Shaw is sold only at Trader Joe's, a specialty retail grocer found in just nine states, where bottles fly off the shelf and walk out the door by the case—by the millions of cases each year, actually. But all this bargain-buy frenzy has Charles Shaw, our dentist and vintner, a tad miffed. Or at least, it has challenged him to resurrect his name and polish it off with a grander reputation, on which he's now working. Shaw is making subtle label changes and producing small quantities of true Napa Valley wines that refute the "Chuck" we know. Wine lovers, stay tuned.

158

Shopping for the Wine Lover on Your List

WINE LOVERS COULDN'T BE any easier to shop for, whether for an everyday gift or a special occasion. When you think to yourself, "My friend loves wine, what should I get her?" the answer shouldn't be coaster, carafe, or other wine accessory. An expensive corkscrew becomes grist for the corkscrew drawer, so unless you know the person really needs one, avoid it.

Here's a little secret: Wine lovers want wine! It is so simple that people miss it. Of course, the only situation more anxiety-provoking than buying pricey wine for yourself is buying it for someone you consider a connoisseur. Will it be the right bottle? Too much? Too little?

To alleviate this anxiety, focus on assembling two or three medium-priced bottles of wine that match each other rather than picking one expensive, nerve-wracking, cellar selection.

Instead of a legendary Châteauneuf-du-Pape, for example, group a good Côtes-du-Rhône, a good Gigondas, and a nice bottle of dessert wine from Beaumes-de-Venise in a gift basket. Add a wedge of raw-milk blue cheese or a great, big piece of Belgian chocolate (Caillebaut is my favorite, the most affordable, and the easiest to find). You may not end up spending less money, but you give the wine lover a suite of options, a move that's sure to please.

Wine for sale at a market in Loches, Loire Valley, France

Drink Up to Your Potential

WHEN YOU READ the latest numbers from The Wine Institute (see Resources), you realize the planet's tasting glass is half empty, not half full.

The trio of France, Italy, and Spain top almost every wine category—total consumption, per capita consumption, acres (hectares), exports, you name it. Roman vintners planted these premier wine nations thousands of years ago. They are the oldest in western Europe, and it makes perfect sense that they lead the world.

In total wine consumption, the United States ranks third. In per capita wine consumption, it ranks thirty-fifth. Americans consume only eleven bottles per person per year, about a glass a week, while the French consume about eighty and the Italians, about seventy.

In short, the U.S. market could double consumption and then double it again, and still need to almost double it again just to equal France.

An optimist looks at Europe as an example of wine's growth potential for the rest of the world (though Luxembourg's two bottles of wine a week per capita seems to be an outlier). Not too surprisingly, the big wine-consuming nations represent cultures that have promoted drinking wine each and every day for the past 2,000 years. Just a few centuries ago, Puritans and bootleggers founded the United States, which explains its neophytic, slightly ambivalent relationship with wine. Who says you can't override tradition?

Albariño

THE ALBARIÑO GRAPE thrives in cool, windy, rainy climates. That's often the weather report in the Galicia region of northwestern Spain, the grape's homeland. In Portugal, the grape is called Alvarinho and is blended into Vinho Verde. Growing interest in Albariño has resulted in some experimentation at California and Oregon wineries.

To thrive in a cool, wet environment, Albariño vines are trained—by pruning and providing a support, such as trellis, that will guide the plant's growth—to grow high so the plants do not trap moisture and cause rot, mildew, or fungal diseases.

But then wind dries out the tall-in-stature vines, so the grape skins thicken to thrive in such conditions. This enhances the intensity of Albariño's aroma, which can exude scents of almond, apple, peach, citrus, flowers, and grass.

Albariño wine is highly acidic, making it a perfect partner for seafood. Drink this wine quickly. It does not age gracefully; within months of bottling, aromas can fade.

Recipe: Mushroom, Bacon, and Riesling Stuffing

THIS RECIPE CALLS FOR RIESLING, but feel free to substitute any affordable Gewürztraminer. Turkey with earthy mushrooms and smoky bacon pairs beautifully with the rich, flavorful G'vertz. This recipe works for one 8- to 12-pound (3.6- to 5.5-kg) turkey. Double the recipe for a larger bird.

4 garlic cloves, minced

¼ pound (113 g) smoked bacon, diced

¼ cup (60 ml) olive oil

1 large onion, chopped

1 cup (100 g) celery, chopped

2 cups (140 g) fresh mushrooms, chopped

4 cups (460 g) sourdough bread crumbs, dried and cut into ½-inch (1¼-cm) cubes

½ teaspoon (3 g) sea salt

½ teaspoon (1 g) fresh ground black pepper

3 tablespoons (5 g) fresh rosemary, minced

3 tablespoons (8 g) fresh sage, minced

5 tablespoons (20 g) fresh parsley, minced

2 cups (475 ml) Riesling

In a large saucepan, brown the garlic and bacon in the olive oil, add the onion and celery, and sauté until just clear. Add the mushrooms and sauté for 5 minutes over medium-high heat until they start to release some of their moisture.

Reduce the heat to medium and add the bread cubes and seasonings. Cook for 5 more minutes, stirring frequently. Add the Riesling and stir well.

Reduce the heat to low, cover, and cook slowly for 30 minutes, stirring frequently. Add a bit more Riesling, if necessary, to keep the stuffing moist.

YIELD: Serves 6 to 8

Use an assortment of mushrooms to give the stuffing a variety of flavors and textures. If you don't have fresh herbs, use the dried version, but half the amount. Loosen the skin of the turkey and spoon in your stuffing beneath the skin, around the legs, and over the top of the bird. Stuff the cavity of your turkey with a few apples and celery stems to keep it from getting dry.

Wine Pairing: Castell-Castell Silvaner

GERMANY

Riesling dominates western German wine making, but as you travel east and south toward Bavaria and ultimately Austria, other white grapes come out of the woods, so to speak. Silvaner (Latin for "forest") produces a dry white wine with earthy flavors—perfect for savory food.

Personal Narrative: GPS for Wine

WHEN I MET MY WIFE, she swore to me that she didn't know anything about wine and never would, but I decided to fall in love with her anyway. She knew plenty about cooking, eating, and living—what many people call the good life. She actually knew about wine, too, but like so many people, she just didn't know it.

As we started cooking and eating as a couple, I began to notice that she really loved Châteauneuf-du-Pape, the famous southern French red from the Rhône Valley. This affection worked out well for many reasons. First, Châteauneuf-du-Pape is delicious, every wine's first responsibility. Second, it's ubiquitous: You can find some version in any wine shop and on every wine list no matter where you travel. Finally, it's the least expensive classical French wine almost on a par with the even more famous Bordeaux châteaux.

Once, I was in a wine shop looking for something to serve with dinner that would make her fall in love with me even more. The resident wine expert, Chuck Eldred, was helping me. "If you like Châteauneuf-du-Pape," he said, "try this," and he handed me a bottle of something red from importer Alain Junguenet (see Day 257). "It's the next town over, and it's half the price." We consulted a wine map, and sure enough, this wine's home was a crossroads 1 mile (2 km) away from the crossroads that was Châteauneuf-du-Pape.

That night at dinner, my wife took one sip and said, "I love Châteauneuf-du-Pape!" I told her it wasn't. She said, "Oh, yes it is. It has that special flavor. This is definitely Châteauneuf-du-Pape." I knew then that our relationship in tastes and appetites would be a perfect one. I had fallen in love with a woman who could take in the entire planet, and still place a bottle of wine within a mile of its birthplace.

Early morning at a vineyard in Napa Valley, California, United States

Jeanne Cho Lee

JEANNE CHO LEE WAS THE first ethnic Asian to achieve the distinction of Master of Wine, a notoriously difficult four-day examination by the Institute of Masters of Wine. Lee was born in Seoul, Korea, and her interest in wine began while she studied at Oxford University as an exchange student from Smith College. She went on to graduate from Harvard University with a master's degree in public policy and then began pioneering the wine world, playing up her role as an Asian woman with a passion for grapes.

She attended Windows on the World Wine School in New York City after graduation. She also obtained a Certificat de Cuisine from Cordon Bleu Paris, and earned the Wine & Spirit Education Trust diploma in 1998. But Lee's first career was in business journalism, and she wrote for publications such as *Asia Inc.*, *Far Eastern Economic Review*, and *The Asset*. She moved on to write a weekly wine column for the *Sun Newspaper* in Kuala Lumpur, and contributed to titles such as *Wine Spectator*, *Decanter*, *Wine Business International*, and *La Revue du Vin de France*.

Today, Lee is an international wine judge, writer, speaker, consultant, and certified wine educator. She has authored two books, *Asian Palate* and *Mastering Wine*.

Lee talks of the growth potential of the Asian market for the wine industry, writing in a 2007 *Wine Business International* article, "If every Chinese person were to drink a mere half bottle this year, the European wine lake would dry in the blink of an eye." But, as she observes, as demand increases, so does domestic production. (For more on China, see Day 263.) The wine industry can count on Lee to follow these and other trends with her journalistic propensity to dig and her impressively deep knowledge of the wine industry.

Wine at Brunch

AN ELEGANT BRUNCH always counts as a special occasion, whether or not it takes place on a formal holiday. Extravagant or simple, this leisure meal calls for a beverage that will complement a buffet and add sparkle (sometimes literally) to the event. Yes, spirits are in order! So early in the day, mind the alcohol content and provide a refreshing, light wine or mixed wine drink that will not cause the party to break up early for a nap.

Mimosa is the classic brunch beverage. This mixture of bright and bubbly sparkling wine (or Champagne) and orange juice partners deliciously with brunch foods. Essentially, you're dressing up plain orange juice with a little something special. And because the drink contains only a little alcohol, your guests will appreciate you later.

Bellini is an Italian wine drink using sparkling wine (or Champagne) and peach purée. The same principles as for mimosas apply here: It's festive, fizzy, tasty with breakfast, and light enough that guests can agree heartily to seconds.

You're not limited to mixed-wine drinks at brunch, so branch out from these standards and serve some brunch-friendly wines that pair well with the foods you're serving. A Spanish Cava, for example, is crisp and sparkling, and complements smoked salmon and other rich brunch buffet seafood. Or try a nice Riesling as an alternative to sparkling wine (and a better option if serving tomatoes with that lox). Riesling pairs easily with many foods, in fact. And it is generally lower in alcohol than other wines. Finally, a dry rosé is light enough for breakfast, but provides character.

Growing Old with Wine

THE MOST FREQUENTLY ASKED questions in the wine world are about age, aging, and the age-ability of wine. People are naturally curious whether wine does age, whether it improves with age, and if it does, whether whites and reds age differently. Part of wine's mystery is the very notion that wines from decades ago can pass history down to us as if transported to the present by a time machine owned by a mad scientist with great taste.

Only a tiny percentage of the planet's wine is not consumed within months of its release, so aging wines refers to only the few, the proud, and the expensive reds.

True, reds and whites grow old at different rates. White wine tastes better brand new, young, vibrant, and full of fruit and flowers. Most red wine tastes better this way too, but most of these will at least survive five or seven years and still taste decent. Youth goes first, of course, and that's what makes a white wine delicious. When it comes to aging, white wine is all about the flower and fruit; red wine is about the skins, seeds, and structure.

As a rule of thumb, seven years is a decent age for red wines. Younger is fine, too. Older is a judgment call.

Nero d'Avola

NERO D'AVOLA IS Sicily's most popular red grape, long used in France and northern Italy to boost milder reds. With its exceptionally high alcohol content—up to 18 percent—and strong presence, this grape can overpower if winemakers don't take care during harvest and processing. In recent years, viticuluralists have adopted techniques to tone down the strong (and highly alcoholic) wine. For example, night harvesting and placing the grapes in cooled vats to spark premature fermentation have resulted in rich wines comparable to Syrah.

Nero d'Avola thrives in Sicily's warm, sunny climate, with soil that lends a uniquely Sicilian flavor, something difficult to capture when growing the grapes elsewhere. Nero d'Avola, also known as Calabrese, is truly a taste of Sicily, and the pure varieties not mixed with other grapes offer a big, fruit flavor—just the serious reds many wine drinkers seek when trying to pair wine with a hearty meat dish.

I See the Wines of Summer

WHITE WINES WE IGNORE all winter long become stars during the summer. Vernaccia di San Gimignano, about the color of water and with hardly any flavor, is perfect for summer drinking. Why? Because when chilled ice cold, its explosive acidity and intense mouthfeel pair outstandingly well with almost any summer food, including raw bar, grilled shrimp, and meaty, marinated monk fish.

The challenge of red wine in summer is twofold. First, the extremely strong flavors from grilling are tough to match, almost like matching wine to a machine gun. What will stand up to something so strong? In my experience, only the strongest, reddest wines survive a head-on collision with a charcoal grill.

Second, people like to drink red wine warmer than white wine, but still a little cool. Nothing's worse than hot red wine, and the temperature control on a picnic or up on the roof is nothing to write home about.

In my mind, there's no question about it: Come summertime, you can safely toss your red wines into the refrigerator to cool them before you head out to the deck. Don't let them get ice cold, but cooling them before opening actually serves you well in hot weather.

> Buy a bunch of seedless grapes (green, black, pink, it doesn't matter), wash, and remove them from the stems. Freeze the grapes, then use them in place of ice cubes to keep your wine cold. Put a whole handful into your glass of white wine to really chill it down, or add just one or two to a glass of red, to keep it under control.

Nero d'Avola grapes on the vine

Champagne

ONLY CHAMPAGNE PRODUCED in this region of France, 100 miles (160 km) east of Paris, has the right to call itself Champagne—and you pay for the name. Any other bubbly must be called sparkling wine.

Most of the vineyards in Champagne, France, fall between the cities of Reims and Épernay, where you'll find a sea of grapes growing on the rolling hillsides. This is the home of Veuve Clicquot, Moët et Chandon, Ruinart, Krug, Pommery, and Dom Perignon. In fact, Dom Perignon brought the sparkle to Champagne's tart wines when he realized that bottling wine before it fully fermented resulted in bubbly; natural fermentation produces carbon dioxide (the sparkle in Champagne). (See Days 23 and 89 for more about the Dom Perignon legend.)

Champagne comes from Pinot Noir, Pinot Meunier, and Chardonnay grapes, and you can identify a quality bottle by looking for R. M. (Récoltant-Manipulant) or S. R. (Société de Récolantes) on the label. These initials mean that the grower vinifies, bottles, and markets the Champagne from grapes he grows.

While touring Champagne, you'll find plenty of opportunities to taste Champagne and other delicacies of the region, such as *boudin blanc de Rethel* ("white pudding"), creamy *Chaource* and *Langres* cheeses matured with *marc de Champagne* alcohol, and *biscuits Roses de Reims*.

The Champagne-Ardennes region, in general, is rich in French history. The Cathedral of Reims—a Gothic architectural masterpiece—held the crowning ceremonies of French kings for a thousand years. In Reims, visit Cathedral Notre-Dame de Reims, with its circular stained-glass rose window and set of windows designed by artist Marc Chagall.

A road sign in France pointing to some of the more famous cities in the Champagne region: Épernay, Chouilly, Avize, and Cramant

Miljenko "Mike" Grgich

AN INNOVATOR IN THE wine field, Mike Grgich earned a Lifetime Achievement Award from the California State Fair in 2008 for two key breakthroughs: He pioneered the use of cold sterilization and malolactic fermentation, and he showed the world how oak barrels promote proper aging.

Perhaps his greatest accomplishment was the Paris Tasting of 1976. A Chardonnay he crafted for Château Montelena in California trumped one of the best wines in France, and the win elevated Napa Valley as a top wine-producing region. "Our victory pumped new energy into the California wine industry, particularly in the Napa Valley," Grgich said, "and it energized wine-makers in many other parts of the world, such as Argentina and Chile. They realized if we could do it, so could they."

Grgich was born into the wine industry, son and grandson of Croatian winemakers. He was one of eleven children, weaned from his mother's milk to a fifty-fifty mix of water and red wine. By age three, he was stomping grapes. He eventually attended business college and studied chemistry, oenology, microbiology, soil biology, fruit, and grapes. From a young age, he prepared for his own venture.

Grgich fled Yugoslavia's communist rule in 1954 to West Germany, eventually making his way to Canada. He had heard of California's wine country and arrived in Napa Valley with a small suitcase. He worked for a couple of different wineries, eventually joining Beaulieu Vineyard, where he stayed for nine years. From there, he became chief enologist at Robert Mondavi Winery.

He continued to impress judges at blind tastings in California and Paris. By the time he opened Grgich Hills Cellar in Rutherford, Napa Valley, in 1977, he had earned the nickname the King of Chardonnay. He returned to his homeland, Croatia, in 1996 to open a new winery, Grgic Vina, to introduce modern techniques to the old country.

Grgich continues to innovate and propel his winery forward with technology, including switching to solar power in 2006. The next year, the winery became completely estate grown, meaning wines produced only from grapes grown on the Grgich property. This accomplishment warranted a name change to Grgich Hills Estate. Today, the property includes 366 acres (148 ha) and five certified organic and biodynamic vineyards. The winery produces 70,000 cases of estate wines.

169

Open-That-Bottle Night

You know that special bottle of wine you've been saving, the one you brought home from Bordeaux, the one a winemaker signed as he shared charming stories, the one you received as a gift, the one you swear you'll never open?

There never seems an occasion quite perfect enough to warrant uncorking *that* bottle. As it rests in your collection gathering dust, the bottle grows to celebrity status and you eventually cannot imagine any life event important enough to open it. At the pit of your stomach sits a queasy feeling related to the thought of emptying its contents. You know you do not have a second bottle of the same variety.

Relax and break free! Now you have an excuse to get rid of the stress of deciding when to savor this special selection you've adored for months or years. February 28th marks the annual Open-That-Bottle Night. It's a true holiday, really!

Wall Street Journal columnists Dorothy Gaiter and John Brecher conceived the event to encourage people to break out those special bottles. You won't be sorry you did, especially if you invite friends (and their important bottles) over for the ritual. Every bottle has a memory to share.

Don't want to wait until February 28th? Maybe it's already passed or you have an early meeting the next morning that could spoil the night's enjoyment. Choose your own day and make it a party. The fact is, you shouldn't always save wine indefinitely. If the wine surpasses its peak, you'll wish you opened the bottle long ago.

Remember, you can save the empty bottle as a keepsake, so you don't lose a memento. And meanwhile, you'll create a new memory and perhaps a new tradition as you open and share the significance of that special bottle. Next time you buy a special bottle, purchase three. That way, you'll have backup.

Tools of the Trade

WINEMAKERS, LIKE CAR MECHANICS, have their own sets of tools and technical skills. What they do from day to day is relatively formulaic: taste wine, run tests in the lab, pump wine from one vessel into another, and the constant cleaning. It's more or less the same the world over, and the routine is punctuated infrequently by a few interventionist moments when winemakers break out the toolbox and do things to wine on purpose.

Being able to think and talk about these big hands-on moments in the winemaking process will help you understand the world of the winemakers and what kinds of flavor ideas they may be trying to express with different wines.

PUMPING OVER

During fermentation, juice is slowly but continuously circulated from the bottom of the fermentation tank to the top where it is literally pumped over the skins and solids floating on the surface. Pumping over helps to extract color and flavor more evenly and consistently from the grapes creating a final wine that's smooth and even tempered.

PUNCHING DOWN

In red wine, the juice and skins are fermented together, and naturally the skins tend to rise to the surface forming a cap on top of the fermentation tank. This cap needs to be broken up and pushed back down into the fermenting juice, typically three times a day, a process called punching down. Next time you're at a wine tasting, just say "You can really taste the difference when the cap's been punched down more than three times a day."

COLD STABILIZATION

Wine contains a small amount of tartaric acid that's normally flavorless, odorless, and invisible. When white wine is cooled way down, close to freezing, this acid crystallizes and drops to the bottom of the bottle where it looks like a little bit of sand. Winemakers cold stabilize mainly for aesthetic reasons and quality control. Most consumers, having cold stabilized a bottle in the home refrigerator, would likely return it to the wine shop where they bought it complaining of sediment.

TO FILTER OR NOT TO FILTER

When winemakers filter a batch of wine before bottling, one of the main things they're filtering out is any remaining live yeast cells that might be in the wine. If you fail to snag them all, there's a chance that another fermentation could begin after bottling, ending in bad-tasting wine, exploding wine bottles, and bitter tears. Still, there's this nagging suspicion that filtering removes some of the good stuff too, whether you mean to or not. The word "unfiltered" on the label implies the wine is of higher quality with a higher price, which you pay in exchange for skipping a step in the production process.

Bonarda

UNTIL RECENTLY, Bonarda dominated Argentinean wine (Malbec has since surpassed its yields). It is typically used to produce table wines in bulk. Of course, there are always exceptions—and some in the wine world disagree about what constitutes a "real" Bonarda grape.

Some experts say the Argentine Bonarda is the genuine Bonarda Piemontese, native to Italy but now rarely grown there. Others argue that Bonarda Novarese is the real deal—another Piedmont grape, also known as Uva Rara.

Added to the mix are other varieties sometimes called Bonarda. Argentina wine authorities are clear about one thing: Croatina, a Lombardy grape that also goes by the name Bonarda Oltrepo Paves, is *not* Bonarda.

Semantics aside, Bonarda wine is a palate-pleaser because of its light-bodied, fruity nature. You'll taste plum and cherry, and not too much tannin. When oak-aged, Bonarda gets big, deep in color, and rich with fig or raisin aromas.

Recipe: Herbed Bean Spread

VEGETARIAN RED-WINE LOVERS must look for subtler food pairings. They must bring up the protein in their cooking and bring down the tannin in the wine with which they pair it. This rich Italian bean spread pairs perfectly with a lighter red wine.

1 can (15 ounces, or 425 g) cannellini beans

½ cup (30 g) fresh parsley leaves

1 large garlic clove

½ teaspoon (3 g) salt

1 teaspoon (1 g) fresh thyme leaves

1 teaspoon (3 g) capers, drained

1 tablespoon (15 ml) fresh lemon juice

3 tablespoons (45 ml) olive oil

Drain and rinse the beans. Combine all ingredients except olive oil in a food processer, and blend until smooth. With the food processor running, add the olive oil until incorporated. This is best if made a day ahead of when you want to serve it. Spread thickly on bruschetta and drizzle with good olive oil before serving.

YIELD: Serves 6 to 8

Wine Pairing: J. Lohr Estates Wildflower Valdiguié

UNITED STATES (CALIFORNIA)

How this grape got to California, no one really knows. For years, it was thought to be Gamay, the red grape of Beaujolais, because they share a name. But genetic testing revealed Gros Auxerrois, an otherwise undistinguished red grape from southern France. In California, J. Lohr produces a dark red version that remains extremely light-bodied, low in tannin, and easy to drink in spite of its intense color. Valdiguié tastes very much like cherries and extremely light cranberries.

Rioja, Spain

RIOJA VINEYARDS WERE planted before the Romans moved into Spain. And though other countries produce more wine, Spain has the most acreage (hectares) planted. This is due in part to centuries of stringent regulation and care to preserve the integrity of grape crops. According to the Consejo Regulador of Rioja website, in 1635, carriages were banned from passing along roads next to cellars for fear that the vibration would disturb the juice and aging process.

Rioja contains three distinct wine regions: Rioja Alta, located on the western edge at higher elevations, produces Old World wines; Rioja Alavesa, with a similar climate as the Alta region, produces wines with a fuller body and more acidity; Rioja Baja, with its Mediterranean climate, generates grapes that produce highly alcoholic wines (some at 18 percent) generally blended with other Rioja wines.

Most of the wine produced in this region is red, made from grapes such as Tempranillo (gentle, berry flavor), Garnacha Tinta (peppery), Graciano (blackberry), and Mazuelo (tannin). Rioja white wines come from Viura (tart), Malvasia (nutty), and Garnacha Blanca (heavy). Families or co-operatives run most of Rioja's bodegas—the Spanish term for winery.

If you want to try a Rioja wine, look for "Rioja Calificada" on the label. Rioja is the only Spanish wine that can use this term, which indicates wine bottled in that district.

A worker in the Rioja region of Spain during wine harvest

Eric Asimov

FOR YEARS, THE COLUMN ERIC ASIMOV conceived of and wrote for the *New York Times* helped people eat lavishly in the Big Apple—appetizer, main course, and dessert (beverages, tax, and tip not included)—for a bargain. The popular column was compiled into Asimov's first book, *$25 and Under: A Guide to the Best Inexpensive Restaurants in New York* (Harper Collins 1995–98) before he shifted focus in 2004 to the meal's liquid portion. More specifically, Asimov became the *Times* chief wine critic in 2004.

Asimov now pens two columns, "The Pour" and "Wines of the Times." He doesn't leave out barley and hops, as his column sometimes switches gears to "Beers of the Times." The man knows his beverages.

He writes about them with an easy authority, unwrapping tastes through words, inspiring readers to experience wines and expand their palates. Asimov admires winemakers with passion and vision—those who make what they love to drink rather than blending what's in fashion. In many ways, this sums up his approach to writing about that very topic.

If you love wine, reading Asimov's work will open your tastes to new varieties. You can travel the globe through his writing, come away feeling as if you've experienced wine countries all over the world without leaving home. Certainly, he'll tempt you to introduce new wines to your collection.

Asimov resides in Manhattan with his wife, Deborah Hofmann, editor of the *New York Times* Best Seller List, and has two children, Jack and Peter. He graduated in 1980 from Wesleyan University, and pursued American studies at the University of Texas at Austin. Prior to joining the *New York Times* in 1984 as an editor in National News, he worked for the *Chicago Sun-Times*. Asimov has served various posts there as editor of the Living Section and Styles of the *Times*.

Bookmark and visit his blog at http://thepour. blogs.nytimes.com for a regular dose of wine knowledge.

Around-the-World Wine Party

TOUR THE WORLD OF WINE in one night by inviting guests to bring a bottle from different countries. Provide international appetizers for each, and treat the party like a tasting so everyone can sample the collection. Get creative and make invitations that resemble passports with stamps for each country your tasting will include.

Here's how to pull off this party theme:

• Assign a country to each guest to ensure a variety of wine from different places.

• Prepare the food yourself, or ask your guests to bring a complementary dish to go with the wine they choose. If you're part of a regular dinner or wine club, your guests will understand and be happy to bring the smorgasbord knowing that everyone takes turns hosting.

• Decide whether to stage the party as a formal tasting where you bag up the wines and reveal their labels after everyone has sampled (see Days 125 + 126 for how to host a blind tasting) or simply ask each guest to present the wine and provide a description.

• Go all out and decorate your home with a global theme. Use flags, festive cocktail napkins, or make wine charms (see Days 244 + 245) depicting each country represented at the party.

• Act as ambassador/host and write a wine list including the names of each bottle presented at your party. Give this list to guests as a favor (and shopping list so they can find their favorites to enjoy at home).

The Color of Wine

AS A SPECIES, WE STEREOSCOPIC humans are very visually oriented. Any time wine lovers get together with a few of their favorite bottles, they rhapsodize about the visual content of a glass of wine. They have a full color spectrum for use in their descriptions, from white wines clear as water to red wines black as ink.

Whites can look silver, gold, or green, luminescent or dull, bright or brilliant. Pink wines are pink, salmon, and sometimes rose-colored. Ruby, garnet, and scarlet say more about red wine than just color, as does the fact that Burgundy is both a color and a wine. At the wine-making level, color really comes down to grape. Red grapes yield pink juice used to make rosé, white Zinfandel, and the like.

When a winemaker takes the pink juice, adds back in the red grape skins, and then ferments all of that together, red wine results.

Though color doesn't tell you everything you need to know about a wine, it sets up some expectations. Delicate, thin-skinned grapes such as Pinot Noir typically make lighter red wines; a dark, dense grape such as Syrah acts as the base for deep reds. Vernaccia is the color of the Italian water it stereotypically replaces. Grenache looks purple and velvety in the glass. Mourvedre appears black and opaque.

Of course, there is the odd curveball: Imagine an ultra-dark red wine that tastes thin or a watery-looking white that's as big as all outdoors. Despite these exceptions, color density is usually a good indicator of flavor density.

Leaning Toward Portugal

As ITS NAME IMPLIES, Portugal is a nation of ports. In fact, it's been the Iberian Peninsula's gateway to the Atlantic for centuries. This explains the association between Portugal's most famous (and expensive) wine and British custom in a previous century. According to history/legend, Portuguese wines of the eighteenth century didn't travel well, so winemakers fortified them with a big dose of brandy (probably to mask the damage as much as anything else). In no time, England developed a taste for this high-alcohol concoction, giving birth to port as we know it.

By the time winter settles in to the northern hemisphere, look for a good wine that goes well with that blazing fireplace. Consider port (wine from Portugal) a classic choice. Mainstream port is a powerful late-harvest red dessert wine mixed with brandy. When it's warm, big black port can be tough to take, especially when the high, soaring alcohol becomes hot and piercing. Port comes out of hibernation when the weather turns cold, however, and the coldest nights seem made for its rich, dense, concentrated flavors.

The white paint smudge on a case of wine means "This Side Up" when storing. Port typically contains a significant amount of sediment, and you'll want to store it always in the same direction so as not to agitate any of the wine's sediment.

Wine Suggestion: Quinta de Roriz Vintage Port
PORTUGAL

Delicious dried fruit flavors—everything from date and fig to plum, cherry, and even a little cranberry—dominate this fantastic Quinta de Roriz, a wine admirably in balance. It has a high alcohol content—about 20 percent—but it's not hot on your tongue; there's late-harvest sweetness, but it's not sugary; and deep, resonant black fruit flavors balance the pervasive gripping tannin. Geologically, this wine would be a fjord, not just a port.

Recipe: Beurre Bleu

OF ALL OF THE CHEESES made in France, many of which are quite ancient, Bleu d'Auvergne is a relative newcomer, developed in the mid-1800s. The "inventor" of this cheese, Antoine Roussel, also invented a process called needling. During this process, the surface of cheese is pierced by tiny needles, allowing the cheese to turn very blue as the mold penetrates deeply in through the holes while simultaneously aerating and expelling much of the intensely noxious aroma that the bluing process generates. The result is an extremely blue yet extremely mild cheese, perfect for blending with butter.

¼ pound (112 g) unsalted butter (1 stick)

¼ pound (114 g) Bleu d'Auvergne or other creamy blue cheese

Allow the butter and cheese to stand for 1 to 2 hours until softened to room temperature. Combine in a large bowl and beat together roughly until the mixture becomes slightly smooth but still shows distinct chunks of blue cheese and butter throughout. Serve with a thinly sliced, crusty baguette.

YIELD: ½ pound (225 g)

Wine Pairing: Domaine de l'Oratoire Saint-Martin, Réserve des Seigneurs, Cairanne
FRANCE

Cairanne is a tiny town in the southern Rhône Valley in the south of France, underpriced and overshadowed by its much more famous neighbors Gigondas and Châteauneuf-du-Pape. This wine represents a beautiful blend of sunny Syrah and Grenache fruit, with the perfect overlay of smoke and wood. It's light enough to complement the butter, but gutsy enough to offset the blue cheese.

Johannisberg: The Magic Mountain

ONE WINERY IS NOTED FOR claiming to discover Riesling, a late-harvest wine known for its young and fruity taste. Schloss Johannisberg winery in Germany's Rheingau wine-growing region has been turning grapes into wine for some 1,200 years, since the Dark Ages. Benedictine monks in 1100 decided the land made an ideal site for a winery. There they built a Romanesque basilica and the hill became known as Johannisberg ("John's mountain," for John the Baptist).

The estate has survived generations of war, reconstruction, and changing of hands. The air raids on Mainz in 1942 during World War II almost completely destroyed the buildings. But today, the vineyard thrives as a jewel in Germany's Riesling country.

Because Schloss Johannisberg grows only one kind of grape, it has to harvest through the vineyards a dozen times or more to extract different ripeness at different times during the season. This is a gigantic amount of work, most of it by hand, but it captures and reveals unique wine identities and personalities. This wine is rich in pear, white peach, and guava. It tastes like honey and smells like crisp white linen.

If you want to taste a thirty-year-old wine from Schloss Johannisberg that is alive and full of flavor try 1971 TBA (Raisin Select Harvest). It is harvested after the grapes have hung on the vines so long that they literally became raisins.

Pressing them released a sweet, thick, unctuous nectar that created an identical wine. Amazingly, even after more than three decades, the wine tastes young and fruity, like sweet mulberries. Only the golden color and a stony minerality behind the juice belie the wine's age. This wine essentially challenges a number of ideas about what a good wine should be—young and dry, for two—but it cracks my personal top-ten list of best pure hedonistic pleasure wines.

Wine Suggestions: Riesling

1975 Schloss Johannisberg Riesling Spätlese/Late Harvest (collectors' item), Germany

This white wine does what few red wines can: survive the journey from vine to bottle to cellar for decades and still taste bright, new, and interesting. It's not uncommon for old wines to smell a little like sherry, and this one's got a nice hint of that. The rest is ripe, gold apple and pear.

1971 Schloss Johannisberg Riesling Trockenbeerenauslese/Raisin Select Harvest (collectors' item), Germany

Real sugary dessert wine survives the test of time thanks in part to its syrupy density. Not much can penetrate, so ideally it ages in self-containment for a long time. This ancient Riesling is sweet and rich in mulberry flavors, with the body of light maple syrup. It doesn't go with dessert; it is dessert.

Schloss Johannisberg, Rheingau, Germany

Georges Duboeuf

In his book *I'll Drink to That: Beaujolais and the French Peasant Who Made It the World's Most Popular Wine*, author Rudolph Chelminski charts the rise and fall and inevitable rise again (if he has anything to do with it) of the Beaujolais empire. He writes of Georges Duboeuf, king of the Beaujolais region and the man who singlehandedly created the annual Beaujolais Nouveau phenomenon.

Duboeuf, a small-town boy, attracted the attention of older, more powerful, better connected people who admired his wines and didn't care about the peasant-vintner's lack of pedigree. Oddly, it's not the Beaujolais that turns heads, but the Duboeuf family's Pouilly-Fuissé. "In 1951, when he was eighteen years old, he started his business by sticking two bottles of his family wine—which was, curiously enough, not a Beaujolais but a Pouilly-Fuissé—in his bike's carrying case and pedaled over to the neighboring town where the famous restaurant Le Chapon Fin had two Michelin stars," Chelminski said in an interview. "Chef Paul Blanc liked Duboeuf's Pouilly-Fuissé, and he said, 'I'll tell you what, kid, if you can get me some red wine as good as this white wine, I'll buy that, too.'"

Beaujolais, a relatively small wine region—about 26,000 acres (10,520 ha) of vines compared with 284,000 acres (114,930 ha) in Bordeaux and more than 600,000 acres (242,811 ha) in Languedoc—is composed mainly of small, privately held properties.

At first, no one took Duboeuf's efforts seriously. Then, as now, large dealers dominated Beaujolais, but Duboeuf took a different approach. "In those days, the growers had to come to the dealers, the dealers didn't come to them," Chelminski said. "After harvest, when they had their first samples of wine ready to taste, the growers had to trek out to either Villefranche or Belleville—the two main towns in the southern Beaujolais—and take their samples to these major wine dealers." The relationship between grower and dealer was bureaucratic, bordering on autocratic. "They would leave their bottles with the dealers, and the dealers would say, 'Come back on Monday and we'll tell you whether we'll take it or not and what price you'll get.' With that, it was finished," Chelminski continued. Dealers who bought the wine would bottle and sell it under their own labels. But Duboeuf started selling and labeling each peasant growth individually—a tradition he still carries out today for especially good growths with exceptional terroir.

Today, Duboeuf has overtaken the dealers to become the region's largest single Beaujolais supplier. He sells about 20 percent of total Beaujolais produced—around thirty million bottles a year—and sends seven million of those to the U.S. market.

Duboeuf earned credit for keeping Beaujolais both delicious and affordable. "His cheapest wines aren't necessarily anything to get your head spinning about, but they're good, honest wines," Chelminski said. Beaujolais is often confused with Pinot Noir. Bottles of Nouveau generally release in late November, making a perfect "gift" for your holiday table—though buying a case or two will ensure you have plenty to last you through the year.

Starting a Wine Collection

SOMETIMES A WINE COLLECTION occurs unintentionally. You begin purchasing bottles you fancy, and before long, you have an eclectic selection of wine—far more than you'd drink at a single party or within a month's time. Whether your collection comes to you happenstance or intentionally, here are some tips to help you expand its variety.

RESEARCH FIRST

Rather than taking a one-of-each approach and filling cases from your local retailer, read about wine and attend tastings to find out what you really like. Study reviews, visit wineries (or their websites), and acquaint yourself with the various styles.

PACE YOURSELF

If you're just starting a collection, purchase moderately priced wines so you don't risk too much on your wine investment. As you learn more about wine and discover your tastes, you may wish to splurge on collectors' bottles. Collecting is a lifetime hobby, so don't worry about rushing into the luxe wine aisle.

MAKE A WISH LIST

Plan which bottles you will purchase, and keep a running list of those you have your eye on to add to your collection. You cannot buy everything at once, and the anticipation of one day getting that special bottle adds to the fun. Also, a list will help you categorize wines into different varieties and establish a well-balanced collection.

MIX OLD AND YOUNG

Some bottles you'll want to age and enjoy years down the road. Others you'll want to uncork that night to drink with friends. Try to keep a variety of wines, some casual bottles you can pop at a moment's notice, and some special wines that will sit for months or years before you savor them.

Starter List

Below is a category list to help start your collection. Choose a wine (or several) in each. As you experience these and learn more about wine, expand your horizons.

Whites

- Chardonnay
- Pinot Blanc
- Pinot Grigio
- Sauvignon Blanc

Reds

- Barbera
- Cabernet Sauvignon
- Chianti
- Merlot
- Pinot Noir
- Zinfandel

What I Drank on My Summer Vacation

WINE'S AGRICULTURAL SIDE is essentially seasonal: growing, harvesting, bottling at certain times and selling year-round. For most people, this farming seasonality may be far away, but wine lovers find that their tastes naturally change with the seasons, too.

Come summer, you want a white wine, naturally. White wine generally tastes better when it's cooler, and coincidentally enough, coolness is just what your appetite desires. This is not to say you never drink a monster red wine after late spring. Outdoor cooking is a huge part of summer, and big reds pair perfectly with big red meat and a little sizzle of carbon.

Even though in theory, only six months have passed since the last mostly white wine diet, when you start drinking whites again, there's a moment of thinking, "Where have you been all my life?" Like many other indulgences, occasional breaks can help keep your interest fresh.

White wine feels young and energetic. The citric acid—the same as in lemons and limes—gives white wine a perceived brightness and crispness that's refreshing in the same way lemon soda and sorbet are refreshing.

Allowing your wine tastes to change is part of wine's seasonality. It connects you back to the core rhythm of how wine is made, from the vineyard to the bottle to you.

> Next time you travel, document not only the landscapes you see, the people you meet, and the sites you visit, but also the wines you drink and the food you eat.

Beaujolais: Place, Grape, Wine Name

BEAUJOLAIS HITS THE TRIFECTA for Old World wine: it's the name of a grape, a wine, and a geographical region in France, all at the same time. Beaujolais the grape confusingly goes by other names—Gamay, for instance. The region further breaks down into regions and neighborhoods such as Morgon, Fleurie, Saint-Amour, and at least a dozen others that are hard to keep in your head unless you live there.

Beaujolais the wine is famous for two reasons: a version of itself called Nouveau—"new"—wine made and released the same year within weeks of harvest, and low prices. Really low prices.

Order-now-and-save low prices. The very top of the Beaujolais food chain is still more affordable than wines from many other more famous French regions.

The Nouveau phenomenon isn't limited to the Beaujolais region or to France. Winemakers have always siphoned off a little bit of the early juice to make a quick, easy wine to celebrate the harvest (or those who don't have always wanted to). The Rhône Valley in southern France makes very tasty Nouveau in almost complete obscurity, and many wineries in northeast Italy make self-styled *novello* from an otherwise unknown grape called Teraldego.

A restaurant in Paris, France, announcing the arrival of Beaujolais Nouveau on its banner

Recipe: Marrow Stew

THIS TASTY STEW takes 30 minutes of prep time, and 4 hours in the oven.

4 pieces cross-cut center shin bone of beef (3 to 4 pounds, or 1.2 to 1.6 kg)

1 bottle (750 ml) good Tuscan red wine, divided

Salt and ground black pepper, to taste

¼ cup (60 ml) extra-virgin olive oil, divided

4 garlic cloves

1 can (14 ounces, or 410 g) Italian plum tomatoes, drained

¼ cup (7 g) rosemary, divided

1 cup (235 ml) vegetable broth

½ cup (30 g) chopped flat-leaf parsley, for garnish

Trim the meat off of the bone and cut into 2- to 3-inch (5- to 8-cm) pieces. Save the bones. Now that the knife work is finished, open the wine. Pour one whole glass, drink half, and keep the rest of the wine handy.

Salt and pepper the meat. In a large heavy pot with a lid, heat half of the oil over medium-high heat and brown the meat, 3 minutes a side.

Add the garlic, tomatoes, and half of the rosemary, and stir. Pour the rest of the bottle of wine over the top. Reduce the heat to medium-low and bring to a gentle boil. Turn the heat down very low, cover, and simmer slowly for 3 to 4 hours. Drink the rest of the wine in your glass and relax. Check now and then, but do not stir! If the dish starts to look dry, turn down the heat more and add a little water.

Ninety minutes before serving, preheat the oven to 400°F (200°C). In a medium-small cast-iron skillet (or other heavy skillet that can go in the oven), heat the rest of the olive oil over medium-high heat. Salt and pepper the bones and brown, marrow side down, for 10 minutes.

Turn the bones, sprinkle with the remaining rosemary, add the broth, reduce the heat to medium, and bring to a gentle boil. Baste the marrow bones and put the skillet into the oven. After 30 minutes, baste again and turn down the temperature to 325°F (179°C). Cook another 30 to 45 minutes, or until the marrow becomes soft and spreadable.

To serve, place a marrow bone in the middle of each plate. Pick the whole garlic cloves out of the stew and put one on top of each marrow bone. With a slotted spoon, scoop out the stew meat and arrange around the bone. Garnish with parsley.

Serve with thin toasted slices of baguette. Give each person a demitasse spoon to scoop out the marrow, then spread it on the baguette along with the stewed garlic.

YIELD: Serves 4

Wine Pairing: Capezzana Conti Contini Sangiovese
ITALY

Conti Contini is true to Tuscany: rugged and rustic, full of tangy Bing cherry flavors. It is a real Supertuscan, in fact. The aroma is herbal and aromatic, with hints of rosemary, dill, and even some black pepper. (For more about Supertuscans, see Day 299.)

Napa Valley

NAPA VALLEY, CALIFORNIA, contains more than 300 wineries, adding it to the list of premier wine regions, along with those in France, Italy, and Spain. Drive the roads that wind through Napa County—located just north of the San Francisco Bay Area—and you'll find quaint family wineries and large producers, rolling vineyards, and a landscape of wildflower and mustard fields.

Napa Valley marks one of the top vinicultural areas not only in the state of California but also in the United States. Some of its original nineteenth-century wineries still thrive: Charles Krug, Shramsburg, Château Montelena Winery, and Beringer. Some of the wine world's leading tastemakers hail from Napa Valley.

Take Robert Mondavi, who left his family's Charles Krug estate to found his own venture (see more about Mondavi on Day 12).

There's Ernest & Julio Gallo and their wine empire, still going strong (see Day 131). Sought-after labels originate from Napa and the region, and you can visit many of the wineries and taste for yourself. Or indulge in the fine cuisine the region offers at world-known restaurants such as French Laundry.

Today, Napa grows a variety of grapes, including Chardonnay, Merlot, Cabernet Sauvignon, and Zinfandel, though roadblocks in Napa's wine-growing history challenged production. For one, Prohibition in 1920, then an infestation of phylloxera root louse, which killed many vines in the valley. Many wineries closed their doors, and Napa's growth as a wine leader slowed until after World War II, when the industry experienced a reawakening. Since then, Napa Valley continues each year to draw millions of visitors who travel to experience the premier wine destination.

Wine Controls Weight

ALCOHOL, WHICH GETS metabolized into sugar, mostly determines wine's caloric content. Sweet wines contain some residual sugar that adds calories as well.

In general, dry, low-alcohol wines (with less than 10 percent alcohol) have the fewest calories, seventy-five to one hundred a glass. Light Italian white wines (Pinot Grigio, Orvieto, and Vernaccia, for instance) and Vinho Verde from Portugal are perfect low-alcohol, low-calorie choices.

Super-concentrated, high-alcohol reds go higher and higher, up to 14 percent alcohol or even more. California Zinfandels advertise 18 percent, but at that level, you're more likely to find yourself unconscious before you'll need to worry about weight gain.

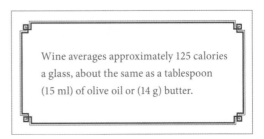

Wine averages approximately 125 calories a glass, about the same as a tablespoon (15 ml) of olive oil or (14 g) butter.

Design a Wine Cellar

YOU STARTED A WINE COLLECTION, and now that your stock is growing, you're stashing bottles in every nook and cranny in your home. Closets, cupboards, crawlspaces—your house is a wild wine country, and it's time for some order. What you need is a home wine cellar.

There are build-your-own books you can buy to learn how to construct the cellar yourself, or you can enlist a professional for the job. Either way, keep in mind these considerations as you plan the space. (Also, check out Days 6 + 7 for some creative places to store wine in your home.)

LOCATION, LOCATION

As long you create the proper conditions to preserve and age wine, you can locate your cellar most anywhere in your home. However, there are some exceptions. Avoid putting wine near a water heater or other heat source. Keep bottles away from vibration, including areas in the home that may tremble when heavy machinery or trucks pass, or even the washing machine. Ideally, choose a dark, cool space that will require minimal temperature and humidity tweaking.

HUMIDITY AND TEMPERATURE CONTROL

Depending on the location of your wine cellar—basement or above ground—you'll need to adjust the temperature and humidity so bottles can age gracefully. Insulation is a must. You are creating a microclimate for your wine that must stay constant. Ideally, you want 60- to 65-percent humidity levels; dry conditions dry out corks. Some basements already have this climate, and if this describes your home, lucky you. Still, you must insulate. Some guidelines for insulation: at least R-13 for walls, R-19 for floor and ceilings. "R" rating, or R-value, is the measure of thermal resistance.

AMPLE STORAGE

Plan for three times more space than you need—really. Building a wine cellar with capacity for 2,250 bottles of wine sounds excessive. But think about it: if you collect 150 bottles a year, with an average five-year turnaround on each bottle, that's 750 bottles. Down the road, at this rate of collecting, you could need a home for a couple thousand bottles. You can wait to install all of these racks and allow wall space to add on to your cellar, but just be sure to give yourself leeway and think big.

FLEXIBLE RACKING

Make sure that racking will accommodate various bottle sizes. Wine ages best in magnums, which hold two regular bottles of wine. Dessert wines generally come in half-bottles. And if you collect Bordeaux, which you may purchase in its original wooden case, you'll need a special spot in your cellar to store these prizes.

Synesthesia

It is said that the Russian composer Alexander Scriabin literally saw flashes of light and different colors when he heard different musical notes. Neuroscientists call this phenomenon synesthesia, and Beatles albums and LSD trips are full of it: tasting colors, feeling sounds, girls with kaleidoscope eyes, and more.

When wine lovers encounter new wines and eccentric flavors they've never before tasted, they fumble through a synesthetic landscape, trying to connect what they taste with what's familiar.

Greeks make a white wine called Retsina that, for reasons complex and historical, is flavored with pine resin (see Day 81). Any carpenter would recognize the delicious aroma of fresh-cut heartwood fir immediately, but you and I might say "paint thinner" and have a very different association.

Mainstream wine flavors—apple, pear, peach, melon, lemon-lime—are all well and good, and they make wine taste delicious. But wine's eccentric flavor profiles, the tastes we don't experience all the time, make it unforgettable.

Mother of All Zins

The Pedroncelli family of Sonoma, California, got into the wine business during Prohibition, when buying vineyard land was cheap and easy. The family has been making wine for more than seventy years.

The winery has a particular plot of grapes assigned "Mother Clone" designation; as it expanded, the Pedroncelli winemakers used grafts from this plot to plant many new vineyards. It is literally the mother of other acres (hectares).

> ### Wine Suggestion: Pedroncelli Mother Clone Zinfandel
> UNITED STATES (CALIFORNIA)
>
> This wine comes from the original Zinfandel vines planted in the late 1920s, when John Pedroncelli purchased the land. According to the winemakers, it has a full body, with subtleties of blackberry and spice, plum, and even black pepper.

Herbes de Provence

A THOUSAND WONDERFUL ASPECTS about the south of France keep people returning to its landscape century after century. For sun-worshippers, it's the unique light of day that's simultaneously bright and soft. For others, it's the warm, Mediterranean climate that connects the French coastal provinces to Italy and Spain. For wine lovers, it's easy to get swept away by the mind-bending, undervalued wines we haven't yet discovered.

Besides the wine, the scent of garrigue, the scraggly herbal underbrush that grows virtually everywhere, defines the south of France. Picture a field of green, only instead of timothy, crab-grass, and dandelion, it has rosemary, thyme, tarragon, lavender, and mint, all of it growing like weeds close to the ground. When you walk through these fields of garrigue, the aroma of the blending herbs rises in the air, and before long, the smell is everywhere, clinging to your clothes and hair for days.

Garrigue in a jar is called herbes de Provence, a blend of all of the herbs above with which you can cook. Try making your own blend with one part each of all of your favorite dried herbs, plus one-half part dried lavender. For recipes that include herbes de Provence, see Day 24, Meat Stew with Garlic Sauce, and Day 80, Rosemary-and-Mushroom-Stuffed Leg of Lamb.

> ## Wine Pairing: Domaine Clavel Les Garrigues Coteaux du Languedoc
> **FRANCE**
>
> Spicy, rich, smoky, and woody, full of delicious herbs and flowers, this wine is worth much more than it costs, but don't tell anyone. A bottle of this wine with a roasted leg of rosemary lamb will transport you to summer.

Herbes de Provence and other herbs and spices offered at a farmers' market in Sainte-Maxime, Cote d'Azur, Provence, France

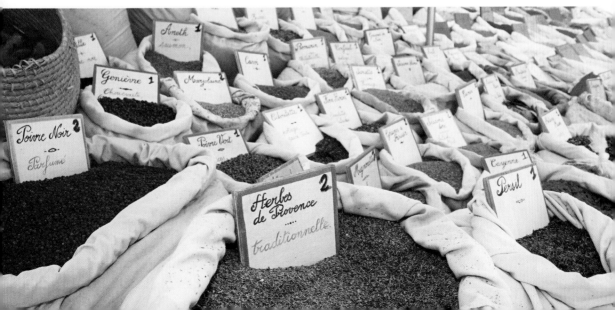

Fine Rhine Wine

THE STEEP HILLSIDE VINEYARDS of Germany's Rhine wine region are home to crisp Riesling wine, and the scenery you'll take in during a drive alongside or a cruise on the Rhine River is out of a fairy tale. Imagine rows of grapes punctuated by centuries-old churches, culturally rich towns with their monuments and alleyways.

The Rhine Valley's warm air, drifting in from the south, provides an ideal climate for grape growing—especially for Riesling grapes, which love mild winters, early springs, and a long growing season through late fall. This area rarely experiences heavy frost—also good for the grapes. The river helps keep the region's temperature in check.

Another winning feature of the Rhine Valley is its slate soil, a prime foundation for growing Riesling grapes. For wine drinkers, this translates into wines with a delicate bouquet, acidity, and mineral overtones, all typical qualities of Rhineland wines.

If you go: A cruise on the Rhine River provides panoramic perspective you won't get while winding through the mountains by automobile (or biking, if you're in shape for some steep hills). You'll make stops in German cities, including Cochem, Bernkastel, Rüdesheim, Heidelberg, Colmar, and Strasbourg.

Heidi Peterson Barrett

HEIDI PETERSON BARRETT, called the First Lady of Wine, is praised for her ability to blend the art and science of wine making. Barrett was only twenty-five years old when she earned the title "winemaker" for Buehler Vineyards in the eastern hills of California's St. Helena wine region. By then, she had worked under Justin Meyer of Silver Oak and Franciscan Vineyards, and worked "crush" (harvest) for Rutherford Hill and Lindeman's Wines, the Australian producer.

Barrett, who has a degree in fermentation sciences from the University of California, Davis, put Buehler Vineyards on the map, increasing production there from 6,000 to 20,000 cases. After five years, she became a wine consultant and in 1988, joined Gustav Dalla Valle to vinify his grapes from the eastern hills of the Oakville wine region. She stayed with him until 1996 and developed the cult wine Maya, a proprietary

Cabernet blend that received two perfect 100s from Robert Parker, renowned wine critic (see Day 57).

The First Lady of Wine then moved on to work at Screaming Eagle, a talked-about California winery where her first vintage, a 1992, earned a 100 from Parker. A six-liter bottle of this wine set a record when it sold for $500,000.

Barrett launched her own label, La Sirena, in 1994. Her latest project is Amuse Bouche, a joint wine venture with John Schwartz. Her wines are fruity yet dense, refined and balanced. Barrett's ability to marry contrary characteristics differentiates her from other fine winemakers. And she pulls it off time and again. According to *Wine & Spirits* magazine, "In the realm of Napa cult wine, Heidi Barrett is the reigning queen . . . Barrett makes gorgeous wines; supple, elegant, generous in flavor and nearly perfect in their composure."

Writing a Proper Toast

YOU ARE ASKED TO GIVE a toast at an important event: wedding, anniversary, retirement, business affair, public meeting, (insert occasion here). You're honored, but now what? You must come up with just the right words to express this person's significance, accomplishments, and so on. Chances are you're the toast-giver because you know the honoree quite well. And if not, you've got some homework to do.

Much has been written about giving a proper toast, and certainly, delivering a powerful toast—"toast" not "speech"—that an audience will remember is an art. Here are some helpful hints when you're the one inviting the crowd to raise a glass.

CONSIDER THE AUDIENCE

Who will be in attendance? Will you address a mature audience, business associates, old college buddies, family? The audience sets the tone for your toast, as does the setting, whether it's formal or casual.

CHOOSE WORDS CAREFULLY

Focus on the most important emotions, a single significant accomplishment, a defining characteristic. Don't try to sum up your entire relationship or the honoree's forty-year career during one toast.

FOCUS ON THE HONOREE

You have the attention of the room, but this toast is *not* about you. Avoid saying "I" and "me" and you'll be safe. Instead, use "we" and speak about the honoree on behalf of the audience.

MAKE IT QUICK

This is a toast, not a speech, a moment of recognition, not a life story. While writing your toast, make a list of points you want to express. Choose the top three and add an anecdote that supports those points. Then stop. Honor the person, and wrap it up.

SAY IT OUT LOUD

Practice your toast by reading it out loud. It's acceptable to read a toast if you cannot memorize it, or to keep some notes on hand so you can stay on track. Just be sure to do a dress rehearsal before the event.

> Save your wine until after the toast. It may be tempting to calm your nerves with a glass of red, but you want to be sharp so you can deliver your toast flawlessly.

First Taste: Is It "Off"?

YOU ORDERED A BOTTLE of wine at a fine res-taurant and the sommelier presents you with the bottle, uncorks it, pours a taste into your wineglass, and looks to you for approval. You uneasily pick up your glass, swirl it, study it, and hope that the attention you pay to this selection is appropriate—but it can be so stressful.

You taste and look up at the sommelier, who awaits your response. Now, here's where many people miss the point of this exercise. The som-melier does not want to know if you *like* the wine, is not asking you whether this is the best Merlot that ever crossed your lips, nor does he or she want feedback such as, "Ahh ... reminds me of a trip to Italy."

The sommelier may acknowledge this pleasant feedback with a smile and courteous reply, but what he or she really wants to know is if the wine is "off." "Off" is the term used to describe a wine's condition. Is it damaged? Not well preserved? Was it stored too hot? Do you suspect the cork failed? You chose the wine variety, so you own that decision. Now it's the restaurant's responsibility to deliver you a quality bottle of that selection.

It's not difficult to tell if a wine is off—you don't need any special training to make this call. A wine is off if:

- Its aroma causes you to pull your head back because of its smell

- It smells like dank newspapers or wet cardboard

- It smells moldy

It doesn't matter *why* the wine is off, and that's not your mystery to solve. All you have to do is politely tell your sommelier, "This wine is off. Could you bring me another bottle of exactly the same?" This shows the sommelier that you are not questioning your choice in wine, but that you are not pleased with this particular bottle's condition.

Beware of subtleties during this quick exchange. The whole drama described here will last less than a minute. If you, at any point, nod at the sommelier, you bought the bottle. Done. So be careful about sending mixed messages and be clear when you speak about the wine. Saying, "This wine is bad," when referring to condition (wet newspaper smell) will confuse the sommelier, who will think you don't like the choice you made.

Be clear and use the term "off" to describe a wine that isn't up to par. Otherwise, nod, pour, and enjoy.

Nebbiolo

FOR ALL THE PAINS viniculturalists go through to raise Nebbiolo and produce the grape into quality wine, it seems fitting that the resulting product should leave a bold impression. It is darker, more tannic, and higher in alcohol than most varieties. And some say it's just as moody as Pinot Noir in processing.

Grown primarily in Piedmont, Italy, where it is regarded as a noble wine, the fruit has a prominent fog that looks almost frosted. (*Nebbia* means "fog" in Italian, another explanation for its moniker.) Depending on where you are in Italy, Nebbiolo also goes by the names Spanna, Picutener, and Chiavennasca.

The only other area in Italy where the grape grows is Valtellina, at the foot of the Alps in the Lombardi region. However, vintners in many places have planted acreage (hectares)—most of them not achieving the quality of Barolo, Barbaresco, and Gattinara wines produced with Nebbiolo. Interestingly, Nebbiolo makes up only about 3 percent of Barolo wine.

So why is Nebbiolo such a temperamental grape to grow? First, it is sensitive to soil, preferring calcareous over sandy, and fickle when grown in different locations. A slight shift in these two variables can result in quite different wines in terms of body, tannin levels, and acidity. Nebbiolo ripens late in the season and requires optimum sun exposure.

That said, if you uncork a bottle of wine containing the Nebbiolo grape, enjoy the cherry-licorice-truffle aroma, and pair it with strong meats and cheeses. Nebbiolo can stand up to foods that may overpower other varieties.

Recipe: Tuna Provençale

PROVENCE IS NOT MUCH of a white wine region, forcing its citizens to get used to pairing red and rosé with seafood, a match at which other cuisines balk. So long as you follow the standard rule—white wine with white fish, red wine with red fish—you can safely go red with tuna in spite of the conventional wisdom.

3 tablespoons (45 ml) olive oil, divided

1 cup (160 g) onions, chopped

1 garlic clove, minced

½ pound (225 g) plum tomatoes, coarsely chopped

1 cup (40 g) loosely packed fresh basil

1½ tablespoons (13 g) capers, rinsed and drained

2 tuna steaks (5 to 6 ounces [142 to 170 g])

Salt and ground black pepper, to taste

Heat 1½ tablespoons (23 g) of the olive oil in a heavy medium-size skillet over medium heat. Add the onion and sauté for 5 minutes, until tender. Add the garlic, sauté until golden, then stir in the tomatoes, basil, and capers. Simmer, uncovered, until the sauce thickens, stirring occasionally.

Meanwhile, heat the remaining oil in another heavy large-size skillet over medium-high heat. Sprinkle the fish with salt and pepper. Add the fish to the skillet and cook until light brown at the edges, 3 minutes per side. At this point, the tuna should be medium-rare. Pour in the tomato sauce. For well-done (or to your taste), cook for 5 more minutes.

Wine Pairing: Saint André de Figuière Cuvée François Côtes de Provence

FRANCE

Typical of southern French reds, this wine contains a broad variety of grapes—Syrah, Grenache, Cinsault, and Cabernet Sauvignon—in almost equal parts. The result: a nicely knit red that's soft and food-friendly. *Figuière* is French for "fig grower," and it's hard not to taste some concentrated dried fruit flavors in this wine.

197

Barossa Valley, Australia

GO DOWN UNDER FOR SOME of the world's renowned Shiraz—down under to Barossa Valley, Australia, which holds rank with Tuscany, Bordeaux, and Napa Valley as a premier wine-producing region. The Barossa, as it is called, sits about an hour's drive from Adelaide and includes four communities: Angaston, Lyndoch, Nuriootpa, and Tanunda, along with a collection of tiny hamlets. The settlement, unlike most other Australian cities, is a true example of preserved British and Prussian heritage.

Wine making dates back to the Barossa's founding in 1857, when hardworking families cleared the land for agriculture, built churches and schools, and planted grapes. After six generations of grape growers, some of those small vineyards still carry the same family names today.

Barossa packs its calendar year with festivals and celebrations. While visiting, stop by artisan butcher and baker shops and indulge in the region's culinary offerings, which equal the reputation of Barossa wine. And where else can you go bushwalking after visiting a winery?

Barossa Valley vineyards in Australia

Jean-Michel Cazes

"I WAS ALWAYS CONVINCED that by making wine, you were making friends," Jean-Michel Cazes once told a *Fine Wine* reporter. The French winemaker and insurance executive managed the wine holdings of AXA Millésimes until 2000, and the Cazes family estates until 2006.

But before settling on the family estate to build the Bordeaux region's famous Château Lynch-Bages into a progressive, contemporary winery, Cazes learned petroleum engineering as a graduate student at the University of Texas, became a sales manager for IBM France, and served as president of STAD (Empain-Schneider Group) in Paris.

Not until he was well into his thirties did Cazes dedicate his time and resources to the wine industry. Upon the passing of his grandfather, after whom Cazes was named, Cazes's father Andre talked about selling the family estate. Cazes, by then married with four children and living in Paris, made a career and life change by moving back to his hometown of Pauillac in 1973, when Bordeaux suffered tough times because of overspeculation in wine futures and the oil crisis.

A determined young Cazes modernized the family winery, drawing on his engineering background as he introduced stainless steel vats for fermenting. He enlisted Daniel Llose—still Cazes's trusted enologist today—to gradually improve all aspects of wine production at Lynch-Bages.

By the early 1980s, Lynch-Bages finally gained a worldwide reputation. Cazes traveled to the United States and hosted wine dinners with other Bordeaux winemakers to introduce their grape to fresh markets. He developed an eclectic following of esteemed fans. A bottle of 1975 Lynch-Bages even ended up in space.

By 1990, Cazes began casual efforts to market his wines in China, and by 2008, Lynch-Bages sold about 5 percent of its output there. He created Michel-Lynch, a 100,000-cases brand. And over time, he created a wine portfolio by investing in French properties and estates in Portugal and Hungary.

Lynch-Bages expanded the family legacy into a tourist destination, complete with a wine school, a nearby luxury hotel, and a restaurant that has earned two Michelin stars, headed by Chef Thierry Marx, a notably innovative culinary talent. Cazes is technically retired, but he keeps an office at the château. His son, Jean-Charles, runs day-to-day operations of the winery, though Cazes's energy prevents him from staying too far from the action.

Too Much Wine …

YOU TASTED YOUR WAY into a tizzy last night. Let's be blunt. You downed way too much wine, kicked moderation out the door, then had a nightcap. Now it's 6:30 a.m. and you lay in bed not moving as your alarm blares. It's Monday morning and you must report to work. Your head throbs like your brain got caught inside a bass drum, and you're sweating even though it's freezing outside. Your mouth is so dry it feels like you ate a sock for dinner. This is not good.

My friend, you have a hangover in the worst way. You likely did not savor each sip of wine. Blame it on your alter ego, Mr. or Ms. Just One More. Regardless, you need a fast recovery. And next time, you need to prevent a repeat of this drama. Here's how:

REHYDRATE

Your head pounds because you chose to drink alcohol rather than water last night. It doesn't help that alcohol is a diuretic, basically sucking the moisture from your body. So drink water, and plenty of it. Add a sports drink to that, which contains electrolytes and sodium and will boost your energy and feed your hurting body. (Don't drink too much sports drink, though—they're also loaded with sugar.)

REPLENISH YOUR BODY

Down some orange juice to help your liver process the wine. Oh, your aching liver. Also, eat a banana. Alcohol depletes potassium levels, a mineral bananas have plenty of.

SNEAK A NAP

Alcohol disrupts sleep patterns, and a full bladder from all that wine doesn't help. You probably didn't sleep well last night, so if you can, sneak in a nap. Don't overexert yourself.

AVOID COFFEE

Remember, you're already dehydrated. Caffeine, like alcohol, dehydrates the body. Reach for juice, a sports drink, or water instead. And do not cure a hangover by having a glass of the "hair that bit you." No sense in that.

Next time, practice the following:

• Eat before you drink wine, and regularly thereafter.

• Drink plenty of water as you consume wine to prevent dehydration.

• Know when to stop drinking—and don't wait to lose your vision and balance before deciding to cut yourself off for the night.

• Savor your wine. You'll enjoy it more if you take the time to immerse yourself in its aromas and pair it with delicious food. If you drink wine this way, you will not need the emergency hangover instructions here. Cheers to being responsible next time!

Wine-Tasting Etiquette

GESTURES ARE LANGUAGE TOO, often just as obscene or genteel as words.

NBC TV's 2003 reality series *The Restaurant* took the camera inside an out-of-control establishment where the unthinkable happened. At the end of a wine-tasting class, one of the waiters actually chugged the spit bucket. A few hundred dollars from a bet with his colleagues does not fully explain his motivation. But the vast amount of wine he'd already consumed during the tasting that generated the spit bucket may.

One year later, in the wine-buddy film *Sideways*, Paul Giamatti's hyper-snob Miles goes into hyper-drive and does exactly the same. It was, without a doubt, one of the most repellant sights crafted for the screen. After the nausea passes, you may start to worry that someone would try that in reality.

Take comfort: of all the people given the opportunity to drink from a spit bucket, true wine lovers are the least likely to do so. You're in good company.

Critique of Pure Riesling

ROUND, RIPE RIESLING, glistening with fruit sugar, tastes like the frosting on the frosting. In a world of dry white wines and big gutsy reds, sweet, easy-to-love Riesling looks a little out of place. At the beginning of the twenty-first century, German winemakers—mostly high-quality Riesling producers—pushed their wine-making skills to produce profoundly dry—that is, sugar-free—Rieslings that do battle with the great white wines of the world.

Once German winemakers tame the sugar in their wines, the grapes begin to show depths of flavor reminiscent mostly of French Chablis and other white Burgundy. Some Rieslings in the fertile Rheingau have so much fruit that even though they're completely free from sugar, they compare to the likes of Sauvignon Blanc and Chenin Blanc.

Dry Riesling is in line to be the next big wine, ready for the pendulum of taste to swing in its favor.

Wine Suggestion: Dry Rieslings

Dr. Loosen Riesling, Germany
Dr. Ernst Loosen (pronounced LOH-zen) engineered a revolution in German Riesling from the best position possible: his family's 200-year-old wine estate. Departing from sweetness, his wines exhibit a whole spectrum of aromatic, earthy, big-time wine flavors ranging from well water to tree sap to rare tropical fruits. Today, Loosen means Riesling around the world, and he has partnered with wine giant Château Ste-Michelle in Washington State to make wine in the U.S.

Leitz Dragonstone Riesling, Germany
The full German name of this wine—Leitz Rudesheimer Drachenstein Riesling—was too long and complicated for a modern, international clientele, so the winery changed it. *Drachenstein* in English means "dragonstone," tribute to the fossils and a giant dinosaur-like footprint discovered on the vineyard. Dry, lean, and bracing, Dragonstone tastes like New World Riesling, attuned to the American palate. If this wine were a musical instrument, it would be all treble; its flavors resonate in the upper register with zippy, lemony fruit.

Harvesting Abundance:
Wine, Cheese, Olive Oil

WINE, CHEESE, OLIVE OIL—these timeless foods all solve the same dilemma of abundance met by farmers and growers: Now that I've had the good fortune of a harvest, what do I do with it all? In the millennia before mechanical cooling, people answered with diverse and interesting solutions.

Grapes aren't like other fruit. They will not ripen further after they're picked. The moment a grape is picked, it begins a relentless descent into spoilage and disintegration. Making the grape juice into wine slows its aging considerably. Raw grape juice at room temperature will last a week or so before the cork starts to pop. In the form of wine, it can persist for years, even decades.

Cheese comes from gallons (liters) of milk in easily transportable pounds (grams) of a delicious food you can eat later, sometimes much later. Similarly, olive oil is both a preservative and an extractor of maximum calories. The meat of an olive contains oil and juice, but 30 percent of an olive's oil comes from grinding and pressing the hard pit. The oil extraction process, separating the sediment and water, then clarifying it renders the oil long-lived and resistant to deterioration.

It's no real surprise that wine, cheese, olive oil, and the de rigueur bread pair together in otherworldly ways. In many religions, this food and drink represented a god: Bacchus of the Romans, Ceres the grain goddess, and the little-known Aristaeus, Greek god of cheese making and olive growing.

Washington State

RELATIVELY SPEAKING, Washington State is a newcomer to the wine world. Wine grapes grew in Washington beginning in 1825, but it wasn't until after Prohibition that the Northwest's first bonded winery was founded on Puget Sound's Stretch Island. By 1938, the area had forty-two wineries, with the first large-scale plantings starting in the 1960s. These efforts set the groundwork for influential wineries such as Château Ste. Michelle. Today, Washington produces more than thirty different grape varieties (nearly a fifty-fifty split of white and red), and has more than 32,000 vineyard acres (12,950 ha) planted.

Washington takes its wine seriously—grapes are the state's fourth largest fruit crop. Now tourists are bolstering the state's wine economy as they visit Washington's various wine appellations, including Walla Walla Valley, Puget Sound, Rattlesnake Hills, Columbia Gorge, and others.

This Pacific Northwest state's wine-growing region is growing fast, with a new winery opening nearly every two weeks. And the quality of wines these wineries produce has earned international acclaim; winemakers from Italy, Australia, and other wine regions are starting to establish wineries in Washington because of the state's ideal geographic growing conditions. The region earns consistent high ratings from wine media. Keep your eyes out for Washington State wines.

Goose Ridge Estate Vineyards and Winery, Columbia Valley, Washington, United States

Jorge Ordoñez and Spanish Wines

JORGE ORDOÑEZ singlehandedly reintroduced Spanish wines to the United States, period. Beginning in 1987, this importer who has twice won the praise of influential Robert Parker as Wine Personality of the Year, began paying careful attention to Spain, which, despite the country's lush vineyards, had heretofore produced mediocre wines. When no one cared about Spanish wines, Ordoñez did.

Ordoñez grew up working in his family's distribution firm, learning hands-on by loading trucks and visiting wineries. He settled in the Boston area with his wife, Kathy, after attending University of Cordoba, and in the 1980s began making trips to Spain to visit small family wineries.

Ordoñez helped the wineries improve their wine selections one by one. And then one by one, he introduced the new Spanish wines to the growing wine market in the United States. Today, Ordoñez has the deepest Spanish wine portfolio, with 130 wines from forty wineries. His green monogram appears on every bottle in his collection. He emphasizes the artisan craft of viniculture to wine-making families and partners with them to succeed.

Tireless in his pursuit to uphold the quality of Spanish wines, Ordoñez puts great energy into celebrating the character of Spanish wines, making friends along the way. He spends winter and spring visiting bodegas in Spain to unearth new wines. Ask Ordoñez anything, *anything* about Spanish wines, and he will answer you with great enthusiasm and not a drop of pretentiousness.

Repurpose Empty Wine Bottles

THERE ARE COUNTLESS creative ways to repurpose empty wine bottles into practical glassware, interesting artwork, even garden accessories. Some treatments require professional help to alter the bottle's shape with heat or by cutting. Other projects involve using the bottle as is, in unexpected places.

You'll never look at an empty bottle the same way knowing all you can do with it:

GARDEN BORDER

Remove labels and fill empty wine bottles with sand. Push them upside down into the soil along a garden bed, leaving the bottom half exposed. The side-by-side bottles form a glass berm (a narrow path). Choose different-colored bottles and vary the pattern to add whimsy.

SIMPLE STORAGE

Purchase a stopper for a bottle, then fill it with olive oil. Save half-bottles, which can come in handy for preserving wine if you open a bottle but don't finish it.

GLASSWARE

With a glass cutter (available at craft stores), remove the bottle neck and cut down until the remainder of the bottle leaves a desirable drinking glass height. Smooth the top, cut edge using a ceramic knife sharpener. Voilà! You've created unique tumblers with the punt in the bottom (see Day 246). Note, be careful when cutting the glass.

CANDLESTICK

Insert a drip candle in the bottle opening and allow the wax to trickle down and decorate the bottle. Repeat this with different-colored candles for an artistic effect.

You Are What You Drink

PEOPLE NEW TO DISCUSSING WINE use their own vibrant vocabulary to describe what they taste. For example, artists describe wine with particular flair. Great cooks and audiophiles seem always to grasp first what's behind or going on with a wine, placing different sensory components in quick relation to each other.

Architects speak of wine in, predictably, architectural terms. They taste deep, foundational elements. Further in, they note other structural flavors, high and decorative.

Painters and photographers taste wine and talk about intensity of color, foreground and background, focus or not. Musicians understand and speak about wine as music, referring to high notes, low tones, and deep resonating flavor passages.

The wine lover with every score memorized can't hold a candle to the person who can explain, "If wine were music or a landscape or a sports car, my favorite wine would be like this." You don't need to be a skilled artist to have nuanced taste in wine; if you can describe wine in a nuanced fashion, you're golden.

Muscat of Alexandria

WHILE AUSTRALIA DOMINATES with Shiraz, it dazzles with eccentric grape varietals such as Petite Verdot, Verdelho, and Muscat of Alexandria. Muscat is one of the ancients, a white grape from the Middle East whose name lives on as the name of Oman's capital city on the Arabian Sea. (The city of Shiraz, by the way, exists only 600 miles [965 km] northwest of Muscat in southern Iran.)

Muscat has spread across the globe, taking different forms in different lands. In northern Italy, for example, you'll find Moscato and the bubbly Moscato d'Asti. Muscat of Alexandria is one of the three official grapes of Spanish sherry. And in the New World, there's Muscat Canelli, orange Muscat, black Muscat, and many more.

What they all share is a tremendous citrus fruit core that smells like orange and guava and tastes the way that orange blossoms smell. You can almost taste the flowers and fresh green leaves.

Wine Suggestion: Alice White Lexia Muscat of Alexandria
AUSTRALIA

Alice White's Lexia (which means "the law") is ripe and rich, a little sweet, but still nice and crisp when you chill it. The alcohol is low at only 10 percent, perfect for casual summertime sipping. Serve it with a basket of fresh ripe peaches and farmer's cheese on crusty bread.

Recipe: Red Wine Risotto

ARBORIO RICE, NAMED FOR the Italian town of Arborio in the Piedmont where it originated, is delicious in flavor but a little boring visually. To make up for this monotony, introduce dry red wine as an ingredient and the rice comes out a festive purple-pink color.

2½ cups (570 ml) chicken stock

1½ cups (355 ml) dry red wine

1 tablespoon (15 ml) olive oil

8 tablespoons (112 g) butter (1 stick), divided

2 garlic cloves, crushed and chopped

2 red onions, chopped

10 ounces (285 g) Arborio rice

8 ounces (225 g) sliced mushrooms

Salt and ground black pepper, to taste

6 ounces (170 g) grated Parmigiano-Reggiano cheese

Heat the stock and the red wine in a large saucepan to a gentle simmer.

Heat the olive oil and half of the butter in a heavy saucepan. Add the garlic and onions and sauté until tender. Add the rice and coat the grains with oil and butter. Add the hot stock to cover the rice.

Simmer and stir, adding about a ½ cup of stock at a time as the liquid absorbs. After adding half the hot stock-wine mixture, add the mushrooms and season with salt and pepper. Continue adding the remainder of the stock, stirring and allowing time for the rice to absorb the liquid. Add the cheese and the remainder of the butter and mix well.

YIELD: Serves 6 to 8

Wine Pairing: La Scolca Rosa Chiara Rosé

ITALY

On its own, a nice rosé from the Piedmont is perfect: not too citrusy like a white wine could be, with a lighter touch than a neighborhood red such as Dolcetto or Barbera—grapes a little too strong for the risotto's delicacy.

209

Muscat grapes hang at a vineyard

Chile

RETAILERS LOVE CHILEAN WINES because wine lovers can have their cake and eat it, too. The price is nice, and Chile today produces some internationally competitive varieties.

Chile's signature grape, Carmenere, produces the Chilean version of Merlot that's becoming a retail staple. Carmenere is a Bordeaux red variety that is an anonymous blending grape back in France but that thrives on its own in Chile. Also, phylloxera, a pest that feeds on vine roots, nearly wiped out this grape in Europe. But to this day, Chile remains phylloxera-free, and no one is quite sure why. In fact, during the 1800s and into the twentieth century when the world demanded European wine exports, the root louse phylloxera had wreaked havoc in the old country, and Chile stepped in to supply quantities of the desired wine.

Through the years, Chile's wine industry has confronted obstacles preventing its growth, including periods of export restrictions and production limits. But since the late 1980s after the country opened its doors to trade and began investing in modern wine-making technology, such as facilities with temperature-controlled stainless steel tanks, gravity-flow infrastructure, modern low-impact crushers, presses, and small oak barriques, the wine growers began to improve their fruit and raise Chile's reputation in the wine world.

Today, Chile exports its wine to more than ninety countries on five continents, and sales continue to climb.

Here's a quick tour of Chile's wine country:

• North of Santiago sit vineyards that produce the Pais grape, which essentially makes table wine or wine made for distillation, and it is known as Chilean white lightning.

• Cabernet Sauvignon grows in the Aconcagua Valley north of Santiago.

• Southwest of Santiago is Casablanca Valley, prime land for Sauvignon Blanc and Chardonnay.

• Maipo Valley is a warmer territory where Cabernet and Chardonnay thrive.

• Colchagua Valley is home to powerful Cabernet and Carmenere.

• In Curico Valley, Merlot and Sauvignon Blanc grow strong.

Chile's wine industry is booming. It's a country to keep an eye on as its wineries develop and introduce labels to the market.

Map of the Colchagua Valley, Chile, painted on ceramic tiles

Ann C. Noble and the Wine Aroma Wheel

WANT TO ENHANCE your ability to describe complex wine flavors? Not sure exactly how to put your finger on a taste you experience with a first sip? Help is on the way with Ann C. Noble's wine aroma wheel. Developed in 1990 by Noble, a retired professor and sensory scientist/flavor chemist emerita at University of California, Davis, the wine aroma wheel tool and its three tiers of terms can help you concisely express yourself in the wine world.

When tasting wine with others, it's nice to have the vocabulary to comment about it other than saying, "Not bad," "pretty bold," "seems fruity," "too sweet." But capturing the best adjectives to describe the aroma of a wine—and, as you've learned, tasting is more about smell than flavor—can be difficult because each wine offers a bouquet of different notes.

Noble's aroma wheel is a user-friendly guide on which beginners and wine connoisseurs alike can rely. Most important, the wheel helps you recognize and remember specific characteristics about wines.

She says the fastest way is to make physical standards to illustrate important and major notes in wine aroma. You can pick up most "standards" at the grocery store. Here's how it works: it's a circular chart with descriptions that go from the most basic on the wheel's exterior (e.g., fruity, chemical, etc) to the most specific at the center (e.g., grapefruit, strawberries, etc).

The wheel is chock-full of common tastes that describe wine, and to begin recognizing those tastes, you can easily train your brain and nose to connect and link terms with aromas.

For example, standards for white wine include asparagus, bell pepper, vanilla extract, butter, clove, citrus, peach, pineapple, honey, and a base wine, an unadulterated wine used for making standards. Noble recommends a neutral, inexpensive white wine for this purpose.

Prepare each standard in labeled wine glasses covered with disposable plastic Petri dish lids or plastic wrap. This helps increase the aromas' intensity. From this point, in this order, smell the wine you're evaluating, then smell the standards. Which smells do you recognize? Repeat the exercise with different standards for red and sparkling wines.

Noble based the wine aroma wheel on her research on sensory and chemical factors that affect perception of flavor and acceptance, with an emphasis on wine.

The wine aroma wheel can guide your learning as you experience new flavors. Rather than tasting a wine and saying, "Smells like fruit," you'll be able to specify exactly what kind of fruit. And then, if it's apple, what kind? Granny Smith? Golden Delicious? The more you practice describing wine in this way, the more comfortable you will grow using this terminology.

This aroma wheel was developed by Ann Noble at University of California Davis, in collaboration with people in the wine industry for winemakers to improve both sense of smell and vocabulary. (Wine Aroma Wheel ©2002 A C Noble www.winearomawheel.com)

Making Wine Charms

AVOID THE GLASS GUESSING GAME when entertaining with wines by providing guests with handmade wine charms easy to craft. These are great gifts for wine lovers, and you can customize the colors to suit a wine party theme or holiday. All you need is some earring hoops (1 inch, or 2.5 cm) and beads or crystals of your choice in various sizes. Choose one focal-point bead larger than the rest so it dangles from the hoop. Otherwise, you'll end up with a ring of beads.

Simply place beads on the earring, making a color pattern using different-size beads for interest. Place your focal-point bead in the center, with an equal number of smaller beads or "seed beads" on either side. Continue this way for each wine charm, varying the design and bead colors to make each charm distinct.

When complete, the wine charm will fasten onto the stem of a wineglass by the earring clasp.

Place beads and/or crystals on an earring hoop, placing a focal-point bead in the center. When finished, the wine charm will clasp around the bottom stem of a wineglass.

Why the Punt?

EXAMINE THE BOTTOM of a wine bottle and you'll notice that it curves inward, as if someone molded the molten glass over a golf ball or clementine and formed an indent. This is called a punt, and while some new manufactured bottles do not have this characteristic, you'll find at least a slight punt in most bottles.

The punt served a purpose when bottles were handblown. Imagine a craftsperson handblowing a bottle, then pulling it off of the hot rod. At the bottom formed a peak where the glass stretched slightly when removed from the rod.

The glassblower would push that warm, excess glass up into the bottle, forming the inward bump you see today. This allows the bottle to sit flat on a surface, and serves a greater purpose for wines under pressure such as Champagne: The punt helps distribute pressure over a greater surface area to prevent the bottle from stressing.

Next time you see a punted bottle, imagine a glassblower expertly removing his or her work from a hot rod and molding the bottle's bottom so it sits evenly and preserves delicious bubbly.

Dolcetto

PIEDMONT, THE FOOTHILLS of the Alps in northwest Italy, grows three red grapes: expensive Nebbiolo (see Day 226), famous for high-price Barolo, Barbaresco, and others; mid-range Barbera; and in third place, a still-undiscovered red called Dolcetto. The name means "little sweet one," as it is the first of the three grapes to ripen come fall, and it makes the lightest colored and flavored of the wines. Overshadowed by Barbera and Nebbiolo, Dolcetto sells unnoticed and a little underpriced most of the time, a great third-place finisher in a strong field.

Workhorse grapes such as Dolcetto are sometimes considered everyday wines, and that's no criticism. If you drink wine every day, as more and more people do, you need a few of these, and their place is not front and center but in the background, as part of the meal. Flamboyantly expressive wines can be astounding and delicious, but Dolcetto tastes delicious without the burden of being astounding, and it will please every time.

Dolcetto has adopted myriad aliases over the years. Its location at the crossroads of Italy and northwest Europe has certainly helped it spread around the world and pick up its many names. Below, several of its monikers:

- Acqui
- Bourdon Noir
- Charbonneau (also known as Charbono)
- Chasselas Noir
- Dolcetta Nera
- Gros Plant
- Nera Dolce
- Plant de Savoie
- Ravanellino
- Savoyard
- Uva d'Acqui
- Uva del Monferrato

Recipe: Crème Brûlée

CRÈME BRÛLÉE IS ONE OF those mystique desserts that people hesitate to make themselves, but in reality, it is a fairly simple dish that does not require a huge amount of active time. This version uses a bit of Molina vanilla from Mexico, plus a vanilla bean for more depth of flavor.

1 quart (950 ml) heavy cream

1 vanilla bean

⅛ teaspoon salt

1 teaspoon (15 ml) Molina vanilla extract

8 egg yolks

¾ cup (150 g) sugar, plus additional for finishing

Preheat the oven to 300°F (150°C) and start boiling a whistling teapot full of water on a back burner.

Place the heavy cream in a medium saucepan. Split the vanilla bean by cutting off the ends and slicing the bean down the middle. Gently scrape the seeds from the bean, and add them with the bean husk and the salt to the pan. Bring to a simmer, but do not allow to boil. Remove from the heat, let steep for 5 minutes, and add the vanilla extract.

While the cream steeps, separate the eggs, setting aside the whites. Whisk the sugar into the egg yolks until mixed well. Whisk the cream mixture into the egg mixture, ¼ cup (60 ml) at a time.

Strain the mixture through a fine sieve to remove the bean husk and any lumps that may have formed. Divide the mixture among 8 ramekins (7 ounces, or 205 ml each), filling approximately two-thirds of the way, and place the ramekins into a roasting pan the height of the ramekins. Add the boiling water to the pan until it reaches halfway up the ramekins. Bake for 55 minutes, or until set, then allow to cool.

Serve the crème brûlée at room temperature or refrigerate it up to one day in advance. When ready to serve, preheat the broiler. Sprinkle the top of each ramekin with sugar to form a thin, even coating. Place the ramekins on a cookie sheet and place the sheet on the top rack of the oven. Check every 30 seconds until the tops brown to your liking.

YIELD: Serves 8

Wine Suggestion: Mionetto Prosecco Brut

ITALY

Sergio Mionetto, the latest in a long line of family to make some of Italy's greatest sparkling wines, readily compares his wines to renowned French Champagne. "Prosecco is not as famous or as expensive," he is known for saying, "it simply tastes better." This Brut is the leanest and edgiest of the Mionetto Prosecco line, and even at that, it's soft and lightly bubbly and easy to pair with food. The trick with this dessert combo is to get a little crème brûlée in your mouth, chew it but don't swallow it all. Then add a sip of this sparkler and let them blend for a moment.

Austria

AUSTRIA IS EMERGING AS a more significant wine player, churning out a range of styles and quality that *Wine Spectator* notes "is better than ever, so there's plenty to try." It also helps that in 2003, Austria put into place a classification system for its wines similar to those of France and Italy. Four major wine regions in Austria produce mostly white grapes (about 70 percent), though more vintners are now uncorking reds from Blaufrankisch and Blauer Zweigelt grapes.

Austria is most known for its range of Rieslings and sweet wines.

Though Austria's wine industry has taken off recently, it actually dates back 4,000 years. An antifreeze scandal in 1985, during which some greedy wine brokers were caught adding diethylene glycol to bulk wines, destroyed Austrian wine sales and forced many of the country's winemakers into bankruptcy.

The lesson learned from this snafu? Get high standards on paper and enforce them. (Hence, the new wine classification.)

It took a decade for the country to convince the rest of the world of the safety of its wines. Today, morale and prices are high, and Austria indeed is experiencing a renaissance.

As a side note, if you're seeking extravagant wineglasses, Austria is the place to find them. The country is home to Riedel, which creates some of the world's most expensive ones.

Manfred Jager seated with his son, Roman, just outside of their cellars in Weissenkirchen, Austria

The Bartholomaus Family

LILLIANA BARTHOLOMAUS lost her battle with breast cancer in 2000. To commemorate her life, her two sons, Alex, a wine importer, and Erik, a tattoo artist, created a label in her honor. Her sons sought a creative way to pay homage to their mother and raise money for cancer research.

Enter Two Brothers Winery Big Tattoo Red, a Chilean blend, and its companion, Big Tattoo White, a Riesling blend from Germany. About 5 percent of the proceeds of each bottle goes toward the cause, and as of this writing, the brothers have raised more than $1.3 million for charity.

The Bartholomaus family has a rich history and recently experienced the wine world's turbulent times firsthand. Alex took over Billington Wines that his father, Alfredo, started in 1985. The Chilean emigrant put South American wine on the world map, and his company was one of the first quality importers to spring up in the thriving Washington, D.C. market. Alfredo brought Catena Zapata wines to the U.S. market, with its big-taste-on-a-budget Argentinean Malbec.

The wine industry is not immune to consolidation. When Catena Zapata moved its value-priced wines to E & J Gallo, Billington Wines lost a 40,000-case customer—one-third of its sales. So Alfredo and Alex joined Winebow, which emerged as the new representative for Catena Zapata.

The Bartholomaus story paints a picture of how the wine industry works behind the scenes— the entities involved, the tough competition, and the high stakes that can put a longtime distributor out of business with a single buying decision. It's also a story that shows how wine can act as a form of community outreach for people, through Bartholomaus's Big Tattoo Red and White labels. This is just one example of the wine-for-a-cause you'll find on retail shelves, many with catchy names and appealing labels. What wine lover wouldn't raise a glass to the concept of drinking *and* giving back?

A bottle of Big Tattoo Red by Two Brothers Winery

Growing Grapes in Your Backyard

TRY YOUR HAND AT viniculture by planting grapes in your backyard. You can purchase plants from nurseries or start them from cuttings taken from a mature plant during its dormant period. This is how vintners all over the world experiment with new grapes, and how *vitis vinifera* (European wine grapes) first traveled.

First, choose which type of grapes you will plant, and consider the location on your property where the grapes will grow. Grapes love full sun, so try to select a south-facing area. You've heard the rule, "Put the right plant in the right place." One key to success is simply digging the hole in the right spot.

Grapes can present a challenge to grow because they require careful pruning; neglecting this chore can produce weak fruit that becomes disease-susceptible, or many leaves and no fruit. Here are some tips for planting and caring for grape plants. As you learn more, explore blogs and websites devoted to this passion. You'll pick up tips from your own experience, and prevent mistakes by reading about others' garden toils.

SITE PREPARATION

Till the soil, remove weeds, and add compost or a soil amendment if necessary. While grapes aren't overly picky about soil condition, they'll grow better if you provide the ground with some nutritional reinforcements to give your grape plant a healthy start.

Dig a deep hole for the plant, allowing ample space for the root ball, and moisten the hole with water. Dampen the root ball and place it in the hole. Fill with soil and pack down gently. Place a supportive structure such as a trellis, an arbor, or a stake to help control and train the vine as it grows.

PRUNING POINTERS

Grapes require hefty but careful pruning. Grapes produce fruit the second year of growth, from the previous season's wood. Prune too much and you'll wind up with no fruit. Prune too lightly and the fruit will be overabundant and weak. Here are some pruning tips:

- Prune during winter once, but never during a severe frost, and always before the sap begins to rise after leaves develop.

- Identify coarse, dark wood, the wood from which next year's grapes will grow. Follow the growing tip back to the older wood from the year before. Then come forward, leaving four or five buds. Cut the vine there using pruning shears.

- Do not allow spring shoots to get unruly. Remove thin, weak shoots and leave the strongest. Flowers from this shoot signal fruit for the next year.

- Prune regularly during the summer, and train vines to climb arbors, trellises, or some supportive structure. Prune back to the third or fourth leaf after fruiting. Remove all leaves from around fruit clusters so they receive full sun.

PICKING GRAPES

Simply because your grapes changed color doesn't mean they are ripe. Taste the grape before picking it. If not ripe, wait for the fruit to develop. Grapes will not ripen after harvest, so be sure to pick them at their peak.

Garden pathway in Montefioralle, Chianti, Tuscany, Italy

First Things First

WHETHER YOU'RE HOSTING a blind tasting or wine dinner, or will sample several wines at a winery, there are some rules for what to drink when. Chemicals affect the human senses, and to fully experience each wine, you don't want to overpower the taste buds with a selection that will cancel out the flavor of the wines you sip afterward.

These guidelines are ranked in priority order, and each rule establishes an order.

DRY BEFORE SWEET

Sweet has a long aftertaste, so drink dry first. Otherwise, your sweet will taste sour. For example, drink a Chardonnay before a Riesling.

LIGHT BEFORE FULL

Full-bodied wines dominate light ones, so drink light first. That way, you can savor the flavor. Drink Pinot Noir before Cabernet Sauvignon, for example.

WHITE BEFORE RED

This is the rule that most of us know. Notice, however, that it isn't top priority. It's more important to drink light before full or dry before sweet. Drink a light Pinot Noir before a full Chardonnay, for example; the light-before-full rule supersedes white before red.

OLD BEFORE YOUNG

Younger wines are fruiter, more acidic, more tannic, and can overpower older wines whose notes have matured and softened. While you'll be tempted to hold until last the mature bottle you've been saving, don't.

Putting these rules into practice, you would drink an old, dry red before a young sweet white. Why? Because dry before sweet is more important than both old before young and white before red.

What's in a Grape?

WHEN IT COMES TO headaches and wine, everybody has a different story. For some people, it's red wine that kicks it off. For others, it's Champagne. Some people can only drink Champagne, because everything else gives them headaches! Of the hundreds of scientifically verifiable chemical compounds that give flavor to wine, which one or two in the Frescobaldi Chianti gave you that blinding headache? Maybe it wasn't even one or two but a combination of forty or fifty. No one knows for sure.

A couple years ago, manufacturers yanked a mess of European jug wine off the market after some bottles contained traces of automotive coolant, of all things. Sadly, this sort of tampering reinforces the image that even fine wine is manufactured, an unnatural processed food, if you will, subject to who knows what. Wine is a complex substance.

All wine contains alcohol, usually between 10 and 15 percent, and in the right hands, it's not a problem. In the wrong hands, of course, it can be a big problem.

Also, all wine contains sulfites. Some asthmatics report reactions from sulfites, but this typically only happens to the highly asthmatic (who know better than to drink wine). Sulfites are naturally occurring sulfur-oxygen compounds from fermentation. Many reputable wineries add sulfites or subject their grapes to a sulfur "bath" as a preservative. In moderation, it's not a worry. Simply avoid cheap jug wine that's often overprocessed, mishandled, and highest in those unappetizing additives and preservatives.

Finally, all wine contains a little bit of the turf in which it grew up. It's the same with any produce or edible. If the soil contained a little pesticide, herbicide, or fungicide, the grapes and wine will, too. The key, again, is to buy quality wine, in which these elements are almost always at a minimum.

Regional Cuisine and Wine

A REGION'S FOOD SPECIALTIES often pair intuitively with its local wines.

Red Bordeaux for example, usually comes from a blend of Cabernet Sauvignon and Merlot, two strong red grapes ideal when paired with red meat. Not too surprisingly, Bordeaux is a tremendous cattle-farming region and has been for centuries.

Alsace produces almost exclusively white wines such as Gewürztraminer, Pinot Blanc, and the lesser known Silvaner.

Alsatian cuisine—pork, cabbage, smoked Gouda, freshwater fish—lends itself perfectly to these wines. One of Burgundy's most famous dishes—beef bourguignon—calls for a whole bottle of Pinot Noir in the recipe, so if you drink the same wine with which you cook, you really can't miss.

Despite these examples, the question remains, which came first, the wine, the cuisine, or the match?

India

THE CONTEMPORARY WINE STORY in India differs much from those of the old countries where grape growing dates back to medieval days.

Take Kanwal Grover, owner of Grover Vineyards, who made a fortune in high-tech equipment, the space program, defense production, and machine tools that he imported primarily from France to India. He wasn't born on a vineyard, but trips to France inspired the entrepreneurial spirit he needed to start his own in the Nandi Hills.

Another example Ranjit Dhuru, owner of the Château d'Ori Winery. He amassed his wealth in the software business, bought land outside of Nasik, north of Mumbai, and is part of India's fast-growing wine industry.

This transition from technology to viniculture has perhaps driven the growing investment in Indian wine business, which has increased by 73 percent during 2008. The upward trend continues. Consumption is also increasing in India, though the 2006 annual per-capita consumption of wine there equals about a tablespoon. Still, that's four times what Indians drank in 2000. And some winemakers think that within the next ten years, as India's economy continues to grow at such a rapid pace, a group of the population will start to desire local wines. The country is already seeing interest.

India's climate makes for interesting grape growing because wineries prune vines in September and harvest grapes in February before the scorching summer heat sets in. This heat pumps up the body and alcohol content in Indian wines, something some vintners are playing with to keep levels in check. Currently, most Indian wines are sold domestically.

Harvesting grapes at Sula Vineyards and Winery in Nasik, Maharashtra, India

Alain Junguenet

BEFORE HE BECAME ONE OF France's leading *vignerons*, Alain Junguenet made a name for himself as a Grand Prix race driver. Junguenet's storied wine career won him more notoriety, even from Robert Parker, who wrote in 1991, "The name Alain Junguenet on a bottle is an indication of a fine wine that is probably undervalued in terms of its quality."

To be sure, standouts in Junguenet's portfolio have gained recognition in the wine community—in particular, wines from Châteauneuf-du-Pape, a wine village in the heart of the Rhône Valley long overshadowed by Bordeaux and Burgundy. Junguenet represents some big Châteauneuf-du-Pape wines. Big, as in alcohol content (12.5 percent or more), flavor, and impact.

Junguenet's wines have earned *Wine Spectator* Wine of the Year recognition, and he continues to import winners. As a wine importer, his portfolio of high-quality Rhône Valley (France) estate wines continues to impress the world's wine enthusiasts and critics (including Parker). Junguenet is credited with persuading Rhône Valley estate owners to sell wine in the United States for the first time.

Junguenet likes to introduce new tastes to wine lovers, and he imports up-and-coming labels such as those from Languedoc-Roussillon, France, fast becoming known as one of the world's most productive wine regions.

Fresh Themes for a Wine Party

IT'S POSSIBLE YOU'VE ALREADY hosted a blind tasting, or invited your friends to an around-the-world wine party. Here are some offbeat themes that will keep guests coming back for more. These themes are all BYOB—bring your own bottle—so invite as many guests as you want. As the host, provide appropriate food and keep the local cab driver's number on hand in case any party-goers overindulge.

CRITTER CRAWL

Ever notice how many labels feature animals: cats, dogs, llamas, monkeys. Ask guests to bring a bottle wrapped with their favorite critter label.

SCORE

Everyone's a critic at this party. Create score cards in advance, and establish a numbering system (one through ten, four stars, etc). Give guests the opportunity to taste and rate each wine, write down their comments, and vote on a favorite. To reward the guest who brought the winning bottle, give away a welcome prize: a bottle of wine!

VALUE VINO

Everyone has his or her go-to value wine, one he or she doesn't feel guilty uncorking to drink with a frozen pizza or have just one glass. There are many quality, inexpensive labels available today, so invite your guests to bring their favorite and host a tasting. The real treat of the night will be finding out there's another value bottle you enjoy.

The Big Chill

THE ICE BUCKET has evolved tremendously, and today's wine enthusiasts can choose from an array of chilling devices that range from tops that fasten onto bottles to cool wine as you pour, to single-bottle devices that bring a wine to temperature in minutes. Here's a taste of what the market offers:

COOL MARBLE

A naturally cool stone, this thick marble sleeve keeps chilled wine cold.

INSTANT CHILL

Freeze this special top and fasten it to the bottle. As wine passes through the steel chamber and pours into your glass, it chills to a desirable temperature. It's the same premise as an ice cream maker: A frozen canister turns liquid ingredients into ice cream. Adjust the serving temperature with an air inlet.

BOTTLE COOLER

These high-tech chillers generally come with adjustable temperature controls and a database so you can find the wine you plan to drink and select a preset chilling temperature from the menu. Many come with a fast-chilling mode so you can cool down a room-temperature bottle in minutes.

WINE REFRIGERATOR

Keep an entire collection cool with a wine refrigerator. Some come with different temperature zones for storing red and white wines. These appliances range from basic mini-fridges to extravagant cases built into a bar or kitchen. With a glass panel front, they double as a showcase.

Seven Deadly Zins, Part I

RED ZINFANDEL GRAPES produce robust wine with berry, anise, and pepper notes. White Zinfandel is the mildly popular, slightly sweet rosé of Zinfandel; it has a little residual sugar and a healthy alcohol level, both of which people love. Zinfandel's relative is Primitivo (see Day 275), and it grows in warm climates where fruit ripens early.

What's interesting about Zinfandel is the grape's uneven ripening. One bunch may turn to raisins while another contains juicy, green grapes far from ready to pick. Some Zinfandels cost so much because some vintners hand-harvest bunches, allowing them to pick each bunch at optimum ripeness.

They may actually pluck single berries from a cluster, leaving the rest to age appropriately on the vine. Other vintners may vinify bunches with overripe and barely ripe grapes.

Some people criticize red Zinfandels for their high alcohol content, though some producers will use reverse osmosis and spinning cones to make the wines less "hot" (alcoholic). Purists say these processes tamper with the wine's terroir (i.e., the flavor it derives from soil).

For a wine-buying guide to Zinfandels, see Day 268.

Zinfandel grapes in Amador County, California, United States

Recipe: Plum Galette

THE PLUM HARVEST bridges summer and fall, and this free-form tart works equally well on a hot August day or a cool September night. Serve with a fun, summery sparkling wine.

For the crust:

2 ½ cups (300 g) flour

½ cup (100 g) sugar

1 teaspoon (6 g) salt

1 cup (225 g) cold unsalted butter (2 sticks)

1 teaspoon (5 ml) vanilla extract

1 egg yolk

1 teaspoon (5 ml) lemon juice

For the filling:

2 ¼ pounds (1 kg) red plums

⅓ pound (160 g) blanched, slivered almonds

½ cup (50 g) powdered sugar

1 teaspoon (2 g) aniseed

1 tablespoon (14 g) unsalted butter, melted

To make the crust: In a food processor, combine the flour, sugar, and salt and pulse for 30 seconds. Chop the cold butter into tablespoon-size chunks and add to the flour mixture. Pulse 12 to 15 times until incorporated. In a bowl, beat the vanilla, egg, and lemon juice, and add to the flour and butter mixture with the food processor running. If the mixture does not form a ball, add 1 to 2 tablespoons (15 to 30 ml) of ice-cold water with the processor running. Turn out the mixture onto a floured surface and shape into a ball. Do not knead the dough; this will make it tough. Wrap in plastic wrap and refrigerate for 1 hour.

Preheat the oven to 375°F (190°C).

To make the filling: Wash and cut the plums into 6 to 8 wedges each and set aside for galette assembly later.

Place the almonds in a small skillet over medium heat, and stir until fragrant and just beginning to brown. Do not overcook. In a food processor, combine the almonds, powdered sugar, and aniseed until finely ground but not a paste.

Roll out the dough until it is a 15- to 16-inch (38- to 40-cm) circle. It is hard to work with, but worth it. Transfer the dough to a large cookie sheet covered with parchment paper. Spread the nut mixture in the middle of the rolled dough, leaving a border of 2 to 3 inches (5 to 8 cm). Mound the plums on top of the nut mixture, making the middle slightly higher than the sides. Fold the sides of the dough over the plum mixture. Brush with the melted butter to ensure even browning. Bake for 35 to 40 minutes, or until the dough browns lightly and the plums bubble.

YIELD: Serves 8

Wine Suggestion: Grande Maison "Cuvée Mademoiselle" Monbazillac
FRANCE

Dessert wines from France's Bordeaux region typically hail from the towns of either Sauternes or Barsac, but there's a third town off the beaten path called Monbazillac (pronounced mon-bah-ZEE-yack). It grows the same white grapes and makes the same sweet style wines at a fraction of the retail price. The color of Cuvée Mademoiselle is very golden, and behind the delicious sweetness it tastes like ripe pear and apple. It's a great fruit contrast with the darker plums in the gallette.

China

If CHINA EXPERIENCES the wine Big Bang that some esteemed wine merchants suggest, the quality of Chinese wine will eventually match that of Bordeaux, France. Not until after 2000, when China's economic boom put disposable income into the hands of some Chinese, did residents actually purchase and consume the locally produced wines. Before that, most Chinese wines were exported abroad.

Meanwhile, in 1980, China imported its first wine—from France—which led to joint ventures between Chinese and French companies and, subsequently, awards and notoriety locally and abroad. It makes sense that China now enters the wine scene with gusto, just as the country has aggressively embraced globalization and a world economy.

Though China has a long history of fermenting and distilling Chinese wines, these ventures and the focus on grape wine now found on shelves outside of the country is fairly new.

At the same time, the Chinese consider wines produced in Europe and the United States a luxury, representing great market opportunity for winemakers everywhere.

An interesting note: The Chinese serve wine differently than other countries. They often mix red wine with lemon/lime sodas and white wine with colas. Also, iced red wine is popular there.

A farmer harvests grapes to sell in Beijing, China

The d'Arenberg Family

LOCATED IN MCLAREN VALE in Australia, d'Arenberg became known as such in 1959, when Francis d'Arenberg Osborn (known as d'Arry) returned to help his ill father run the family winery business. After taking over full management at age eighteen, he launched his own label, d'Arenberg, in honor of his mother, Frances Helena d'Arenberg.

Today, the name lives on as one of the region's most significant wineries, with a rich history dating back to 1912 when teetotaler Joseph Osborn purchased 62 acres (25 ha) of vineyards. His son, d'Arry's father, Francis Ernest Osborn, left medical school to help run the business, increasing the vineyard size to 193 acres (78 ha) and constructing cellars. The winery then started exporting its dry red table wines and fortified wines to Europe. Under d'Arry's management, the winery began winning trophies. The fashionable wines captured international attention, and the family continued to stick to its Old World wine-making values and principles.

Today, the fourth generation runs the business—d'Arry's son, Chester d'Arenberg Osborn. D'Arry's daughter, Jackie, lives in Sydney and sells d'Arenberg wines to its distributors, Inglewood wines. Chester took over the reins as chief winemaker in 1984 and returned to the family's traditional grape-growing practices to achieve natural soil flavors and low yields: minimal inputs and no fertilization, cultivation and irrigation wherever possible. All grapes are basket-pressed, the winery's reds fermented with the grape skins submerged in open lined concrete fermenters using foot-treading.

Robert Parker called Chester one of the Top Forty Wine Personalities in the World, writing, "His wines have been gobbled up by an insatiable American audience looking for value and individuality, and he's one of an increasing maverick breed of Australians who have done unbelievably well in this marketplace."

Wine Suggestions: Two d'Arenbergs

d'Arenberg The Dead Arm Shiraz, Australia

The name comes from a disease that afflicts the old vine vineyards that produce this wine—*eutypa lata*, Latin for "dead arm." One branch of the grape vine slowly dies off, and the remaining branches produce tiny amounts of intensely concentrated, flavorful grapes. Wine lovers say a wine like this has a long finish, which means you can literally taste it for minutes after you've swallowed.

d'Arenberg The Hermit Crab Marsanne Viognier, Australia

This blend of the relatively unknown white grapes Marsanne and Viognier produces a tart, extremely dry wine with great citrus and explosive acidity. Save it for seafood.

Planning a Vineyard Tour

IF YOU'RE LOOKING FOR an adventure beyond the wine-tasting room, consider booking a vineyard tour—essentially a backstage pass. You'll experience what it's like to walk among the rows of trellised grape vines, feel the soil underneath your feet as you traipse through the property, imagining the excitement of harvest time. A vineyard tour provides total immersion in the wine-making experience. You get an up-close-and-personal view of where all wine begins: on the vine.

Connoisseurs and beginners alike learn a great deal on vineyard tours. Your guide will share information about growing grapes, the terroir, the climate, challenges in the vineyard, and successes with certain varieties. When you taste the wines produced in the vineyard you tour, you'll have a heightened appreciation for the labor and love imbued in every ounce (milliliter).

Prices range for vineyard tours. Smaller outfits may host less formal complimentary or nominally priced walkthroughs. More involved tours may include a tasting on site, transportation to different sites within the vineyard (if it is large), and a heftier price tag.

Find out about cost and vineyard tour times before your visit and keep the following in mind:

SPIT DISCIPLINE: You show respect and get respect on a winery tour by really using the spit buckets. You may notice quickly that the more wine you spit, the more different wines people will pour for you.

WINE NUTRITION: Most wineries feature crackers or bread or a little something to nibble on while you taste, but make sure you plan time for deliberate food and water breaks.

A TASTE OF REALITY: In other words, don't try to do too much or drive too far on one tour. However many vineyards you think you'll visit in one day, subtract one.

CALL AHEAD: Schedules change and private events happen at wineries all the time, so always call ahead to double check the tasting room and tour schedules.

If you've visited wineries but never walked among the vines, you'll appreciate this fresh perspective on the wine world. It's highly recommended. Bring a camera, and journal about your experience.

Horse-drawn wagon tours at Sonoita Vineyards in
Elgin, Arizona, United States

Virtually Meet a Wine Pro

YOU CAN SPEND THE WEEKEND as an armchair tourist, virtually visiting wineries across the world and even "meeting" the winemakers there. All you need is Internet access and you'll gain a wealth of information from spending time on a winery's website: its history, regional climate, varieties grown, wines processed, special events, and more.

Now that many wineries have a home online, tap into the knowledge of professionals by contacting them via email, or directly through the winery website. Do you have questions about the winery's wines? Want to know more about the grapes, their processing, and the availability of vineyard tours? Most winemakers respond to inquiries. It's a hospitable industry, and they are just as interested in telling their stories as you are in hearing them!

Taking correspondence a step further, you may decide to enroll in online courses to learn more about wines. Or you can tune in to Webcasts, join chat rooms, or become a regular commenter on a blog—even start your own blog (see Days 279 + 280). These are just a few ways to reach out to other wine lovers and professionals in the industry to ask questions and deepen your appreciation for and understanding of wine.

A simple Internet search will turn up hundreds of options to explore. The world of wine is vast, and technology brings exotic grape regions right into your home. Take advantage of online tools, and build your knowledge by engaging with experts online.

Seven Deadly Zins, Part II

READY TO TASTE BOLD, red Zinfandel? Consider these selections, which vary in price.

Alexander Valley Vineyards Sin Zin,
United States (California)
Not as sinful as the decadent label makes it out to be, this wine still tastes quite delicious, with fruit and spice, smoke, and great tannin.

Robert Biale Vineyard Monte Rosso Zinfandel, United States (California)
This wine is a beautiful monster from one of California's most famous Zin vineyards.

Bogle Vineyards Old Vine Zinfandel,
United States (California)
One of my favorite affordables, this wine is full of personality, ripe fruit flavor, and loads of oak.

Cline Ancient Vines Zinfandel,
United States (California)
This wine is awesomely dark and rich, with explosive overripe plum and fig flavors everywhere.

Cline Zinfandel, United States (California)
This entry-level Zin is rough and ruddy, dark and inky, with pungent, almost sweet fruit, and wonderful funky aromas of earth, leaves, bark, and sap. Its flavor profile is aggressive, which makes it good with strong, aromatic foods such as garlic and meat.

Dry Creek Vineyard Heritage Clone Zinfandel, United States (California)
Raspberry, blackberry, and black raspberry dominate this wine, which also has a hint of menthol and rosemary. Wait for sundown and open it with your favorite barbecue sauce.

Fife Zinfandel, United States (California)
Bold, graphical presentations on the outside of the bottle promise much, and Fife delivers. Huge tannins and a big fruit bomb balance each other perfectly. The Red Head Zinfandel is especially over the top.

Folie à Deux Zinfandel and 1998 Folie à Deux Bowman Vineyard Zinfandel,
United States (California)
Amador County, way inland and due northeast of Napa and Sonoma, has a very hot and dry climate, producing Zinfandels of extreme density and concentration.

Michael David Vineyards Seven Deadly Zins Zinfandel, United States (California)
Seven Deadly Zins comes from California's Lodi appellation, a hot inland wine region due east of San Francisco. This wine's raspberry-blackberry flavors are superripe and concentrated, and it contains a nice dose of smooth, toasty oak. Its alcohol level is a sinful 15 percent.

Murphy-Goode Liar's Dice Zinfandel,
United States (California)
This wine is full of cinnamon, brown sugar, and vanilla. You could call it crème brûlée in a glass.

Peachy Canyon Dusi Vineyard Zinfandel,
United States (California)
Don't be shy about buying anything from Peachy Canyon, from its low-priced generic red up to its top single-vineyard wines.

Pedroncelli Mother Clone Zinfandel, United States (California)
Thank history for the Italian-Americans who kept many vineyards and much wine making alive in California during Prohibition. Thanks to the Parducci, Mondavi, Pagani, Foppiano, Pedroncelli, and other families, we have old-vine Zins such as this Mother Clone, presumably the mother of all Pedroncelli Zins, both literally and figuratively. Stately, dense, and concentrated with raspberry and blackberry flavors, its style is Bordeaux and its core is 100 percent California.

235

Recipe: Parmigiano Black Pepper Biscotti

BISCOTTI GETS ITS NAME from the medieval Latin *bis coctus*, meaning "twice cooked," which is the main technique of this recipe. Parmigiano-Reggiano is perhaps Italy's most famous cheese, but you could substitute Grana Padano in the recipe, a similar cheese that costs about half as much.

1½ tablespoons (14 g) whole black peppercorns

4 cups (500 g) all-purpose flour

2 teaspoons (9 g) baking powder

2 teaspoons (12 g) salt

4½ ounces (128 g) Parmigiano-Reggiano, finely grated

¾ cup (170 g) cold unsalted butter, cut into cubes

4 large eggs, divided

1 cup (235 ml) whole milk

Preheat the oven to 350°F (180°C).

Crush the peppercorns with a mortar and pestle or use an electric coffee/spice grinder.

Whisk the crushed pepper, flour, baking powder, salt, and cheese. Blend in the butter with a pastry cutter. Whisk 3 of the eggs with the milk, and add to the flour mixture and blend until a soft dough forms.

Turn the dough out onto a lightly floured surface and divide into quarters. The dough may be sticky so flour your hands well to form each quarter into a 12-inch (30-cm) flattened log. Place each log on a baking sheet at least 3 inches (8 cm) apart. Whisk the remaining egg and brush over the logs. Bake for 30 minutes. Reduce oven temperature to 300°F (150°C).

Let the logs cool for 10 minutes. Cut each into ½-inch (1¼-cm) slices and place on a baking sheet, cut side down. Bake for 35 to 45 minutes, turning each slice once.

YIELD: 5 to 6 dozen biscotti

Wine Pairing: Castello di Poppiano Vin Santo Della Torre Grande
ITALY

Vin Santo, the traditional dessert wine of Tuscany, like so many Tuscan wines, is a great match with strong, flavorful cheese such as Parmigiano-Reggiano and others. Although late-harvest white grapes produce this wine, its color often appears quite dark, thanks to long aging in oak, chestnut, cherry, and sometimes juniper wood barrels. It smells like date-nut bread, with suggestions of cinnamon and allspice.

Puglia

PUGLIA (PRONOUNCED POOL-yah) is this region's generic name. It starts at the Gargano Peninsula in the north (an outcropping that looks like a disturbing Achilles tendon injury) and runs all the way south to the end of the earth.

Winemakers grow three important grapes here: Primitivo, the genetic parent of our modern Zinfandel; Negroamaro, whose name means "black and bitter"; and Malvasia Nera, an easy, flavorful red grape.

Stick to the ripe, mouth-filling, big-boned reds from Puglia. They are tremendously food-friendly, and they show off best with tangy, exciting foods such as sautéed olives (see recipe, Day 66), spicy tuna, and baked rosemary chicken.

Wine Suggestion: 2001 Feudo Monaci Salice Salentino
ITALY

Feudo Monaci (pronounced fay-YOU-dough moan-AH-chee) is the name of the winery, and it comes from the same root as our word "feudal." It loosely translates to "monastery farm," what the place had been until 1480, when the winery took over.

Salice Salentino (saw-LEE-chay saw-len-TEE-no) is where the wine comes from, a small sunny town on the tip of the heel of the Italian boot, south of ancient sailing towns Bari and Brindisi, south of almost everything but the sea.

Salice Salentino blends Negroamaro and Malvasia, a combo that results in a delightful, sunny, radiant red that seems to capture a blast of summertime in the bottle.

237

Gargano Peninsula, Viesta, Puglia, Italy

Bill Blosser and Susan Sokol Blosser

BEFORE A WINE INDUSTRY existed in Oregon, Bill Blosser and Susan Sokol Blosser planted their first vines. That was 1971. Today, their state boasts more than 300 wineries and 13,000 acres (5,260 ha) of vineyards, and you can buy Oregon wines at retailers all over the world. Sokol Blosser winery, too, has thrived and remained a family-owned operation involved in shaping Oregon's wine culture.

At Sokol Blosser, sustainable practices are a priority; the winery follows the Natural Step principles and figures the environment into all vineyard practices. Its estates are farmed organically and received full United States Department of Agriculture organic certification in 2005.

Going a step further, Salmon-Safe certified the estate as a vineyard that protects and restores salmon habitat. Its farm tractors are powered by 50 percent biodiesel, and the winery uses unbleached paper products for its labels, wine boxes, and gift bags. And everything there gets recycled, down to pallet shrinkwrap and office paper. Sokol Blosser was the first winery in the country to earn Leadership in Energy and Environmental Design (LEED) certification for its "green" building characteristics—a difficult designation to earn.

Currently, children Alex and Alison Sokol Blosser are co-presidents of the winery, and Mondavi-trained winemaker Russ Rosner runs the Pinot Noir program.

Wine Suggestions: Sokol Blosser Selections

Sokol Blosser SB Select Chardonnay and Pinot Noir, United States (Oregon)
SB Select represents the power of the second label concept in the hands of the right people. Both the Chardonnay and the Pinot Noir deliver true fruit, good structure, and plenty of depth. Best of all, they just feel well made.

Yamhill County Chardonnay and Pinot Noir, United States (Oregon)
The Yamhill County signature cuvée is a major step up in flavor and intensity. Like many Oregon Chardonnays, Sokol Blosser is lean and steely with deep mineral flavors. The Pinot Noir holds back the oak a bit and has stately Pinot fruit flavors.

Make a Cork Wreath

LOOKING FOR A WAY TO PRESERVE and display the special corks you save from your favorite wines? Create a wreath. You choose the size. All you need is a straw wreath to serve as a base, a hot glue gun and glue sticks, twine (for hanging), and all the corks you can find. Then, follow these five simple steps:

1. Separate corks into two piles: special and ordinary (no offense to the wine, of course!). You'll build two layers of corks for this wreath, so save corks with interesting imprints for the top layer. Plain corks make a practical foundation.

2. Prepare the straw wreath by tying a piece of sturdy string or twine and making a loop that's wide enough so that there's slack between your fingers and the wreath. When complete, you will hang the wreath from this loop.

3. Using a hot glue gun to fasten corks to the wreath, start from the inside edge and glue corks in even rows, butted up against each other, completely covering the wreath. Do not glue corks to the back side. You want the wreath to lay flat against a door or wall.

4. Vary the pattern of your corks on the second layer, positioning them at angles to create interest (see illustration at right). Continue adding corks until you are satisfied with the design.

5. Hang your wreath and begin collecting corks for your next project! Cheers!

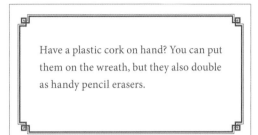

Have a plastic cork on hand? You can put them on the wreath, but they also double as handy pencil erasers.

Save the most interesting corks for the second layer and glue them at different angles to each other on top of the base layer of corks.

Wine Components

THE NUMBER ONE INGREDIENT in wine is water; it makes up 80 to 85 percent of most bottles. What remains are alcohol, tannin, acid, and sugars. These are called components, and they give a wine its character. Here is how wine components balance and complement one another to create a pleasing experience:

ALCOHOL

Alcohol is the product of fermentation, and wines with much alcohol have more body. Alcohol can make a wine "big."

TANNIN

These bitter compounds are extracted from grape skins, pips (seeds), and stems during and after fermentation. Tannins are pigments, so the more tannin, the darker the wine. Tannin helps balance out the alcohol.

ACID

This tart component of wine balances alcohol and sugar. It cuts through fats and oils in the mouth, partly why acidic wines pair well with many foods.

SUGAR

As mentioned above, acidity or tannins balance out a wine's sugar component. Sometimes these components mask the sugar's sweetness, leading the drinker to believe a wine is dry when it actually contains quite a bit of sugar.

Primitivo: The Ancient One

RECENT SCIENTIFIC TESTING reveals that Italian Primitivo is the genetic parent of California Zinfandel. The family resemblance is strong, with those same dark fruit flavors and great tannins.

Primitivo is known for its prevalence in southern Italy, where the grape has grown for thousands of years. It actually originated in Croatia under the name *Crljenak*. (Leave it to the Italians to give the grape a more grandiose name.) Primitivo is known for its spicy, plum, fruit flavors. So is Zinfandel. That brings us to the whole Zin/Primitivo relationship and what it means to the wine world.

The "family" connection has sparked quite a bit of tension among California winemakers who invested a huge effort in creating the grape from scratch and creating a world following for Zinfandel, only to learn that Primitivo is the same fruit. Californians worry that Italian "Zinfandel" (good, old Primitivo) will flood the market and dilute the reputation of the wine they've worked so hard to escalate as a premier selection.

You can imagine how this drama might play out. Italians will claim their Primitivo is the high-quality Zinfandel. California winemakers will argue that theirs is superior. All you need to know is that you'll get that same rich taste regardless of which you choose, and the prices just may come down as a result of the genetic discovery.

Wine Suggestion: Pervini Archidamo Primitivo di Manduria

ITALY

Granted, this wine is a ringer, so to speak, tossed into the mix to keep life interesting. Archidamo was an ancient Greek warrior-king who laid waste to this part of Italy some millennia ago. All seems forgiven having tasted this beauty. It's great with sautéed olives and artichokes with a little crumbly feta cheese on the side.

Primitivo grapes in Maduria, Apulia, Italy

Recipe: Mussels Marinière

FOOD APPEALS TO SO MANY of our senses—sight, smell, and taste, obviously—but when it comes to mussels, you introduce touch—people must pick up and pluck the meat from the shell by hand—and sound, that cacophony of dull clicks a pot of mussels makes when you take it off of the stove and pour it into its serving bowl. Make sure each person feasting has a big piece of crusty baguette for sopping up the wine sauce.

2 tablespoons (30 ml) olive oil

2 garlic cloves

½ cup (120 ml) dry white wine

2 pounds (900 g) mussels, scrubbed and debearded

Salt and ground black pepper, to taste

Handful of chopped parsley, for garnish

Heat the oil in a large ovenproof casserole, add the garlic, and cook but do not brown. Add the white wine and bring to a simmer. Add the mussels, and season with salt and pepper. Mix well, cover with a lid, and bake for 8 minutes. Check the mussels and discard any that have not opened. Sprinkle with parsley and serve.

YIELD: Serves 4 to 6

Wine Pairing:
Château Coucheroy
FRANCE

The wine region of Bordeaux is as much about water as it is about land. Two rivers come together at the Atlantic Ocean to form a giant estuary called the Gironde, filled with mussels, oysters, and clams for millennia. White Bordeaux is almost exclusively Sauvignon Blanc, and not surprisingly at all, it matches perfectly with the abundance of seafood that the citizens harvest from the sea. The name *Coucheroy* means, idiomatically, "where the king sleeps," a tribute to the respect this wine region receives.

Piedmont

PIEDMONT MEANS "foot of the mountain" in Italian, and this region's location—landlocked and mountainous—produced distinguished Nebbiolo grapes found in renowned Barolo, Barbaresco, and Battinara wines. If you looked on a three-dimensional map of Italy, you'd see that in the north, the foothills of the Alps, called the Piedmont, rise up and face south and west, toward the setting sun. Picture this geography as an avid sunbather on the beach propped up in a chaise lounge in order to catch the rays at a more direct and intense ninety-degree angle. This geologic attitude about the sun, among other things, makes the Piedmont one of the world's most famous wine regions.

Piedmont is known for its rich reds, and has been noted as the region that produces the largest number of renowned, prize-winning wines. After all, Piedmont is home to Asti Spumante, thanks to Carlo Gancia applying Champagne knowledge he picked up in Reims, France, to Italy's Moscato grapes. Piedmont is also home to the birthplace of the classic martini ingredient Vermouth, in a wine shop near the Turin Stock Exchange. You may recognize the name Martini & Rossi.

Piedmont is a dynamic region beyond its grape-growing. It was one of the first Italian regions to embrace the Industrial Revolution with the introduction and founding of Fiat, the Italian car company, there in 1899. The rise and fall of empires—the rise of the Celts, then their fall and takeover by the Romans; the rise of the Roman Empire, then its fall when the French feudal family Savoy occupied Turin in Piedmont in the thirteenth century—appear throughout its history. The Savoy family ruled the region until the end of World War II and the birth of the Italian Republic.

Wine Suggestion: Dezzani Monfrigio Roero Arneis
ITALY

This Italian white is subtle, golden, and rich with nice flavors of ripe pear and peach. It comes from northern Italy, where white wines traditionally focus more on complex depths of flavor than on ripe explosiveness. Monfrigio tastes deep and wide, like fresh well water, leaves, and flowers.

Michel Rolland

MICHEL ROLLAND IS A French winemaker cast in the role of Satan in the 2004 documentary *Mondovino*, which attempted to expose the negative effects of globalization on the wine world. He is known in the wine business as the "flying winemaker" because he consults for clients on literally every wine-producing continent.

Director Jonathan Nossiter tried to blame him (and the Mondavi family, among others) for everything that's wrong with the wine industry today. Allegedly, that amounts to wine tasting too good and people liking it too much, thanks to the efforts of wine criminals such as Rolland.

Put another way, it sounds like Nossiter was trying to say that wine was better when it was more rare, precious, incomprehensible, and unattainable.

Now modernists such as Rolland have handed anybody and everybody the key to a private wine clubhouse.

> ### Wine Suggestion: Clos de los Siete
> ARGENTINA
>
> This delicious red blend (40 percent Malbec, 20 percent each of Cabernet, Merlot, and Syrah), called Clos de los Siete (pronounced kloe-duh-lahs-see-YET-ay), is soft and approachable yet stands up to big, red meat or spicy barbecue.

Start a Wine Blog

THE WEB IS FULL OF wine enthusiasts like you who post their musing about winery tours, interesting labels, exciting varieties, and wine excursions on blogs. Blog is short for Web-log, an online journal that allows bloggers (i.e., writers) to share their thoughts about any subject.

Conduct an online search for "wine blog" and you'll get staggering results. Fascinating anecdotes or interesting wine trivia will flood your screen. Some blogs are managed by wine professionals, and others are written by wine enthusiast magazine journalists, consultants, importers, wine and food writers, vintners, and so on. These blogs offer reliable sources of information that will quench your thirst for wine knowledge as you continue to learn about and love wine.

You don't have to be a wine professional to start a wine blog. Treat it like you do a notebook journal, using this forum to describe your wine journey, whether tasting or touring. Remember that the public can search and find your blog—and once you press that "publish" button, it's online for good. This is great for wine lovers interested in connecting with other enthusiasts. You'll "meet" some talented and interesting people who may visit your blog to read and comment.

Texture Vocabulary

WINE IS A LIQUID. How can it have a texture? A typical wine is 80 to 85 percent water, and the rest is a wine's composition, which includes alcohol, tannin, acid, sugars, and so on. Within the composition, you discover a wine's texture and structure. This is where terminology gets creative. Here are some words to describe wine texture:

GRIP

This alludes to a wine having a "grip" on the palate—a traction, a bold statement. This usually relates to a wine's acid or tannin. Wine without grip feels wimpy or too light.

JAMMY

Use the word "jammy" to describe wines with a sticky, fruity texture that may not have the structure to stand up to their own sweetness.

LAYERED

If a wine has complex, dense layers of flavor that coat the palate, use this word.

RICH

This is as it sounds: concentrated, dense, and not thin, watery, or bland.

SILKY

Describe a wine as "silky" if it tastes fine and smooth—like silk.

UNCTUOUS

This translates to having "a greasy or soapy feel." It describes wines with rich, creamy textures that coat the palate.

VELVETY

Call wines that feel smooth in the mouth, yet a bit more coarse than silky "velvety."

A Whiter Shade of Pinot

IN THE FIELD, Pinot Blanc grapes look much like Chardonnay because of their similar leaf structure. In fact, many vineyards in Europe intentionally intermingle the two varieties, though the grapes come from decidedly different families and produce entirely distinct wines. Pinot Blanc has a light aroma with apple and almond notes, and it can be high-acid or full-bodied depending on its processing. Some winemakers will use oak barrel fermentation, copying a common Chardonnay method.

Pinot Blanc's family history goes like this: It is a clone of Pinot Gris, which is a clone of Pinot Noir. In Italy, where Pinot Blanc is planted extensively, the grape is known as *Pinot Bianco*, and is also used for blending with Muscat in Spumante.

You'll find Pinot Blanc grapes in Germany and Austria, where some call the grape Weissburgunder. Pinot Blanc also grows in Eastern Europe, Uruguay, and Argentina. Most of California's Pinot Blanc grows in Monterey County.

Wine Suggestion: Pinot Blanc

Adelsheim Pinot Blanc,
United States (Oregon)
Adelsheim is a major Pinot Noir producer in Oregon, but the winery also makes a few whites including Pinot Gris and this wonderful Pinot Blanc. This wine is full-bodied and nicely viscous on the tongue, with fruit flavors of pear, white peach, apple, and honeydew everywhere.

Lucien Albrecht Pinot Blanc,
France (Alsace)
Crisp, clear, clean white fruit flavors dominate this dry white from beginning to end. Serve it with grilled seafood or chicken sausages.

Recipe: Chicken Jerez

SHERRY, A POPULAR WHITE WINE from south-west Spain, is fortified with aquavit—distilled spirits—to bring it up to 15 percent alcohol. Its flavor is typically extreme, with intense nutti-ness, strong alcohol, and unfamiliar fruit flavors. Eating food with sherry, especially dry white sherry, is essential. It's an acquired taste, like many fortified wines, but with the right dish, such as Chicken Jerez, you begin to understand how it works as a wine.

2 tablespoons (30 ml) olive oil

4 to 5 pounds (1.8 to 2.3 kg) chicken, cut into 6 to 8 pieces

Salt and ground black pepper, to taste

1 cup (160 g) sliced shallots

2 garlic cloves, minced

1 cup (235 ml) dry sherry
(any affordable Fino or Manzanilla will do)

1 cup (235 ml) low-salt chicken broth

1 orange, halved lengthwise, each half cut into 5 wedges

1/3 cup (33 g) brine-cured green olives

Preheat the oven to 425°F (220°C).

Heat the oil in large ovenproof skillet over high heat. Sprinkle chicken with salt and pepper. Add the chicken to the skillet and brown. Transfer the chicken to a plate. Reduce the heat to medium-high, drain all but 2 tablespoons (30 ml) of the drippings, and add the shallots, letting them cook until soft and beginning to brown. Then add the garlic.

Add the sherry, let it come to a boil, and reduce the liquid by half. This will take a few minutes. Add the chicken broth and bring to a boil. Return the chicken to the skillet, then place the orange wedges and olives among the chicken pieces. Transfer to the oven and braise, uncovered, for 20 minutes, or until chicken cooks through.

YIELD: Serves 6 to 8

Wine Pairing: La Gitana Manzanilla Sherry

SPAIN

The alcohol in this sherry is at the whisper level, and that's what makes it so easy to drink. Hard white fruit flavors such as pear and apple are behind it all, though the wine is bracingly dry.

Château Recougne

Situated in the French wine mecca of Bordeaux sits Château Recougne, an estate with more than 400 years of recorded history on a hillside in Fronsac, near Pomerol. It is home to Meacutelen Milhade, whose family makes wines from several châteaux they own around Pomerol and Saint-Émilion.

Because a visit to the Bordeaux wine region can be such an overwhelming experience—so many châteaux to visit, so much wine to taste—you may choose to skinny down your agenda by choosing a selection of wineries.

If you want to experience Bordeaux Superieur done right, Château Recougne is your stop. The winery was supposedly named in the early seventeenth century after France's King Henri IV. Then, the estate was honored for its red claret. Today, you'll get to know it for its fantastic, budget-minded Bordeaux.

Château Recougne is mostly Merlot, and that makes it lush, easy, and drinkable. The tannic grip is super, prickly, and pervasive. It is probably best with big red meat, and it may be worth trying with something like lamb shanks with pomegranate glaze.

The Trentadue Family

ACCORDING TO LEGEND, thirty-two French people moved to the Italian city of Bari sometime during the Renaissance, and their number—*trentadue* in Italian—became their name. Relocated yet again to northern California's Sonoma Valley, this branch of the family has, for decades, possessed some of the region's most superb ancient vineyards. The oldest patch of vines on the property was planted in 1896, and you can taste an example in Trentadue's La Storia estate wine.

Andrew Bouton first developed the Trentadue winery property in 1868, where he ran a business propagating and selling fruit trees. In the late 1950s, the Trentadue family purchased the property and began planting new vines. In 1962, the vineyard established the Carignane vines—the oldest example of this varietal in the United States.

Next, the Trentadues took on Sangiovese, planting the grape during the 1970s and growing it quite successfully despite its reputation for being tricky. In 1984, Trentadue earned praise for being the first American producer to make a 100 percent Sangiovese wine.

Today, Trentadue's winemaker Miro Tcholakov sources grapes from all around Sonoma and recreates the spirit of the old patch in the winery. Zinfandel, Carignane, Petite Sirah, Sangiovese, and Syrah all go into the mix, resulting in an exciting, vivacious wine that's consistently interesting and tasty, with dense, dark, radiant color and rich, ripe fruit.

The "Old Patch Red" originally came from an exquisite "old patch" of mixed vines. The winery's wine-making focus continues to be on intensity, extraction, and dynamic explosive fruit. And if you ask, Tcholakov will tell you about the stand of minty bay laurel trees near the vineyard.

> ### Wine Suggestion: Trentadue Petite Sirah
>
> UNITED STATES (CALIFORNIA)
>
> Trentadue Petite Sirah is a favorite: dense, purple-black, and opaque, it is a huge mouthful of tooth-blackening wine that's full of plum, date, fig, and blackberry juice flavors.

Reading Up on Wine

FROM HISTORY BOOKS to biographies that tell the stories of renowned vintners, tasting guides to travel resources, the wine category in bookstores is rich with material to nourish the wine geek in you. Here are a few:

Windows on the World Complete Wine Course by Kevin Zraly: Pick up the twenty-fifth anniversary edition and this will fast become a staple in your wine library.

The Wine Bible by Karen MacNeil: This book is broken down by country, covering major and small wine producers in each region. MacNeil is a teacher, and her clear writing style will appeal to wine beginners and connoisseurs alike.

Great Wine Made Simple by Andrea Immer: Learn to differentiate the qualities of the big six varieties, brush up on terminology, and read other practical information such as Stupid Label Tricks. This is wine straight talk.

The Oxford Companion to Wine by Jancis Robinson: While esoteric at times, this is the go-to guide—the authority, the be-all-end-all when it comes to wine terminology, with more than 3,000 encyclopedic entries.

Wine for Dummies by Ed McCarthy and Mary Ewing-Mulligan: This husband-wife team wrote a book that breaks down wine in the simplest manner. (Consider it the opposite of the Oxford guide listed above.) This book is a helpful orientation to wine.

The House of Mondavi: The Rise and Fall of an American Wine Dynasty by Julia Flynn Siler: This book tells the captivating story of famous vintner Robert Mondavi, his estate, and his effect on the wine world.

The Emperor of Wine: The Rise of Robert M. Parker, Jr. and the Reign of American Taste by Elin McCoy: Learn how famous wine critic Robert Parker shaped America's palate.

The Widow Clicquot: The Story of a Champagne Empire and the Woman Who Ruled It by Tilar J. Mazzeo: Barbe-Nicole Ponsardin was widowed at age twenty-seven, took over the family winery, and helped build the famous Veuve Clicquot brand. She was a prominent female leader in a male-dominated industry, building an empire during the political unrest of the Napoleonic Wars. This book tells the story of Champagne's Grande Dame.

Spelling Out Wine Acronyms

WHILE EXPLORING THE world of wine, undoubtedly you have confronted acronyms on labels, in reviews, or even in conversation with a learned wine drinker. There's an alphabet soup for every hobby, it seems. Wine is no different.

Most countries have wine co-operatives, almost always referenced on a label with an acronym (e.g., CV for Cooperative de Vignerons in France). Here are other acronyms you may come across and what those letters mean.

• ABC: Anything But Chardonnay or Anything But Cabernet. The term comes from Randall Grahm of Bonny Doon Vineyards in Santa Cruz, California.

• ABV: Alcohol by Volume. It's listed on a wine label along with a percentage.

• AOC: *Appellation d'Origine Controlée* or Appellation of Controlled Origin. These French laws specify where a wine can originate and what processing methods are acceptable.

• AP: Number *Amtiliche Prüfungsnummer.* An official testing number displayed on a German wine label that means it passed quality-control standards.

• ATTTB: Alcohol and Tobacco Tax and Trade Bureau. The U.S. government agency responsible for regulating wines sold and produced in the United States.

• AVA: American Viticultural Area. U.S. laws, similar to those in Europe, regulate the use of place-names on wine labels. However, there are no restrictions on grape variety, yield, or wine-making practices. There are more than 140 AVAs.

• BOB: Buyer's Own Brand. A private-label wine owned by the restaurant or retailer.

• QPR: Quality Price Ratio. Day 22 offers a detailed explanation. Briefly, the ratio of quality and taste of a wine compared to its cost.

• TBA: *Trockenbeerenauslese.* A very sweet German dessert wine made from late harvest, raisined grapes. *Trocken* means "dry" and *beeren* means "berries."

"V" is for Viognier

THE APPEAL OF VIOGNIER is difficult to explain, but California winemakers are pushing this richly textured white grape. Lean and hard, acidic and full of subtle fruit and flower aromas, Viognier is reminiscent of a strong-willed Italian Tocai in overdrive.

California vintners have been giving Viognier a test-drive for a decade or so already, and Australia winemakers—open to exotic whites and always looking for the next big affordable grape—have started to embrace it as well. But even by New World wine standards, the grape named Viognier (vee-o-NYAY) is new to the game. Back home in France, it occupies a little more than 250 acres (100 ha) in the northern Rhône Valley, forgotten and hemmed in by better reds all around.

This rising popularity is interesting because just a few years ago, Viognier seemed an endangered variety. Fewer than 35 acres (14 ha) were planted in France in the 1960s; forty years later, California had in excess of 2,000 acres (800 ha), and winemakers in other states including Colorado, New York, North Carolina, Oregon, Texas, Virginia, and Washington, are readily planting the grape. Meanwhile, Australia and Brazil have embraced Viognier, and the result is a wider selection of wines for consumers (see recommendations at right).

Viognier the grape is drought-tolerant, but it can be difficult to grow because it is susceptible to diseases such as powdery mildew in damp, humid climates. It has a tendency to develop high sugar but low acid, which yields wines that go down easy but have an alcoholic kick. Its apricot-orange-acacia aromas do appeal, and because the wine is dry, it can please a palate that normally savors Chardonnay.

Wine Suggestions: Viognier

Yalumba Viognier, Australia
Yalumba has dabbled in Viognier for a long time, ever since then-winemaker Peter Wall got hooked in the 1970s in France. Yalumba planted its first Viognier in 1980. This wine represents a great balance between flavor and texture. Its fresh fruit and citrus flavors are bright, clean, and a little bracing, and there's an underlying smooth roundness to the wine that makes it elegant and complete. Yalumba Viognier is a fine, supremely affordable type-O white wine: it will go with practically any food.

Renwood Viognier,
United States (California)
This grape came from southern France, where it's grown in a remote area called Condrieu. Now New World winemakers are running with it, outstripping the original in price and quality. The best characteristic of this Renwood is its texture: rich, round, viscous, and almost oily.

Viognier grapes growing at a vineyard at Puddicombe Farms in Hamilton, Ontario, Canada

Recipe: Parsley Pesto

In Latin, *PESTA* means "to crush by pounding and grinding." The kitchen tool pestle gets its name from the same root. Aromatic greens, nuts, herbs, spices, oil, salt, and pepper that are ground into a paste is pesto, pistou, pâté, chimichurri, or a hundred other names.

The grinding releases oils, acids, and aromatic esters that combine in the semiliquid medium and begin reacting with each other on a chemical level. The result is a batch of flavors and aromas that, just like wine, would never have happened on their own.

¾ cup (110 g) whole almonds

1 cup (60 g) fresh Italian parsley, whole sprigs (leaves with first stem)

2 garlic cloves, crushed

3 tablespoons (45 ml) olive oil

3 tablespoons (45 ml) lemon juice

1 teaspoon (4 g) sugar

1 cup (235 ml) boiling water

Toast the whole almonds under the broiler until golden brown.

Chop the parsley finely in a food processor. Add the whole almonds and grind to a fine consistency. Add the garlic, olive oil, lemon juice, sugar, and water. Blend until it produces a sauce. Spread on crusty bread or bruschetta.

YIELD: Makes 1 cup (260 g)

Wine Pairing: Argiolas Costamolina Vermentino di Sardegna
ITALY

Windswept Sardegna (Sardinia) produces some rare great white wines. The Mediterranean is generally too hot for white grapes, but thanks to cooling sea breezes—*costamolina* means literally "windmill hill"—Vermentino grows well and produces the signature wine. It tastes lean, zippy, crisp, and green, like fresh-cut grass.

Jumilla, Spain

THE SPANISH WINE REGION of Jumilla and its bodegas (wineries) have blossomed, and even the esteemed wine critic Robert Parker is taking note. Located in southeast Spain between La Mancha (mountain range) and the Mediterranean Sea, Jumilla has a hardy grape-growing climate, surrounded by wine country, with France to the northeast and Spanish sherry territory to the southwest. Jumilla carves its niche in the wine world by producing red wines from the Monastrell grape, with a strong purple-red color and fruity aroma. Monastrell is also grown in southern France where it is called Mourvedre.

Phylloxera spread in 1989 and destroyed Jumilla's grape vines, but the area today is experiencing a comeback. Surrounding regions had suffered long before Jumilla and already replanted. Jumilla growers decided to replant with different varieties, such as native grape Monastrell that appreciates the region's drought-prone climate. They also planted Petit Verdot and Cabernet Sauvignon, and the region shucked its bulk-wine reputation. Some Jumilla wines include Finca Omblancas, Casa de la Ermita, Pedro Luis Martinez, and Silvano Garcia.

Wine Suggestions: Jumilla

Panarroz Jumilla, Spain
This wine blends Monastrell (Mourvedre in France), Syrah, and Grenache, a combination familiar to wine lovers. It's approximately the same grapes found in the best Côtes-du-Rhône wines from southern France. This wine is bright, sunny, and full of ripe fruit flavor, smoke, and spice.

Castana Solanera Monastrell, Spain
Its name may mean "black sun," but the flavors of this wine are all red fruit, blackberry, and raspberry.

257

Geerlings & Wade

THE WINE BUSINESS is tough under any circumstances. Margins are tight, relationships critical, and hardest of all, states in the U.S. individually regulate the wine business unlike anything else but tobacco and firearms. In fact, the federal Bureau of Alcohol, Tobacco, Firearms, and Explosives (known as the ATF) regulated wine down to the ad copy on the label for decades. Today, the ATTTB—Alcohol and Tobacco Tax and Trade Bureau—does this work.

It's this level of regulation that tripped up so many would-be online wine merchants. The Web knows no boundaries, the government knows nothing but delimitation, and the stage is set for a conflict that the law is destined to win. Geerlings & Wade (with its headquarters in Canton, Massachusetts) has survived the bubble by predating it: Long before the Internet came into the picture, this company was selling wine through print catalogs and newsletters by attaining licenses and permits everywhere possible.

Geerlings & Wade started in 1986 as one of the first direct-mail wine clubs, specializing at that time in French wines. Phillip Wade sold the wine in the U.S. that his partner Huib Geerlings selected in France. Today, G&W has warehouses in sixteen states, and thanks to legislative reciprocal agreements, sales in twenty-nine. These guys did it the hard way, which turned out to be the right way, and they're still in business, selling 350 different wines a year.

G&W wine director Francis Sanders is not a gentleman-farmer like so many in the wine business. He pays attention to various tastes in wine, and does whatever he has to to sell wine that appeals to his wide-ranging audience.

In broad terms, this translates into a company flavor profile that favors ripe fruit, oak, and butter in white wines, and ripe fruit, oak, and soft texture in reds. In more than one instance, Sanders said he got involved directly in the blending process to bring wines—especially French wines—more in line with his vision of delicious drinkability.

Create Cork Coasters

REUSE OLD CORKS by cutting them crosswise and using the coin-shaped pieces to make coasters. You can piece them together in different designs. All you need are wine corks, a sharp knife, a hot glue gun and glue sticks, a newspaper or plastic tablecloth to protect your work area, and some craft glue for extra reinforcement. Then follow these four simple steps:

1. Cut the corks. Using a sharp knife, cut the corks crosswise into ¼-inch (½-cm) pieces. How many pieces you'll need depends on the size of your coaster, and whether you will set a wineglass or a wine bottle on the coaster.

2. Plan a design. Play with the cork pieces and try different designs before you get out the glue. For a simple circle shape, you will need approximately six cork pieces.

3. Apply glue. Hot glue the edges of the corks, pressing them together into a circle (or the shape of your choosing). If you will use the coaster for wineglasses, this may be just the right size. For wine bottles, make two additional cork circles. Then attach the three circles.

4. Secure the bottom. Cover the bottom of your cork coaster with craft glue and allow it to dry. This will provide the coaster with extra stability. And don't worry, it should dry clear.

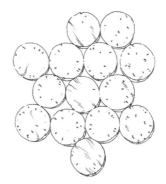

Lay out the cut cork pieces and plan a design, from a simple circle, to a more interesting shape, keeping in mind the size of the glass it is intended for.

The (In)Efficiency of Cork

WHEN YOU SEE HOW SMALL, light, and compact some of these new wine closures are, you have to wonder why a cork is so big. It's doing the same job as the screw cap or the glass cap, but in comparison, it's huge.

Technically, the traditional cork is the size it is because of the pressure it needed to exert over its relatively large surface area and to maintain its seal. The screw cap, in comparison, focuses its seal on just the very top surface of the bottle's mouth. In surface area alone, it's a tremendously smaller job, and that makes it much easier to get right almost every time.

Cork represents a preindustrial analog solution to closing a bottle of wine. Although it's sealing only a small opening slightly larger than a fingertip, it's a critically important seal, so we throw some bulk at it, 2 or more inches (5 or more cm) of cork sometimes, and maybe dip it in wax, just to make sure. Finally, winemakers seal it with a foil or plastic capsule for good measure. In all, we have to overcompensate just to feel secure.

From the industrial, almost postindustrial perspective, this sort of problem solving is quaint, and there's no wonder it doesn't work that well. In fact, cork is a terrible way to seal a bottle of wine. Despite cork's size, more than 1 percent of them fail, an absurdly high figure for something mass-produced.

Chenin Blanc

CHENIN BLANC IS ONE OF the main white grapes of France's Loire Valley in the northwest, and it came to California early in the United States' wine history. Like most wines, it's had sufficient periods of being tremendously popular and then falling out of favor. Wine lovers certainly have variable and fickle tastes.

Chenin Blanc has a tendency to ripen very sweet, a characteristic that made it popular in the first place. It is known for its floral, honey character and acidity. When American tastes turned toward dry wines, however, Chenin Blanc's natural sweetness doomed it in the market.

Chenin Blanc the grape is highly disease-resistant, and its hardiness perhaps explains why it is so wildly grown in California and France. The grape breaks bud early and ripens late, so it grows best in climates too warm for many vinifera. It also isn't picky about soil.

It will grow vigorously in sandy or clay loam, and generally produces five to eight tons of grapes per acre (hectare). In fact, after a few years, vines will overproduce. The downsides to Chenin Blanc are its susceptibility to bunch rot and, because of its early bud break and late harvest, sunburn.

Wine Suggestions: Chenin Blanc

Dry Creek Vineyard Chenin Blanc, United States (California)
In the sunlight, the wine Chenin Blanc shows off colors of pale green and silver. It smells lively and vivacious in the glass, almost effervescent, with zippy, bright citrus fruit.

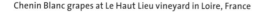

Chenin Blanc grapes at Le Haut Lieu vineyard in Loire, France

Recipe: Zinfandel-Braised Beef Short Ribs

THE KEY TO MAKING this recipe really work is to use a half-bottle of rich, ripe, high-alcohol Zinfandel in the braise to really crank up the Zin-ful flavors. Check the label and go for 15 percent alcohol, as long as it's affordable.

2 tablespoons (30 ml) olive oil

Salt and ground black pepper, to taste

4 boneless short ribs of beef (2 pounds, or 910 g)

1 medium onion, diced

2 carrots, diced

2 celery stalks, diced

4 garlic cloves, peeled

2 tablespoons (3.5 g) rosemary

1 can (28 ounces, or 810 g) Italian plum tomatoes, drained

½ bottle (375 ml) red Zinfandel

¼ cup (15 g) chopped fresh flat-leaf parsley, for garnish

Preheat the oven to 400°F (200°C).

On top of the stove, warm the olive oil in a large Dutch oven (or other heavy baking dish with a lid) over medium-high heat. Salt and pepper the short ribs, brown them on both sides in the olive oil, and remove to another plate. Add the onion, carrots, celery, garlic, and rosemary. Brown for 5 minutes, stirring now and then. Return the short ribs to the pot, add the tomatoes and wine, reduce the heat to medium, and cover.

Cook on top of the stove until the ingredients bubble nicely, then put the dish in the oven. Immediately turn the heat down to 275°F (140°C) and cook for 4 to 6 hours. Serve over polenta, risotto, or your favorite pasta. Garnish with parsley.

YIELD: Serves 4

Cooking tips: Check the dish now and then once it goes into the oven and add more wine if it's drying out. Look but do not stir! When you serve, pick out the garlic first, and make sure everyone gets a whole clove right on top.

Wine Pairing: Gnarly Head "Old Vine" Zinfandel

UNITED STATES (CALIFORNIA)

If you prune a grape vine from the top, called head-pruning, it grows like a small bush, and the shoots and grapes issue from what's now called the head of the vine. This is the gnarly head the name of this Zinfandel refers to. Its gnarliness is a product of age and exposure to sun, wind, weather, you name it, over many decades. Any wine called "Old Vine" or any variation thereof comes from grapes much older than thirty-five years, the age at which most vineyards are replanted because of declining production. California Zinfandel and Petite Sirah called "Old Vine" can be from vines as old as eighty or one hundred years.

The Douro Valley, Portugal

HIGH IN CENTRAL SPAIN, the headwaters of the Douro River circle lazily to the east, then the river turns sharply west and runs in almost a straight line through northern Spain and Portugal to the Atlantic Ocean. Each day, the sun sets along the length of the river, bathing the hillsides to the north and south in warm afternoon light.

By the time the Douro reaches Portugal, its vineyards and wineries start to fall under the wonderful warming influence of the ocean downstream. Sea breezes keep the grapes dry and cool in summer, and the warm water nearby creates a long autumn and a soft, moderate winter. After more than 2,000 years of grape growing and wine making, Portugal's wines other than port are strangely unknown outside the country. (This may be partly due to political repression by the former dictator António de Oliveira Salazar.)

Wine Suggestion: Douro

Sogrape Douro Reserva, Portugal Sogrape is the largest winery in Portugal and produces a broad spectrum. This delicious Reserva is black and concentrated, intensely oaked and tannic, big and robust and full of spice and vanilla. It is blended from three grapes: Touriga Nacional (the main grape in the world's great ports), Jaen (a tasty red table grape), and Tinta Roriz (the Portuguese name for the Spanish Tempranillo).

Piero Antinori

FOR MORE THAN twenty-six generations—since 1385—the Antinori family has been in the business of creating fine wines that earn international recognition. The company has remained family owned and operated, and is today directed by Marchese Piero Antinori.

"More things have changed in the past twenty years than the previous 200," Antinori said. "We know that using a combination of our own Chianti traditions, coupled with innovation, we can produce wines with qualities they didn't have before, wines with unique complexity, charm, and personality."

As one of the largest Italian wine families, the Antinoris and their innovations in the 1970s played a significant role in the Supertuscan revolution.

In fact, many credit Piero Antinori with creating the first Supertuscan by blending Sangiovese and Cabernet Sauvignon.

Then in 1985, after the family business was 600 years old, he first laid eyes on Atlas Peak Vineyards in Napa Valley, California. He began planting the new vineyards with cuttings of Sangiovese—the main grape of Chianti—taken from original Antinori vineyards in Italy. Twenty years later, Atlas Peak is the undisputed leader in growing Sangiovese in California.

Careful investments and research have allowed the company to produce quality wines from Tuscany and Umbria, Italy. In the wine world, the Antinoris are known as leaders and trendsetters.

Barges carrying wine in the River Douro in Portugal

Decorative Wine Bags

You don't need a sewing machine to craft an attractive fabric wine bag. These come in handy when giving wine as gifts. Use remnant fabric, recycle a cloth place mat, or purchase fabric with colors that complement the season. To dress up the bag, tie cording with tassels or a beautiful ribbon around the neck.

You'll need only a hot glue gun, fabric scissors, material, and a ribbon (or other embellishment). Then follow these three simple steps:

1. Measure and cut. From top to bottom, measure the bottle, and figure you'll need to double this length plus add 1 extra inch (2.5 cm) for a seam at the top of the bag. Repeat this step for the width of the bottle, allowing 1 extra inch (2.5 cm) on either side so the bottle can easily slip into the bag. Cut a piece of material two times the bottle's length, plus the seam allowance, and the bottle's width, plus the seam allowance.

2. Flip and glue. With right sides together, fold the cut fabric piece in half. At the top, fold 1 inch (2.5 cm) down, toward you, and secure with hot glue. Repeat this for the other top/side. Now, open the strip of fabric so the right side faces up. Run a strip of glue along each side, from the top to the halfway point. Then, fold the bottom up to secure the sides, pressing down on the glued edges. At this point, right sides will be together (with the wrong side of the fabric facing you). Let dry.

3. Turn in and embellish. Turn the wine bag so right sides face out, with your seam neatly concealed on the top and sides of the bag. Now, finish the project by slipping a wine bottle into the bag, and tying a cord with tassels or pretty ribbon around the neck.

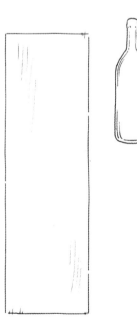

Begin with fabric that is approx. 3 inches (7.6 cm) longer than twice the length of the wine bottle.

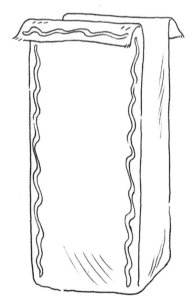

Apply hot glue beneath the fold of the fabric and along each edge (on the wrong side).

Wine Glossary, Part I

HERE ARE SOME common terms to become acquainted with as you explore the world of wine. The second part of the glossary appears on Day 309.

Astringent: A mouth-puckering feeling caused by tannins and accentuated by acid in wine

Balance: When no single wine component (e.g., alcohol, tannin, acid, sugar) overwhelms the wine

Blanc de Blanc: French for "white from white," meaning white wines made from white grapes; generally used to describe Champagne made entirely from Chardonnay

Blanc de Noirs: French for "white from black," meaning white wines made from red grapes, such as Champagne made entirely from Pinot Noir

Bodega: Spanish for winery or aboveground wine storage

Bouquet: A wine's smells or aromas

Cap: Solid parts of the grape, including skins, seeds, and stems, that rise to the top of the fermentation tank during red wine making; cap must be broken up so the elements can impart characteristics on the wines

Cloying: Too sweet

Cooked: Wine exposed to and damaged by heat

Co-operative: A member-owned central processing facility where vineyard owners can take their grapes to be made into wine or bottled

Crush: English for "harvest"

Cuvée: A vat or tank; usually refers to a batch of wine; used on wine labels to specify that the bottle came from a specific (special) batch of wine; also refers to a blend of wines

Enology (or oenology): The science of wine production

Esters: Components in wine formed when acids and alcohol combine; contributes a fruity, perfume smell

Fining: Clarifying wine using different agents, such as gelatin, egg white, or bentonite (clay), to add substance to which cloudy particles will stick; upon settling, the winemaker can skim the clear wine off the top

Foxy: The smell of native American grape varieties, such as the Concord grape

Free Run: The highest quality juice that appears just after crushing

Tempranillo

THIS RED GRAPE IS one of Spain's calling cards, particularly for wines produced in the Ribera del Duero and Rioja Alta regions. Tempranillo is blended into port, and in Portugal, they call the grape Tinta Roriz.

Tempranillo means "little early one," and the grape requires a short growing season and ripens early. Its vines thrive in cool climates, though they tolerate heat—the wine drinker, however, may not warm up to the undesirable flavors that result from overexposure to hot weather. In general, Tempranillo grapes have low acidity and sugar, and high tannin, thanks to the dark grape skins. If grown in a cool climate, the grape will produce wine that has a moderate alcohol content and lasts a long time (thanks again to those tannins).

Tempranillo is usually blended with other grapes such as Grenache, Carignane, or Cabernet Sauvignon.

Wine Suggestion: Tempranillo

Pata Negra Gran Reserva, Spain
This affordable Pata Negra is a great introduction to some of the Iberian Peninsula's best wines. Tempranillo is the main red grape in Rioja wines (kind of like Sangiovese and Chianti), but it's typically blended with other grapes as well. An all-Tempranillo formula is very twenty-first century, and the big delicious dose of French oak makes the wine modern as well. Long aging, on the other hand, is very traditional—the current retail vintage is almost ten years old.

Tempranillo grapes in Navarra, Spain

Recipe: Lavender Crisps

LAVENDER IS ONE OF THE main components in herbes de Provence (see Day 220), the traditional southern French herb mixture of sage, thyme, tarragon, rosemary, lavender, and more. Be careful cooking with lavender; it can become potent very quickly. Lavender and the word *livid* share the same Latin root, a tribute to the vibrant color of lavender flowers. You can find lavender in the bulk spice section of your local natural food store, or look for resources online. Try baking these cookies with rose, saffron, poppy seed, vanilla, lemon, or rosemary.

⅔ cup (150 g) butter

½ cup (100 g) sugar

1 egg, beaten

1 tablespoon (4 g) dried lavender flowers (make sure to buy culinary grade)

1½ cups (180 g) self-rising flour (or 1 cup [125 g] all-purpose flour)

Preheat the oven to 350°F (180°C). Grease 2 baking sheets.

Cream the butter and sugar together, then stir in the egg. Mix in the lavender flowers and the flour.

Drop spoonfuls of the mixture onto the baking sheets. Bake for 15 to 20 minutes, until the cookies turn golden. Serve with some fresh leaves and flowers to decorate.

Note: If you use all-purpose flour, the cookies will come out crisper and take less time to cook.

YIELD: Makes 2 dozen crisps

Wine Pairing: Domaine La Garrigue Cuvée Romaine Côtes-du-Rhône
FRANCE

Garrigue is the name for the densely growing dry scrubland and underbrush in southern France near the Mediterranean (see Day 220). During World War II, the French Resistance fighters called their movement Garrigue because it was omnipresent and impossible to root out. This wine is bright ruby red in color and smells like the wild herbs for which it's named. It tastes like black raspberries and figs.

There's No Place Like Côtes-du-Rhône

THE RHÔNE VALLEY (see Day 67) is considered one of the world's premiere wine regions, and its history as an important center of wine production and trade dates back to 125 BCE, when the ancient Greeks used the Rhône to travel to the heart of Gaul, France. Rhône competed with Italy for wine supremacy in the first century CE, and archeological digs have uncovered artifacts that confirm that Côtes-du-Rhône wines have one of the longest French wine-growing histories.

By the seventeenth and eighteenth centuries, Rhône Valley wine production began to pick up, and as early as 1650, regulations were introduced to guarantee the wine's origin and quality. All casks were branded with the letters CDR, for Côte-du-Rhône (later known as Côtes-du-Rhône). In 1937, this designation was updated to Appellation d'Origine Controlée (AOC)—Côtes-du-Rhône. Qualifications to earn this classification included having one or more varieties of a vine, a clearly defined territory, and expert wine production.

Today, Côtes-du-Rhône houses more than 6,000 estates, and it is the second largest French AOC. The Mediterranean climate bestows the region with heavy rains, high temperatures, and much sunshine. Key grapes grown in this region include Grenache (black and white), Syrah, Mourvedre (red), Clairette (white), and Marsanne (white).

Wine Suggestions: Rhône Valley

Cave de Cairanne Grand Reserve, France
Co-operative producers such as Cave de Cairanne make some of the highest quality bargain reds coming out of southern France today. True to form, this red is rustic and gutsy, full of fruit and easy-to-drink tannin.

Domaine Boisson Cairanne Rosé, France
Salmon colored, rich and ripe, this is a pink wine bordering on red. It contains fantastic fruit and much more structure than almost any other rosé.

La Vieille Ferme Côtes du Ventoux, France
Côtes du Ventoux (coat-dou-vonn-TOO) is a little-known region inside the more famous Côtes-du-Rhône in southern France. Mount Ventoux rises from the valley floor and dominates the local landscape. Grapes grow all up and down its slopes and hillsides, and the wine is almost always blended from multiple black country grapes, including Grenache, Syrah, Carignane (karen-YAWN), Cinsault (CHIN-so), and others.

Mas de Gourgonnier, France
This old favorite comes in a funky port-like bottle, and its eccentricity doesn't stop there. Its flavors are explosive and literally wild: rosemary, tarragon, and lavender lead to raspberry, hay, and leather.

A hut in a lavender field in Côtes-du-Rhône, France

The Foppiano Family

THE FOPPIANO FAMILY—five, going on six generations of California winemakers since 1896— doesn't chase after wine fashions. They've been making Pinot Noir under the radar for years while growing famous making the bigger, blacker Petite Sirah in a bold style everyone loves.

Wine fashion always comes full circle, returning to leaner, lighter, more expressive red wines in the form of Pinot Noir, Bonarda, and Nero d'Avola. Thanks to not moving around in pursuit of a trend, the spotlight is unexpectedly on Foppiano's delicious and true Pinot Noir from Sonoma's cool Russian River. It tastes like real Pinot Noir fruit: radiant and red, full of Bing cherry and fresh plum flavors. The tannic grip is delicate and nicely present, in good balance with the lighter fruit style.

Bistro Wines:
Weekends of Drinking Frugally

AS YOU BECOME more of a committed wine lover, wine can cease to be a special occasion beverage and instead become more of a staple, like bread and butter. And just like you rarely splurge on staples (except for that fancy French butter once, maybe twice a year), you stop splurging on wine most of the time, opting instead for affordable favorites—the bistro wines.

Bistro wines, or "bottega" or "tasca" wines, fall into the class of beverage served at most European bistros. The menu lists these simply as either "the red" or "the white." They are stored in a large modern amphora, and sold very cheap by the liter or half-liter. Much like great diplomats, bistro wines get along with all food on and everybody at the table.

Bistro Around the World

Beaujolais is the prototypical bistro red: It's a very soft, fruity juice, with not too much tannin, and moderate-to-low alcohol. It complies with almost all kinds of food. Beaujolais is so easygoing that you can serve it chilled like a white wine or at room temperature like a red.

In Italy, the house white is almost always Pinot Grigio, that great ubiquitous white. Look for Pinot Grigio by the magnum (double bottle size), especially Cavit Pinot Grigio from the wine country outside of Venice.

Wine Glossary, Part II

A CONTINUATION OF THE glossary terms found on Day 302, these are additional common terms with which to become acquainted as you explore the world of wine.

Glycerol: An alcohol resulting from fermentation; usually consists of less than one-tenth of the alcohol in wine

Hard: A tannic wine, perhaps out of balance; some young, "hard" wines soften with age

Hectare: The metric unit for measuring land area; 1 hectare equals 10,000 square meters or 2.5 acres

Lees: Sediment left over from young wines while still in the barrel, tank, or vat

Legs: An overused term referring to the streams of wine seen on the side of the glass after swirling; an indication of alcohol level

Limpid: Transparent; a wine that is clear and bright

Magnum: A wine bottle that holds the equivalent of two traditional-size bottles; used for slowly aging red wines

Mou: French for "soft" or "thin to a fault"

Pipe: A large oak barrel tapered at its ends; twice the size of an average barrel; generally used for port

Plastering: Adding substances such as calcium sulfate before fermentation to increase acidity or adding calcium carbonate to reduce acidity

Racking: Transferring young wine from one barrel (with sediment) to a new barrel to leave the sediment behind; a wine clarification process that exposes wine to oxygen

Rehoboam: An oversized bottle that holds six regular bottles of wine

Short: A measure of how long a wine's flavor stays in your mouth after swallowing; a short wine is of poor quality and does not linger

Sound: Free of defects; a minimum expectation, not a compliment

Split: A quarter bottle of wine, usually Champagne

Topping: Replacing evaporated wine in the barrel to reduce oxidation and ensure quality

Vinification: The process of turning grape juice into wine

Zymurgy: The science and study of fermentation

Aligoté

A vigorous, white grape with a long history in Burgundy, France, the Aligoté grape has larger berries than Chardonnay and produces higher yields. Where soil conditions won't permit Pinot Noir and Chardonnay, Aligoté grows quite happily—and in quantity. The official name of wine sold under the Aligoté name is Bourgogne Aligoté.

As for taste, Aligoté isn't necessarily a big-impact grape. But combined with other varieties—commonly Chardonnay

in Pouilly-Fuissé and Saint-Veran—it makes for a charming blend. You just won't see Aligoté stand alone in a wine.

One prime example of a fine Aligoté blend is the Shooting Star Aligoté. Washington State takes chances with the rare white grape Semillon, so why not with Aligoté? This wine smells unpromising and like mineral water, but tastes almost exactly the opposite: rich, ripe, and almost sweet with a core of banana split and vanilla ice cream.

Recipe: Muscat Ice

WINE DOESN'T GET the freezer treatment very often, but this recipe is about as close to home-made wine sorbet as one can get. Even with wine's modest alcohol content, it is a challenge to freeze nice and hard. Make sure when you select the wine for this recipe that you look for something with low alcohol, preferably in the single digits.

½ bottle (375 ml) Muscat wine

1 pound (450 g) Muscat grapes (substitute seedless white grapes when Muscat grapes aren't available)

Pour the wine into ice cube trays and freeze completely.

Remove the seeds from the Muscat grapes, and peel the fruit. Chill until ready to serve.

Chill serving dishes for a short time in the freezer. Remove the Muscat ice cubes from the tray and put them into a food processor or blender. Crush for 30 seconds.

Serve immediately with the peeled grapes—and do I need to say it?—the rest of the Muscat wine.

YIELD: Serves 4

Wine Pairing: Sipp-Mack Muscat
FRANCE

Muscat is one of the oldest wine grapes known, and it grows around the world under many names: Moscato, Moscatel, Moscophilero, and more. In eastern France, it grows along the west side of the Rhine as simple Muscat, and it's made from completely dry to sugary sweet. Sipp-Mack splits the difference beautifully by creating a Muscat that's got great acidity, like the dry versions, with a little residual sugar to highlight the ripeness of the fruit. Like almost all Muscat, it smells like fresh flowers and honey.

Aligoté grapes in traditional wicker baskets in Pernand-Vergelesses, France

Paso Robles, California

PASO ROBLES WINE COUNTRY is halfway between Los Angeles and San Francisco, along California's central coast, where long, warm days and cool evenings produce wines with dynamic flavors—an ideal grape-growing climate. This burgeoning wine region has more than 26,000 vineyard acres (10,520 ha) and forty different grape varieties. It's quickly gaining steam as one of California's top wine areas—impressive because of how high Napa Valley sets the bar.

The number of bonded wineries in Paso Robles has tripled in the past ten years, and Robert Parker wrote in a 2005 *Wine Advocate* that "there is no question that a decade from now, the top viticultural areas of Santa Barbara, Santa Rita Hills, and the limestone hillsides west of Paso Robles will be as well-known as the glamorous vineyards of Napa Valley."

What's different about Paso Robles compared to other California wine regions is its soil. The region contains more than forty-five different soil series, primarily bedrock soils from weathered granite, marine sedimentary rocks, volcanic rocks, and calcareous shales, sandstone, or mudstone.

A single vineyard block may contain multiple different soil types. This makes for a varied grape crop. The dominant grapes of this region include Cabernet Sauvignon, Merlot, Syrah, Zinfandel, Chardonnay, Viognier, and Roussanne.

Wine Suggestion: Paso Robles Liberty School Syrah
UNITED STATES (CALIFORNIA)

Syrah is the perfect red wine with grilled food, and the new Liberty School is on target with ripe black fruit flavors and plenty of tannic grip, for the right price. Syrah (Shiraz in Australia) continues to dominate the world market in delicious red wine, and this California varietal is every bit as tasty and lovable.

Eberle Winery in Paso Robles, San Luis Obispo, California, United States

Robert Parker

ROBERT PARKER of the *Wine Advocate* is perhaps the most famous wine critic; his wine scores can make or break a bottle. Hard as it is to believe, before Parker, no one had ever thought to apply to wine what's essentially the A-B-C-D-F grade scale from school systems. In Parker's system, 90 to 100 is an A, 80 to 90 is a B, and so on down the list. For more about the scoring system, see Day 57.

Parker had two strokes of brilliance at once. First, he applied this grading scale—something with which everyone in the U.S. is fundamentally familiar. Suddenly, wine came into focus for millions because anybody could understand that a "solid B+ wine" was one that someone liked well enough. Second, Parker immediately carved out a reputation for being the hardest grader of them all, refusing to grade on any curve whatsoever. Normally, an 88 or a 90 is a good score, but not with this professor.

Parker's scoring focuses unrealistic interest on high-scoring wines. You hear it all the time from wine shops: if it gets less than a 90, the shop can't sell it, and if it gets more than a 90, it's impossible to get in the store. Out in the world of wine, eccentric-exotic-rustic wines provide excellent wine experiences, but they score low because they're really just *vin ordinaire*, high Cs or low Bs. They can provide great enjoyment, but they never sell on scores. If they did, they'd have to pull out their vines and plant soybeans, and that would be a shame.

What hath Parker wrought? The great mass of the world's wines have been relegated to a wine netherworld by scoring in the 70s and 80s. But for the cream of the crop, Parker's performed a great service.

If you could create a wine scoring system, what would it be? Try to come up with something concrete but that leaves some room for subjectivity. One wine magazine awards zero to three "glasses," but strangely this doesn't represent how many glasses of the wine in question you'd happily drink; it just means each glass is worth slightly more than thirty-three points.

Your scale could be flexible and expandable, awarding icons instead of scores. For example, one glass means you would drink one glass. Three bottles in a wine rack means you'd buy a few bottles to keep. A wedding ring means you love this wine so much that with it you would happily spend the rest of your days. A bag of coins means the wine works well to clean pennies. Of course, you are free to make up more icons as you go along.

Buy the Glass

ONE BOTTLE OF WINE represents 8,000 years of wine history. That's why it's so hard to choose just the right one. Sometimes it's best to buy wine by the glass.

Fleming's Prime Steakhouse & Wine Bar, with locations in more than twenty-five states in the U.S., has solved this problem. Instead of offering many wines by the bottle and a choice of a few by the glass, the Fleming's restaurants feature a hundred wines by the glass every day and a shorter reserve list of special wines by the bottle.

Buying by the glass at Fleming's offers educational opportunities, too; you could try two or three different wines every time you ate there and never drink the same wine twice. By the time you worked your way through, the list would change, and you'd have to start all over again.

Not near a Fleming's? Most restaurants' menus include at least a few wines by the glass. Next time you dine out, peruse the wines-by-the-glass list at your favorite restaurant and educate yourself all night long.

Why We Sniff

WINE LOVERS GET ACCUSED of much, including snobbery, elitism, and fuzzy syntax, all to which we plead guilty. Every now and then, we have to stand up and explain how seemingly strange behavior—such as enormous amounts of sniffing from the business end of a wineglass—actually makes sense in the grand scheme of wine tasting.

Historically, sniffing was all about keeping bad wine from happening to good people. Picture your college roommate going through the fridge. "Well, it looks OK . . . it smells OK . . . maybe I'll take a little taste." This is the basis for many, if not all, of our most uncomfortable wine traditions, from inspecting the cork to swirling, sniffing, and spitting in front of other people.

At one time, the world's hygiene was far worse than today, and the likelihood of being poisoned by a nasty bottle of wine was far better. If you sniffed your wine and discovered it smelled like kerosene, you could spare yourself the danger of even taking a sip.

Today, few truly damaged bottles of wine exist out there, so most of the wine we sniff these days is good wine. Some people even buy bigger and more specialized wineglasses that allege to deliver more scent molecules per sniff, to maximize the sensation.

Slowly but surely, the incredible aromatic sensation you get from sniffing and attending to wine makes an impression, and sniffing becomes high art appreciation. Wine lovers look critically for whatever they can find in a wine, be it wood, fruit, or flowers, just like they would any other work of art. Needless to say, winemakers love this kind of talk.

Finally, people just love the smell of food and wine naturally. It's part of being a human animal to pursue the scent of food. We civilize it and take the hard edge off by putting the prey in a glass. I think it smells like life.

276

Sangiovese

SANGIOVESE FORMS the base of Chianti wine—generally an average of 70 percent, along with some Canaiolo (red), Trebbiano (white), and sometimes Colorino (red). There are at least fourteen different clones of Sangiovese, which matures slowly and ripens late. The grape thrives in the hot, dry climate of Tuscany; its thin skin makes it susceptible to rot in dampness. Don't try to grow the plant above 1,500 feet (457 m). It won't mature well.

Sangiovese wine tastes fruity with moderate to high acidity, and can be elegant or robust with a bitter finish. Aromas include strawberry, blueberry, floral, violet, or plum. Lately, more winemakers are experimenting with Sangiovese, blending it with Cabernet Sauvignon or Merlot to produce pricey Supertuscan blends.

Wine Suggestions: New World Sangiovese

Ferrari-Carano Sangiovese,
United States (California)
Sangiovese changes a lot when grown under the hot California sun. What's a relatively light but strong red wine in Italy can come out dense and dark when ripened New World style. Ferrari-Carano is made from vineyards yielding a miniscule 2 tons of Sangiovese per acre (0.4 ha), and the concentration of black fruit flavors is amazing. I would drink it with a few friends, a big piece of blue cheese (like gorgonzola dolce), a loaf of crusty bread, and a half-dozen pears or apricots to go around.

Robert Oatley Rosé of Sangiovese ,
(Australia)
This wine is peculiar in a few charming ways. Sangiovese is a quirky choice, but when it's made in Australia? That's doubly quirky. And on top of that, you have the rosé factor. The Robert Oatley marque is a tireless rosé advocate and the Sangiovese is brilliant, salmon colored, and rich tasting with good weight. Serve with any heavier seafood like tuna, swordfish, or salmon.

Recipe: Pears and Stilton

THE BRITISH INVENTED PORT in Portugal (see Day 205), and consequently gave us its culture and traditions. The classic match with port is Stilton cheese, toasted nuts, and pears.

4 ripe pears

3 tablespoons (45 ml) olive oil

1 tablespoon (15 ml) lemon juice

½ tablespoon (4 g) toasted poppy seeds

Salt and ground black pepper, to taste

3 ounces (88 g) Stilton cheese

3 tablespoons (40 g) large-curd cottage cheese

8 to 10 toasted walnuts, for garnish

Cut the pears in half lengthwise, scoop out the cores, and cut away the bottom flower. Make a light dressing by combining the olive oil, lemon juice, poppy seeds, salt, and pepper.

Beat together the Stilton and cottage cheese, and add ground black pepper to taste. Divide this mixture among the pear slices. Spoon the dressing over the pears and garnish with walnuts.

YIELD: Serves 8

> ## Wine Pairing: Prager Royal Escort Port
>
> UNITED STATES (CALIFORNIA)
>
> The Port Works has been making wine in St. Helena, in the middle of Napa, since 1979. The style is classic, full of sweetness and soaring alcohol. This Royal Escort comes from Petite Sirah grapes.

278

Discovering New, Old Tastes

WINE INNOVATION COMES FROM old grapes grown in new places, classic wines made in new styles, or previously unimagined wine blends. There will always be new trends in wine, but no matter where you look, there are "new" wines to discover—new to you, that is.

Part of the joy of learning about wine is unearthing a label you never tried from a place you never dreamed grew grapes. We make these discoveries every day just by touring the aisle of our local supermarket or corner boutique wine retailer.

We hear immigrant tales of an underappreciated grape in a new country. For example, Malbec and Carmenere, nearly unknown in France, both

flourish in South America and exhibit exciting new flavors impossible in the old country. See how it works? Countless examples show how wine in its place (all of this book's Thursday entries) can excite new flavors.

As you explore wine countries from an armchair, a laptop computer, or on foot during winery or vineyard tours, consider the most important element in every bottle, that secret ingredient that no one really talks about: place. With every sip, you taste a sense of place that captures a region, history, and culture.

Dan Goldfield and Steve Dutton

WINEMAKER DAN GOLDFIELD was getting passionate about topography. On our restaurant table and a good bit of the next lay maps of the Russian River. Goldfield pointed to the Pacific Ocean and then to the California hills. "Cold air comes off the ocean and east up the Russian River," he said. "And down here's something called the Petaluma Wind Gap, and cold air flows east through it." He pointed at the map. "Right here where they come together," he said, "the Green Valley. Our grapes and our winery."

Steve Dutton's family at Dutton Ranch—or ranches, actually, because the family owns more than one—has provided top-quality grapes for years. Now that he and Goldfield have joined business forces, they have a seemingly perfect symbiotic relationship. "I'm a farmer, not a winemaker," Dutton supposedly declared at the beginning. Goldfield answered, "My dream was to spend my life on my bike or on my skis. I never thought I'd be a winery owner."

Dutton-Goldfield Winery sits at the western end of the Russian River Valley, nearest to the cooling ocean. Russian River is rightly famous for creamy full-bodied Chardonnay with the crisp, snappy finish of a lighter white wine. Dutton-Goldfield fruit exploits this valley's coldness to get a unique finish in the winery's Chardonnay, one good enough and distinctive enough to be a signature.

According to his own legend, Goldfield was on a mountain-bike adventure one day, turned a corner, and stumbled upon one and a half acres (a little more than half a hectare) of pre-Prohibition old-old-vine Zinfandel (maybe as old as 120). According to Goldfield's research, the remaining plot was part of more than 100 acres (40 ha) well established long before the turn of the previous century. From there, Dutton-Goldfield took shape.

Wine Suggestions: Dutton-Goldfield

Dutton-Goldfield Dutton Ranch Chardonnay, United States (California)
This wine looks gold and bright, with a little silver tinge, and smells creamy and spicy, with well water aromas. It tastes like caramel, almost sweet, with round, ripe, tropical flavors, and a perfect finishing balance of citrus and crisp acidity. It tastes great with food such as shellfish or freshwater trout, even a roast chicken.

Dutton-Goldfield Morelli Lane Vineyard Zinfandel, United States (California)
This wine, subdued for a Zinfandel, but full of super-concentrated red fruit, has dense, dark, black juice. It has an earthiness like Old World Syrah, but ripe, bright fruit that's perfectly California. Morelli Lane is the westernmost vineyard in the Green Valley, and thanks to being closest to the ocean, it's also the coldest and breeziest of the neighboring hillsides, accounting for some of this wine's restrained personality.

There's No Business Like
Wine Show Business

HAVE YOU EVER ATTENDED a weekend wine show? In two whirlwind days, consumers get to taste a vast range of wines they could likely never hope to taste otherwise, even if they spent an entire year going from wine shop to wine shop. Hundreds of wineries pour thousands of different wines. The problem with many wine shows, however, is that they are often so vast and full of great wine experiences that you could find yourself wandering and tasting aimlessly for upwards of four hours if you're not careful. Here are some tips to get you through:

GO ON DAY TWO

As swirling, noisy, upbeat, and busy as Day One is, Day Two is comparatively laid-back. Sunday's crowds are reduced, and winemakers and salespeople feel relaxed and unhurried, really able to spend time talking you through what you're tasting.

ATTEND A SEMINAR

Some shows have grown immensely over the years and have evolved beautifully to include seminars and celebrity chefs. Take a break from tasting by sitting in on one of these sessions.

EAT FIRST, THEN DRINK

Going to a wine show on an empty stomach is a big mistake. Eat like you were about to run a marathon: lots of carbs, protein, and water.

DRESS FOR A MESS

Basic black is a good wardrobe choice for a wine tasting. You can spill almost anything on it and still look untouched. European winemakers favor the busy sports coat with a pattern so elaborate you could spill an egg on it and not see the stain.

SIP, SWISH, SPIT

It's undainty and undignified, but you have to spit, not swallow. There are spit buckets everywhere, and everyone else is spewing wine like crazy, so don't be shy. Besides, doing this will allow you to taste more wines.

Display of wine bottles at an open market in Lyon, France

The Art of the Wine Label

FOR THE PAST EIGHTY or so vintages, the ultra-famous Château Mouton Rothschild label has literally featured a work of art designed by many of the twentieth century's greatest visual artists: Dali, Chagall, Warhol, Kandinsky, and Picasso have all been paid in wine—not a bad deal.

For the 2001 vintage, the Baroness Philippine de Rothschild tapped the genius of experimental theater director Robert Wilson. Apparently without experimenting, however, Wilson delivered a label featuring not one but two pictures of the Baroness herself, a former actress.

Granted, we all have to give our bosses what they want sometimes, but it would have been nice if Wilson could have done so without assuring this wine bottle's place one day in the Museum of Safe Art. The good news: The wine itself is unaffected.

Psychedelic Label

Randall Grahm from Bonny Doon Vineyard bends the rules of wine and wine making to a Hendrix-like breaking point whenever he can. He introduced the Cardinal Zin Zinfandel, which sells successfully based much on the massive weirdness of its label—psilocybin-reminiscent and created by English artist Ralph Steadman.

Steadman illustrated many of drug-eating gonzo-journalist Hunter S. Thompson's more notorious works, so it makes you wonder what's in the bottle. Overall, the wine is hallucination-free. There's a big blast of fresh fruit at first, a dash of sugar, and then good strong tannin comes through on the swallow. I'm not sure I would have made this wine a Zinfandel, which is tough to rationalize at the price. In a couple of years, maybe the Zin-ful essence will assert itself. Until then, consider looking at the label and drinking the wine only under black light.

Rare Château Mouton Rothschild wine bottles painted and signed by some of the great modern and contemporary artists: Roberto Matta (1963), Bernard Dufo (1963), and Bernard Sejourne Mouton (1986)

Trebbiano: The Great Unknown

AMAZINGLY, THE MOST widely planted white grape in both Italy and France—the world's two biggest wine producing nations by far—is not one of the usual suspects. Chardonnay, Sauvignon Blanc, Riesling, and especially Pinot Grigio come immediately to mind, but no, it's none of these famous mainstays of the wine world. In fact, one of the reasons no one knows its name is because this grape is so ancient and widespread that it goes by many. The ancient Roman naturalist Pliny the Elder wrote about the white grape variety vinum trebulanum more than 2,000 years ago, and now it's grown around the world.

Today in Italy, this grape is generally called Trebbiano plus a dozen or so different place names: Trebbiano Toscano, Trebbiano di Lucca, Trebbiano d'Abruzzo, di Tortona, di Soave, and so on. Italians also call it Greco, Lugana, and Procanico for good measure. Trebbiano is so ubiquitous it is found in lots of white wines with their own semi-famous names: Orvieto, Verdicchio, Soave, Frascati, even into red Chianti at one time, though relatively rarely in the twenty-first century. No wonder the humble every-grape Trebbiano gets lost in the shuffle.

Across the Alps in France, Trebbiano has its own particular names and uses. Known mostly as Ugni (pronounced oon-YEE) Blanc, it's also Hermitage Blanc, Clairette Ronde, Clairette de Vence, Saint Émilion, Blanc de Cadillac, Charentes, and more. Most French Ugni Blanc goes into the production of the much more familiar brandies called Cognac and Armagnac. Ironically enough, the few still white wines produced from Ugni Blanc are inexpensive, light, and generally disregarded for being one-dimensional; yet the famous brandies of France, also made from Ugni, charge sometimes three and four figure prices.

Italian wine makers have taken and planted Trebbiano around the world with varying degrees of success. In California, the grape teeters on the edge of novelty, with many wine makers going to Pinot Grigio for a dependable Italian-style white instead. Trebbiano in Australia is called both White Hermitage and White Shiraz, and production is so tiny it's in the White Grapes/Other category.

Wine Pairing: Masciarelli Trebbiano d'Abruzzo

Its color is not as clear as water but almost, and for words to describe the aroma, you have to think about the smell of rain, or a fast-flowing river, or clothes drying on the line. It's either what you love about Italian white wine—the lightness, the brightness, the refreshingly simple flavor— or what you hate—too light, too simple, no depth. Serve with a light white cheese such as mozzarella fresca, ricotta, or farmer's cheese and fresh fruit.

Recipe: Anchovy Butter

ANCHOVIES ARE FISHED along the entire Italian coast, but Sicily is the reputed home of the Mediterranean's best of these small oily fish. Popular since at least ancient Roman times, anchovies are cured, canned, and served fresh, ranging in flavor from strong and fishy (a by-product of the curing process) to mild and light tasting when fresh. A Sicilian white wine is the perfect match in flavor—lemon-lime, what we like to sprinkle over seafood of all kinds—and in geography.

½ cup (8 tablespoons or 112 g) unsalted butter

2 teaspoons (8 g) anchovy paste

¼ teaspoon (1.3 ml) onion juice

½ teaspoon (2.5 ml) lemon juice or ½ garlic clove, crushed

Ground black pepper or cayenne, to taste

To start, soften the butter by creaming then beat in all the other ingredients. Serve by spreading on bruschetta, or use it as a sauce over light seafood for a blast of ocean flavor.

YIELD: about 1 ½ cups (120 g)

Wine Pairing: Fondo Antico Grillo Parlante

ITALY

Grillo mean "grasshopper" in Italian, and the name of this indigenous grape speaks to its high-pitched flavor tones, full of citrus and tropical fruits. Fondo Antico is fermented in steel, a technique that preserves the wine's intense acidity.

Malbec grapes from Familia Zuccardi in Maipú, Mendoza, Argentina

Argentina

EUROPEAN WINE GRAPES came to Argentina early in the 1500s, a three-century head start over California.

This South American country is primarily known for wines made from one red grape: Malbec. This grape came to the area from France, where it grows widely around Bordeaux and in a relatively unknown region called Cahors, not far south of Bordeaux.

Malbec is to Argentina what red Zinfandel is to California or what Shiraz is to Australia, but even more affordable. Though in its native land, Malbec went ignored or was blended with other grapes, the South American climate did it wonders, and it has flourished in its adopted land. Today, Malbec represents Argentina's wine face to the world: modern, enjoyable, approachable, untraditional, tasty, and cheap.

Incidentally, Argentina consumes 337 million gallons (1.3 billion L) of wine each year. Its per-capita consumption of 9 gallons (34 L) a year is nearly five times that of the United States.

Wine Suggestions: Malbec

Trapiche Oak Cask Malbec, Argentina
Its fruit concentration is great, and it has enough abrasive tannic grip to deal with strong food. Note in the wine's soft toasted aroma the strong presence of the oak cask to which its label alludes.

Trapiche Iscay Merlot-Malbec, Argentina
This joint effort by winemakers Angel Mendoza and Michel Rolland deliciously overflows with wood flavors after more than a year in nothing but new French oak barrels. Iscay is thoroughly modern, competing more with California wines than any Old World ones do.

Eileen Crane

YOU CAN START YOUR OWN wine genome project, one sip of wine at a time, thanks to Eileen Crane. Crane is the president of and winemaker at Domaine Carneros, located in the southern part of California's Napa Valley.

Domaine Carneros, owned by the Taittinger family, is naturally most well known for its sparkling wine. And Crane has extensive experience with sparkling wines. Then, when she made her first Pinot Noir sometime around 1992 on a whim, as a holiday gift for the staff, the Taittingers were so impressed that they decided to develop the wine as part of their product line. "People warned me that Pinot Noir is the hardest wine to make, but it's actually the second hardest," Crane said. "The hardest wine to make is sparkling wine, which I'd been making for years."

Because the Carneros region has a history of growing successful Pinot Noir since the mid-1800s, winemakers there have a good deal of experience with different clones that have yielded favorites. "We think of these as Carneros heirloom clones," Crane said. "They give us very consistent vintages, and we treat them very much the same way we do the sparkling wine grapes: gentle pressing and lots of blending."

Crane began her wine-making career in a roundabout way. She's a New Jersey native with a master's degree in nutrition who moved to Venezuela to pursue social work. She returned to the United States, did graduate work at the University of Connecticut, then attended the Culinary Institute of America (CIA) in Hyde Park, New York. Her next stop was California. After an introduction to wine at CIA, she spent four months at the University of California, Davis studying viticulture and enology. Though she hadn't before studied it, Crane grew up appreciating wine, thanks to her father, a former military police officer who became interested in wine during a tour in Europe and later built a wine cellar in their New Jersey basement.

In a 2007 *Wine Spectator* article, Crane described her wine-making style: "Like Audrey Hepburn in the perfect little black dress. It's not just a black dress—it's a *perfectly lined* black dress with the *perfect* strand of pearls, the wrap, the whole thing. It's not fancy, it's not overdone. In wine making, I do that . . . I make wines that you need to pay attention to . . . layers come to you piece after piece."

Back to Wine School

IF YOU WANT TO LEARN about wine, you have to experience it, taste it, and keep tasting it. Attending a wine school or workshop allows you to immerse yourself in wine history and practice, and to expand your knowledge beyond the bottle. Whether you're just beginning your wine adventure or you're a longtime connoisseur, wine classes have much to offer the enthusiast who wants to feed an unquenchable thirst for knowledge.

Take classes open to the public to learn wine etiquette, wine tasting, grape basics, and some history. Or turn your passion into certification by attending a sommelier school, where you can earn professional standing. Regardless of whether you consider wine your hobby or livelihood (or both), wine schools and seminars offer a learning environment where you can meet other enthusiasts, talk about wine, learn about wine culture, and expand your appreciation for the grape.

What can you expect at a wine school? Of course, that depends where you go. Typically, you'll find classes geared toward various levels and interests: professional, advanced, or intermediate certification; leisure classes such as Wine Tasting 101 or Understanding Classic Grapes; and wine-and-food pairing courses. Seek out a local venue to take classes, or enroll in online courses such as those offered by *Wine Spectator* (though the experience of mingling with other wine lovers is much of the fun).

Where can you find such opportunities?

• Local retailers. Find out about wine classes and other learning opportunities by inquiring at your local wine retailer. Someone there can likely guide you to nearby events.

• Online. Search for classes online at websites such as www.localwineevents.com.

• Restaurants. Tune in to events that wine-savvy restaurants host, such as wine dinners or meet-and-greets with winemakers.

The key is to find a venue where you feel comfortable asking questions. Wine is communal, much more enjoyable when shared. The instructor should be approachable and speak your language—in other words, someone practical who leads a class like a teacher rather than a critic. With a surging interest in learning more about wine history and culture, new wine schools are popping up all over the place. Chances are, there's a classroom with an open seat close to where you live.

Marketing Messages

MANY WINES SUCCEED commercially because they have talented and committed people behind them organizing, selling, and promoting like wild. These salespeople often work for distributors and importers who control much of what is available. Like it or not, their taste and good work habits account for many of the wines on our tables. Usually, their names appear on the back label, small and inconspicuous. The identities of the marketers for Oriel Wines and Tangent Winery, on the other hand, have been expanded and promoted to the front label—where they belong.

Oriel is the brainchild of John Hunt, international winemaker in both Spain and Australia. In essence, Oriel hires twenty or so of the planet's best and most talented winemakers and lets them make a limited quantity of whatever they want. The largest production of any single wine was about 3,000 cases in 2006. Most come in batches of 500 or so cases. Like a talented importer, Oriel has a somewhat wildly diversified stable of twenty-seven wines from twenty-four appellations in eight countries. All the wines share the basic Oriel label identity, but each bottle goes deep into the different region from whence it came.

The Tangent name is figurative, representing the company's pursuit of only white wines and only white wines from eccentric grapes tangential to mainstream wines.

Both Oriel and Tangent represent highly modern, flat-earth business models that depart from current style. In the second half of the twenty-first century, many wine companies will likely operate this way.

Wine Suggestions: Oriel and Tangent

Oriel Palatina Riesling, Germany
The Oriel Palatina Riesling comes from the Mosel River Valley, west of the Rhine, much closer to France, and with much better food than just 25 miles (40 km) east of there. It is bright, zippy, and tropical with plenty of mineral notes. Also, this Riesling is deliciously dry, with reduced sugar revealing a much more interesting world of soil, sky, and sea flavors.

Tangent Paragon Vineyard Pinot Gris, United States (California)
Tangent makes only a handful of wines: explosive Sauvignon Blanc, an exotic Albarino, Pinot Blanc, and Pinot Gris, and an unexplainable but yummy white blend called Ecclestone. There's not a single Chardonnay in the lineup. This full-bodied wine has concentrated peach, ginger, and tropical fruit flavors.

Cabernet Franc

ACCORDING TO LEGEND—or is it history?—Cabernet Franc came to Friuli in northeast Italy with one of Napoleon's generals during the Continental Wars of 1812. In the hours not spent fighting Austrians, the general introduced Pinot Blanc and Cabernet Franc—two cold-climate French favorites—to this cool northern region of Italy. White wine rules the Loire Valley of northwest France, but man cannot live by white wine alone. Right in the middle of the region, where the Loire River takes a lazy southern loop on its way to the Atlantic, sits an island of red Cabernet Franc grapes. Three neighborhoods—Chinon (shee-NON), Bourgueil (boor-GAY), and Saumur (so-MOOR)—produce almost all of the red wine that comes from this place. Cabernet Franc, a distant cousin of the more famous Cabernet Sauvignon, is typically dense and dark, but it is a rare cool-climate red grape. Long, slow ripening and little exposure to oak aging or fermenting produces a soft wine low in tannin.

Wine Suggestions: Cabernet Franc

Domaine Saint Vincent Les Adrialys, France
The grapes grow on fifty-year-old vines, but the wine is named for two of the winemaker's children, Adrian and Alys. Half of the wine is barrel-aged, and all of it goes through barrel fermentation. The result is a fruity, fresh wine with a good dose of oak and barrel tannin. It's super with duck or dark meat chicken.

Domaine Saint Vincent Léa, France
Anyone with children knows the kids are sensitive to being left out, so naturally enough, this offering is named for another daughter of the winemaker. Inky and dense, it smells like cinnamon and pumpkin pie spice with a little menthol. Fruit flavors of fig and plum dominate, and the tannin is hard, bracing, and wonderful.

289

The first vintage in 1978 comprised of 80 percent Cabernet Sauvignon and 20 percent Malbec, Merlot, Syrah, Cabernet Franc, Pinot, and Tannat

Recipe: Clementines in Cinnamon Caramel

ORANGE BLOSSOMS and wine converge in the form of Orange Muscat, a grape the Italians call orange-blossom Muscat because of its pungent citrus aroma. It is a perfect component of this fragrant, seasonal treat.

8 to 12 clementines

1 cup (200 g) sugar

1½ cups (355 ml) hot water

2 cinnamon sticks

2 tablespoons (30 ml) Orange Muscat

Pare the rind from 2 clementines using a vegetable peeler, and cut the peel into fine strips. Reserve for later use in the syrup.

Peel the clementines, removing all the pith but keeping them intact. Place them into a bowl.

Gently heat the sugar in a pan until it dissolves and turns a rich golden brown. Do not stir. Turn off the heat immediately. Pour in the water and bring to a slow boil, stirring until the caramel dissolves. Add the rind, cinnamon sticks, and Muscat, then simmer for 5 minutes. Allow to cool for 10 minutes. Pour over the clementines. Cover the bowl and chill for several hours before serving.

YIELD: Serves 4 to 6 (2 clementines per serving)

Wine Pairing: Renwood Orange Muscat

UNITED STATES (CALIFORNIA)

Intense candied orange rind is the main flavor in this wine, a perfect match with the milder clementines. Renwood grows in California's hot inland Amador County, home to countless concentrated dessert wines.

Vineyard rows in Navarra, Spain

Navarra, Spain

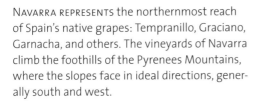

NAVARRA REPRESENTS the northernmost reach of Spain's native grapes: Tempranillo, Graciano, Garnacha, and others. The vineyards of Navarra climb the foothills of the Pyrenees Mountains, where the slopes face in ideal directions, generally south and west.

Navarra is Basque country, an elbow of territory where Spain and France meet on the Atlantic. The people consider themselves neither Spanish nor French. They speak a language more Baltic than Romance, and the Basque influence on food, wine, and culture goes back millennia. The ancient Romans found the territory between Bordeaux and Rioja already inhabited by a tribe of people called Vascones, today's Basques.

The rising tide of Spain's wine reputation has brought attention to many previously ignored wine regions in Spain, including Navarra, which is beginning to enunciate what makes its wines different and interesting.

April Cullom is a certified educator on Spanish wines who organizes events and promotions for Spain. She articulated the difference as such:

"The Navarrans were the first Spanish winemakers to go international. They've been working forever with native grapes such as Tempranillo, Garnacha, and Graciano. But they like to use a lot of international varieties such as Cabernet Sauvignon and Merlot. They're much more international in style and very easy for consumers to understand and enjoy."

Because Navarra's vineyards are nestled in the foothills of the Pyrenees, the region does not have the same heat that other Spanish vineyards face. The Atlantic Ocean's winds and rainfall keep the climate cooler and the land is much greener compared to Spain's central regions, such as La Mancha.

Conventional wisdom tells us that wine grapes make the best wine when they grow at their limits: barely enough water, barely enough solar radiation—that sort of agriculture is good for wine. Craig Gandolf, a wine buyer for the U.S. importer and impresario Jorge Ordoñez, says the wines from Navarra have "more finesse and class" than some of the big reds that other regions boast.

291

Todd Williams

KNOWN AS DR. TOAD for his Toad Hollow Vineyards, Robert Todd "Toad" Williams was an entertainer, the main event—especially if you were lucky enough to earn a seat at one of his wine dinners. But Williams's main act focused on grapes. He was drawn to the wine world after running the restaurant the Whiskey River Inn with his wife in the Sierra foothill town of Arnold in California. That outfit failed, but Williams began to learn about wine through jobs he held afterward: sales for Whitehall Lane and working with American Wine Distributors in San Francisco selling to upscale restaurants. He worked as a national sales manager for Shafer Vineyards and became a marketing guru. He launched Hillside Estates Marketing Company in the 1980s to bring national exposure to small wineries.

Williams's wines from Toad Hollow Vineyards in the Russian River Valley feature bold, catchy labels: a cast of dapper toads; names such as Cacophony and Askew (with a crooked label).

Williams passed away in 2007 at age sixty-nine. In every sense, he left an impression.

> Dr. Toad's showmanship runs in the family. His brother is actor Robin Williams.

Ordering Wine for a Crowd

YOU'RE DINING OUT with friends and, as the host who organized the event, are confronted with a server ready to take your beverage order. Your crew includes some beer drinkers, some lovers of red wine, and a few who only tip back white. You can't vote on what type of wine to order— definitely a mood killer.

You must place the order, and there are a few different ways you can handle this task and still please everyone. (The beer drinkers can order for themselves.) Servers today are more knowledgeable about wine than ever before, as restaurateurs recognize the drink's growing popularity and waitstaff learn how best to help customers. When in doubt, ask the server for suggestions.

Another tip: follow that wonderful cliché, "When in Rome, do as the Romans do." Order an Italian

red and white wine while dining at your favorite trattoria. If you're in an ethnic restaurant, choose wines that originate from the region that complements the menu. Don't fight your gut instincts by ordering a French wine at a Mexican restaurant.

You're always safe ordering a high-acid white and a moderate-tannin red because these wines pair well with most foods. Ask the server to direct you to these options, which will include Sauvignon Blanc, Riesling, and Merlot varieties. Order one each of white and red, get them on the table in a hurry, and allow your guests to pour their preference.

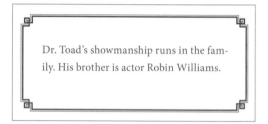

Sunset at Seven Hills Vineyard in Umatilla County, Oregon, United States

The Word of the Law

ATOP THE WINE NEWS heap these days is fallout from the May 2005 U.S. Supreme Court ruling that effectively ended interstate limits on buying, selling, and shipping wine. Some states, in what looks like a fit of unattractive pique, proposed new wine control laws even more punitive than before but that would satisfy a loophole in the case. Let's be honest: this case happened because time has passed, business has changed, and people just want to be able to buy, sell, and deliver wine like anything else on the planet.

One winning argument centered on the unfairness and anti-competitiveness of state laws that allow in-state vineyards and wineries to ship direct and sell wholesale direct, yet require out-of-state wineries to go through a distributor. This was economically harmful behavior, and wine lovers wanted it to stop.

In 2004, before the case got to the courtroom, Michigan politicians (and others) were already threatening that the state could vindictively rewrite the law to ban all direct selling and shipping, even by in-state wineries, and then it wouldn't be unfair anymore, would it? This is exactly what a number of states have attempted since, and in fact, it is still unfair, maybe even worse for wine lovers than before.

Constitutionally, Prohibition represented such an extreme infringement on people's rights that it required an amendment to enact. Thirteen years later it earned the distinction as the only Constitutional amendment ever repealed, an act that itself required yet another amendment. Part of the compromise to get this whole thing off the books, so to speak, was that localities would exercise liquor control, which is why we still have the odd dry town or county today.

After decades of unfair controls, some states now propose to level the playing field by expanding the unfairness and distributing it more equitably. That recent Supreme Court ruling sent a message that state governments purposefully aren't receiving: wine is food, not booze, and should be regarded and respected as such.

Carmenere

WITHOUT THE BENEFIT OF high-tech genetic testing, it's actually pretty difficult to identify different grape varieties with any accuracy just by looking at them, which has been the extent of the identification system for 8,000 years. Leaf structure is a visual clue. The physical shape of the grape cluster is another. When the grapes ripen in the fall—early, middle, or late fall—is a major differentiator, too.

Carmenere, a relatively unknown and little-planted, red blending grape from Bordeaux, came from France to Chile sometime in the latter half of the 1800s. Thanks to a leaf that looks a lot like Merlot and a tendency to ripen late, also like Merlot, the two became confused. Carmenere in Chile was essentially renamed Merlot for more than a century, until DNA testing in 1994 confirmed what made Chile's Merlot so special: it wasn't Merlot. In an instant, Chile's Carmenere industry was born.

Wine Suggestion: Santa Rita 120 Carmenere

CHILE

This delicious red grape is a new contribution to the wine world from Chile, where it grew for years and was confused with Merlot. It has the best of two worlds: deep chocolate richness like Merlot but bright, lively, spicy fruit like Zinfandel.

Collecting harvested carmenere grapes at the Clos Apalta winery in Chile

Recipe: Blueberry and Crème Fraîche Tarts

THIS IS A BEAUTIFUL, simple dessert, perfect for a summer dinner party. Serve with a perfectly matched blueberry port.

3 tablespoons (45 g) salted butter

5 tablespoons (38 g) pistachios

1 tablespoon (20 g) brown sugar

4 sheets phyllo dough, thawed

1⅓ cups (195 g) fresh blueberries

1 tablespoon (20 g) honey, divided

1 tablespoon (15 ml) lemon juice

1 cup (225 g) crème fraîche*

1 tablespoon (15 ml) vanilla extract

1 tablespoon (6 g) fresh mint, julienned, for garnish

*Note: If you can't find crème fraîche easily, you can substitute lightly whipped heavy whipping cream or plain whole milk yogurt. You can also make your own crème fraîche. Combine 1½ cups heavy whipping cream with ¼ cup buttermilk in a clean glass jar with a tight lid. Cover and shake the mixture vigorously for 30 seconds, and refrigerate till ready to use. This should be used within two or three days of when it is made.

Preheat the oven to 375°F (190C°). Butter 4 cups of a muffin tin and set aside.

Place the pistachios in a small skillet over medium heat, and stir the nuts until fragrant. Be careful not to overcook. The nuts will burn in a matter of seconds. In a food processor, combine the cooked pistachios and 1 tablespoon (10 g) of the brown sugar. Pulse until finely chopped.

Lay out the first sheet of phyllo dough, and keep the others covered with a damp paper towel. Cut the dough to make an even, relatively large square. Brush with the melted butter and sprinkle one-third of the nut mixture on the dough. Place the next layer of Phyllo on top, and again trim to a square, brush with butter, and sprinkle with one-third of the nut mixture. Repeat with the third and fourth layers of phyllo. Do not top the last layer with the nut mixture.

Cut the square into equal quarters. Place each quarter into a buttered muffin tin, with the bottom of the dough against the bottom of the tin, and the top of the dough sticking up or folding over toward the outside. Bake for 10 minutes. Immediately remove from the tin and cool on a wire rack.

While the phyllo-pistachio pastry cools, in a bowl, combine the blueberries, 1½ teaspoons (10 g) of the honey, and the lemon juice. In another bowl, combine the crème fraîche, vanilla extract, and remaining honey.

Assemble just before serving. Place ¼ cup (56 g) of the crème fraîche mixture in each cup, top with the berries, and garnish with fresh mint.

YIELD: Serves 4

295

Wine Pairing: Duckwalk Vineyards Blueberry Port
UNITED STATES (NEW YORK)

Made from Maine blueberries, this strong dessert wine—from Duckwalk Vineyards on Long Island's North Fork—is a great counterpoint to the lightness of the phyllo tarts. Blueberries actually make great wine, and this one has nice bristling tannins like a red grape wine. It's supremely sweet.

Grapes That Grow Down to the Sea

THE OCEAN IS GOOD medicine for vineyards.

It moderates the temperature, delivering warmer breezes than some inland regions experience, and provides cool evenings that allow grapes to thrive. Something about the ocean makes wine grapes grow especially well on land that once was ocean, even land that hasn't been underwater for several million years, such as Burgundy in France. Dig down a few feet and in no time, you turn up seashells hundreds of miles (kilometers) from the nearest ocean.

Ancient beach soil provides effective drainage. Rather than suffocating clay soil, the broken down seashells and kneading of the ocean on the land for centuries creates a supple foundation for growing wine grapes. The sandy, gravely alluvial soils from ancient ocean floors can store more water than rocky, hard soil.

Matyas Vogel

WHEN WINEMAKER MATYAS VOGEL thinks of the wines of his youth in southwest Hungary, he smiles as he remembers wine on every table, as automatic as salt and pepper. Vogel was born on a vineyard—"surrounded by vines," as he puts it. His family grew Chardonnay, Riesling, and a few reds. He studied winemaking in Hungary and came to the United States in 1987 to make wine on the East Coast, at that time nearly the most undervalued and ignored winemaking region in all of North America.

Vogel brought with him a sense of reality and a touch for strong, practical winemaking. Free from any dewy-eyed romantic vision of what it means to make wine, he merely made the best wine he could every time with whatever his bosses harvested or bought from New England's few vineyard acres.

"I try to make the wine the old-fashioned way," Vogel said. "To preserve the fruit, we want as little physical involvement with the wines as possible… no unnecessary filtering, no over-manipulation. This preserves the pure taste of the fruit, as if you picked a grape right now right off the vine and ate it. It should taste just like that in the wine."

Even in his early days of working at Via della Chiesa Winery in Raynham, Massachusetts, all of his wines were famous for being extremely well made: clear, clean, true to the grape, and well balanced. Vogel's Cayuga was bottled as Cayuga "Supreme" and it had a good deal of spritz, with fresh, explosive fruit, and a flavor similar to an Italian Tocai, but much more light-hearted in personality. At the time, it was one of the best, most distinctive wines the region had ever produced.

Vogel continues to make wine at Truro Vineyards on Cape Cod in Massachusetts, dealing patiently and effectively with the fruit New England's variable seasons produce. Today, he works just 5 pampered acres (2 ha) of hand-picked Chardonnay, Cabernet Franc, and Merlot. The winery also makes Sauvignon Blanc, Pinot Grigio, and a Riesling-style white called Vignoles (pronounced veen-YOLL), all grown under their direction by their vineyard partners. Regardless of any other factors, the Vogel Principle still applies: make the best wine you can every time. It's the tiny winery's only recipe for success.

Make Wine at Home

Recipes for wine can be found online or from a wine supply shop. Ask home winemakers to share successful recipes, if they are willing. It's always better to start with a tried-and-true formula. Here is an overview.

Supplies

bottle brush (for cleaning equipment)

2-gallon plastic bucket with secure lid

spoon for stirring

enamel or aluminum pan (for boiling ingredients, if the recipe calls for this)

funnel

mesh sheet for straining juice extract

demijohn (large, narrow-necked bottle) or fermenting vessel with a rubber bung and airlock

plastic tube for siphoning

bottles with corks or stoppers

Note: Avoid metal pans, stainless steel, or colored plastics for fermentation and long-term storage; these materials can taint the wine.

Basic Ingredients

Fruit (fresh, canned, or frozen concentrate)

Water

Sugar

Yeast

Pectin enzyme

Grape tannin

Potassium sorbate

Yeast nutrient

Campden tablet (for before fermentation and bottling)

1. Sterilize equipment. Bacteria can infect wine and spoil the product at any stage. Take care to use boiling water to sterilize all tools and bottles. You can also sterilize your supplies with products used for sterilizing baby bottles.

2. Choose your fruit. Using fresh fruit or concentrate depends on your recipe (fresh fruit produces better-quality wine with more flavor). Find orchard grapes from farmers' markets, or ask for a resource at a local wine store. Concentrates can be found at wine supply shops. Mix fruit and water in the bucket with lid.

3. Extract the flavor. Most homemade wines need to be diluted with water. This formula is called "must." Dissolve sugar in the must, and add yeast by using a funnel to "pitch" it into the mixture. (Follow your recipe for amounts.) Sugar converts into alcohol during fermentation, and yeast jumpstarts fermentation.

4. Allow the wine to ferment. Yeast consumes the sugar and produces alcohol. During the aerobic stage of fermentation, yeast builds up a colony to consume sugar, which occurs during the second stage when alcohol is produced. This process takes place in the same bucket from extraction.

5. Wait and strain. The recipe indicates how long to wait before straining the liquid (raking) and pouring it into your demijohn with a fermentation lock. The lock blocks air and prevents bacteria growth. The bubbling is the yeast using up remaining oxygen. The bubbling stops when oxygen is gone and a slower fermentation takes place.

6. Siphon and age. The yeast has done its job when it drops to the bottom of the demijohn and wine starts to clear. "Rake" it again with a siphon and pour wine into a clean jar to age. Secure the jar tightly.

7. Transfer to a bottle. After wine has aged (check recipe for time), bottle it and continue the aging process. A corking machine is a convenient gadget that can help seal the bottles. After the wine ages in the bottle, it's ready to drink!

297

Writing a Better Wine List

MOST WINE LOVERS confess to feeling daunted by the task of ordering wine in a restaurant and navigating an incomprehensible wine list. People report confusion, intimidation, and worst of all, a nagging certainty that the same pricey bottle of wine they're about to order sits in the bargain bin at their local wine shop.

Charmingly, most wine lovers actually blame themselves for feeling discombobulated. "If only I knew more about wine," they think, "or could speak the secret language of the sommelier, then I could get a good glass of wine every time." Consumer education is important, but frankly, the people in the wine and food industry are to blame.

Restaurant management seems to focus more on the etiquette of serving wine than on the practical aspects of selling it. Self-styled wine masters hide wine's inherent subjectivity behind a veil of experthood and gibberish. And servers—often just as confused and intimidated as their customers—recommend the same safe wines over and over again.

Here's a short list of how I'd like to see restaurants improve their wine games.

MORE COPIES OF THE WINE LIST

Imagine handing a party of eight only one food menu to share. Utterly ridiculous, right? From now on, wine lists for everybody!

MORE WINE TRAINING FOR SERVERS AND COOKS

Every person in the front of the house and the kitchen needs to know the wine list inside and out. That means tasting, talking, and thinking about wine all the time. When salespeople from importers and distributors show up, make sure everyone present tastes the wines, not just the beverage manager. Schedule regular, mandatory wine training. That way, chefs will design dishes and specials with wines in mind, and servers can go out and confidently sell both.

A STREAMLINED WINE LIST

Most wine lists are just too long. Take a less-is-more approach. Focus on a dozen whites, a dozen reds, and a half-dozen rosés on one page. Put everything else in a leather-bound reserve list.

A WINE LIST ON THE FOOD MENU

Don't make people guess which wine goes with which foods; put that information right on the menu. Some of the most successful wine lists are literally integrated into the food menu. Seafood dishes in the left column, seafood wines listed to the right, red meat dishes with red meat wines, desserts with dessert wines, and so on. This approach makes wine pairing simple, and it reinforces the idea that food and wine go together.

EXPERIENCED SERVERS WHO READ THE TABLE FOR WINE

When a customer points to a wine on the wine list and asks, "What's this wine like?" the best response is, "It's delicious, of course, but what are you like?" With that, a conversation is underway and the server is selling wine, not just serving it.

Wine list at the restaurant Aux Lyonnais in Paris, France

V P
Apéritif CERDON 5 20
BLANCS
2000 Coteaux Lyonnais
2000 Beaujolais
2000 Macon village
2000 Viognier
ROSÉS Tavel 2000
ROUGES
2000 Chiroubles
2000 Vin de Pays
2001 Regnie
2000 Mazis Chambertin
1999
PRIX NETS

White Wine from Red Grapes

RED GRAPES GROWN IN cold climates—either far north in Europe and North America or far south in the southern hemisphere—are notoriously hard to get ripe, especially the color of the skin. How intensely black a red grape becomes as it ripens is partly a function of how much sun the grape gets. More sun produces a darker color and a thicker skin.

Pinot Noir—the Italians call it Pinot Nero—is not nearly as black as the name suggests. In fact, it's one of the lighter red wine grapes, more of a cherry color; and Pinot is known for being thin-skinned, literally. Cold-climate Pinot growers embrace the opportunity underripe fruit presents by making Vin Gris (gray wine, pink really) or even white wine from red grapes when nature delivers it.

Wine Suggestion: Pinot Nero

Cavallotto Langhe Pinot Nero Bianco, Italy
This quirky, charming Italian white wine comes from northwest Italy near Barolo and Barbaresco, and is made entirely from Pinot Nero. This Pinot Nero Bianco tastes deep, woodsy, and intense with a dense, delicious acidity that really brightens up the shadows.

Recipe: Fresh Figs in Honey and Wine

TODAY, THE RULE for cooking with wine is simple: if you wouldn't swallow it, don't cook with it.

1 3/4 cups (410 g) dry white wine

1/3 cup (115 g) honey

1/4 cup (50 g) sugar

1 small orange

8 whole cloves

1 pound (455 g) fresh figs

1 cinnamon stick

Combine the wine, honey, and sugar in a heavy saucepan and heat gently until the sugar dissolves. Stud the orange with the cloves and add to the syrup along with the figs and cinnamon. Cover and simmer over low heat for 5 to 10 minutes, until the figs soften. Transfer the figs to a serving dish and let cool. Drizzle a bit of the sauce over the figs and a soft Brie-style cheese.

YIELD: Serves 6 (1/2 cup [75 g] each)

Wine Pairing: Shooting Star Blue Franc Lemberger

UNITED STATES (WASHINGTON)

Don't let the name confuse you. This wine has nothing to do with the ultra-potent Limburger cheese. Rather, it is made from an Austrian red grape called Blaufrankisch (Blue Franc in the name) and it's a mild, low-tannin, low-acid red.

Umbria

IF YOU DRIVE NORTHEAST from Rome and cut across the middle of the Italian peninsula, right in the center is the region of Umbria. The festival towns of Spoleto and Perugia are pretty well known, and St. Francis's hometown of Assisi is here, too, but the rest of the landscape is still very remote and untouched.

In wine terms, Umbria remains comfortably overshadowed by Tuscany just to the north, which may be just as well. Many of Umbria's wines are just as good as those yummy Tuscan reds people go on about, but are usually about half the price.

> ### Wine Suggestions: Umbria
>
> **Falesco Vitiano**, Italy
> This solid, almost chewy red is one-third each of Cabernet Sauvignon, Merlot, and Sangiovese, the traditional grape of Chianti. A nice dose of French oak softens up any hard edges.

Thomas Jefferson:
Celebrity Winemaker

THOMAS JEFFERSON, third president of the United States and overall Renaissance man, was a huge wine lover. In 1807, he embarked on an ambitious planting at Monticello of almost 300 vines from twenty-four different European grape vine cuttings he selected and imported. He imagined that like so many other crops, grapes would flourish in fertile, verdant Virginia. Not only did he anticipate that his vineyards would be as successful as anything else, but also he actually thought he could grow super grapes and make super wine to first equal, then surpass those of Europe.

Jefferson's vineyard experiment failed spectacularly, the first time and each of the six times he subsequently replanted. He discovered that as counterintuitive as it seemed, wine grapes did not automatically flourish in rich soils. Virginia piedmont soils are rich in other things too, such as bugs and bacteria, molds and mildews to which grapes are highly susceptible.

Jefferson never learned what killed his vines—technically, it was black rot and the root louse phylloxera—but the irony was not lost on him. Native North American grapes that did grow made freakishly bad wine; any grapes worth drinking would not even take root.

Luckily, Jefferson was wealthy and well connected enough to own several extensive wine cellars and import all the red Bordeaux he wanted—a bottle of 1787 Château Lafite from his cellar went for $160,000 at auction in 1985—and that may have helped take the edge off his disappointment in the short term. Overall, it was a disheartening, bad first attempt at growing European wine grapes in the New World, and it was difficult not to take the vines' emphatic reaction as a rejection of the whole idea. Jefferson's transformative vision of making great wine in America would persist, but it would take centuries to realize.

Vineyard in Umbria, Italy

Stomping Grapes

MAYBE YOU RECALL the *I Love Lucy* episode where the vivacious and barefoot Lucille Ball is marching, dancing in a vat of grapes during an Italian village's grape stomping ritual. It's a messy scene—and you can't help but wonder, is that really how wine is made? And why on earth would you smash grapes with your feet? There has to be some type of equipment that can do the job.

Grape stomping—the process of trodding grapes—is a practice as old as the vines themselves. The idea is that the seeds (pips) inside the grapes are full of astringent tannin, so you don't want to squish those pips.

The walking motion of your foot will not pop the pips—in fact, you'd have to pierce that pip with something sharp to burst it. Also, during the stomping process, fermentation begins, so the stomping puts the grape juice in contact with the yeast on the outside of the grape.

Some wineries still trod grapes for festivals, but usually the ritual is performed for show because now we have modernized presses so we don't have to get our feet dirty. Call around and you will be able to find local vineyards that stage these events, and even allow guests to get in on the crushing.

Vintage Hype of the Century

CALL IT MILLENNIUM wine hype, century madness, or even ridiculous, but after the 2000 (millennium) harvest, the hype-fest began, albeit very slowly at first. It picked up speed as wine lovers' wishes for a super millennial vintage turned into a self-fulfilling wine-futures market.

Six months after the harvest—during the summer of 2001—2000 Bordeaux went on sale as futures. Don't get me wrong. I love red Bordeaux, especially the most intense, delicious, expensive Bordeaux. But here was the deal: pay now, receive shipment some time in 2003, taste in 2010, drink in 2020. By the time wine god Robert Parker gushed to inordinate levels about its quality, the hype was over.

Meanwhile, wholesalers tried to hold back the 2000 vintage until they sold off more of the delicious but ignored 1998s and 1999s already out there. Sure, 2000 might have been a vintage year for hype—as most first years of new decades are—but that doesn't mean the wines were better. It just meant they were pricier.

Grapes being harvested for Pinotage production on Skoongesig Farm in Firgrove, Cape Province, South Africa

Pinotage

PINOTAGE WAS BORN from an experiment conducted by a professor in South Africa in the 1920s. He crossed Pinot Noir with Cinsault grapes and came up with Pinotage, a fruity and refreshing wine (some say it tastes like bananas) that ranges from young and light to deep and rich. It all depends on where the Pinotage is grown.

The grape did not impress the wine world for years, and it was, for the most part, ignored until 1961, when a 1959 vintage Pinotage won the Grand Championship at the Cape Young Wine Show in South Africa. After that, wineries began to specialize in the grape, but it never took off. Until 1991, that is, when Beyers Truter, winemaker at Kanonkop Estate, entered his Pinotages at England's International Wine and Spirit Competition. He became the first South African to win Winemaker of the Year. Suddenly, Pinotage was hot and prices shot up in a big way.

Eventually, the Pinotage Association was formed and an annual Pinotage Top Ten competition launched. When apartheid ended, new markets opened up for this and other South African wines. Today, the demand for Pinotage continues to grow. The grape also grows in New Zealand, Israel, Canada, Brazil, Zimbabwe, and the United States.

Wine Suggestion: Pinotage

Zonnebloem Pintage, South Africa
This Pinotage from Zonnebloem (Afrikaans—the South African language—for "sunflower") is full of smoke, wood, and leaves, with a fruit component juicy like blood orange and concentrated like cola.

Recipe: Baked Fennel with Parmigiano-Reggiano Cheese

ALTHOUGH THEY'RE ONLY distantly related, fennel and anise both contain the aromatic compound anethole, and their distinctly similar aromas link them in the mind.

Fennel has been associated with wine for thousands of years. The ancient Greek god of wine, Dionysus, and his clan carried clubs made from the stalk and bulb of giant fennel. Prometheus brought stolen fire to humanity in the form of a burning fennel flower. It feels natural to pair this dish with a potent Greek wine.

2 pounds (900 g) fennel bulbs, washed and halved

4 tablespoons (55 g) butter

½ cup (50 g) freshly grated Parmigiano-Reggiano cheese

Preheat the oven to 400°F (200°C).

Cook the fennel bulbs in large pot of boiling water until just soft. Drain well.

Cut the fennel lengthwise into 4 or 6 pieces. Place the pieces in a buttered baking dish.

Dot with butter and sprinkle with grated cheese. Bake until the cheese turns golden brown.

YIELD: Serves 6

Wine Pairing: Megapanos Savatiano

GREECE

Savatiano is one of the principal white grapes of Retsina (Day 81), the famously challenging Greek wine flavored with a little pine resin. This version is not Retsina, but a crisp, clear expression of Savatiano's typically tart green apple.

Sonoma County Line

IN NORTHERN CALIFORNIA, a short distance separates the wine countries of Napa and Sonoma, but their differences are important and distinct. Sonoma Valley is almost directly north of San Francisco, and the southern end begins where San Pablo Bay ends. Napa also begins at the bay, but many miles (kilometers) east, much farther from the cool Pacific and naturally much warmer.

Summertime brings tremendous temperature swings to Sonoma. During the day, temperatures are around 100°F (38°C), but at night they fall to around 50°F (10°C). That's a daily shift of almost 50°F (28°C), and it takes a little getting used to.

Wine grapes, however, love this kind of weather. They get all the sun and heat they could want during the day—this produces rich, ripe, delicious fruit—but they get a breather at night, so they retain their balance and crispness instead of growing and growing.

It's a helpful generalization to say that Napa is Cabernet-centered. Sonoma, thanks to its cooler climate, tends to grow more different kinds of grapes—from Syrah and Petite Sirah to the almost-unheard-of Carignane, Sangiovese (see Day 317), Malbec (see Day 114), and Petite Verdot.

Carry A. Nation

PROHIBITION'S MOST POTENT and enduring symbol was a pinched, violent, disagreeable woman named Carry A. Nation who became famous for attacking saloons armed only with a hatchet and her firm belief that she was striking out at what Jesus "doesn't like." Nation's mother was a known sufferer of psychotic delusions and believed long and actively that she was Queen Victoria. Nation may never have thought she was a member of the royal family, but she did believe her name was an assignment from God, and that it was appropriate to attack people and property in the name of temperance with a hatchet. (A failed marriage to Charles Gloyd, a severe alcoholic, also fueled Nation's passion for the temperance movement.)

Nation and her followers chopped up many bars and barrels and broke bottles with their hatchets of righteousness. And Nation got tons of publicity for doing so. After one of her flamboyant arrests, in Wichita, Kansas, a photographer captured Nation kneeling and praying in her jail cell; the image looks like a well-styled studio shot, her face softly illuminated from above and backlit by prison bars. You can't buy publicity like that, but you can sell official "Carry A. Nation Brand Saloon-busting Hatchets"—exactly what she did, in addition to hiring a manager and traveling the country on a speaking tour as "The Famous and Original Barroom Smasher." Her name was a registered trademark in the state of Kansas.

A book deal in 1905 brought us *The Use and Need of the Life of Carry A. Nation*, an autobiography in which Nation spelled out her quaint views about family, morality, race relations, food, alcohol, pseudo-science, and, strangely, Masons. Nation believed an underground cabal of Euro-centric Masons was encouraging wine and alcohol consumption in the U.S. to further their unspecified but nefarious goals. "I believe the Masons were a great curse to Dr. Gloyd," she wrote, referring to her first husband who died a raging alcoholic.

Nation made no distinction between her diverse enemies. Beer, wine, whiskey, and the Masons were equally evil. She rarely limited her enforced self-improvement to one vice. Nation opposed cigarettes and railed against foreign foods of all kinds, with wine a special target, being both foreign *and* alcohol. She devoted substantial space in her only book to debunking the myth that wine is food, one of the core principles of great European cuisine. The science behind her assertion is an almost medieval vision of two "classes" of food: flesh formers and body warmers. By her frontier science, alcohol is neither, so therefore, it is not a food. If it is not a food, it's a toxin.

Nation did not live to see national Prohibition. Maine enacted state Prohibition in 1851, Kansas in 1880, and five more states in the early twentieth century. But Nation died in 1911. Her epitaph reads, "She Hath Done What She Could."

Join a Wine Club

IF YOU WANT TO LEARN more about wine from fellow enthusiasts, consider joining a wine club. There are wine clubs all over the world, and you can find one that suits you by doing a simple Internet search or asking your local wine retailer for suggestions. (They might even have their own wine club.) Some clubs may offer monthly tastings or even discounts and other perks like vineyard tours. There are clubs that are purely forums for sharing information—the Internet is rich with these.

So why join a wine club? Why not?! Nevertheless, here are some benefits you may enjoy:

- Special pricing available to wine club members
- An opportunity to meet other wine lovers and share favorite vintages and other tips
- Advice on preparing glasses, tasting, winemaking, and pairing wines with foods
- Invitations to early taste tests at wineries
- Behind-the-scenes tours of wineries or harvest tours
- Access to wines that may not be for sale to the public
- Wine suggestions from fellow members
- Travel opportunities

Mnemonic Devices for Wine

AS ANY COUPLE WILL TELL YOU, only one balm can soothe the inevitable frictions of an intense love relationship: communication. You have to talk about "it," and that goes for your wine life as well. This scenario falls at the practical end of the wine-communication spectrum: You're at a wine shop trying hopelessly to remember the name of that delicious wine you drank two weeks ago at a restaurant. Tasting a great wine, then forgetting its name is the worst disappointment.

Because most people aren't in the wine business and don't make a point of remembering vintages and vineyards, why not try a good mnemonic device? The easiest memory technique for most people is to alphabetize their favorite wines, and study them in that form. Then they naturally associate wines with the letters of the alphabet: B reminds them of Beringer, which reminds them of Byron and Byington and Benziger. You get the picture.

Another trick is to make absurd, memorable word-play associations. Lolonis is a great California winery, and anytime you can't remember the name, just think of the little town of Hohokus, New Jersey. Looking for a nice red Bordeaux? Think Loudon Wainwright and enjoy Château Loudenne.

Finally, simple visualization often works effectively. Get an empty wine box, the kind with the twelve-bottle cardboard insert. Put in a few of your favorite wines. Then, take them out one at a time, hold them, read them, and then put the bottle back. Later, when you try to remember them, think about being with the box and the wines and what it was like to remove, replace, and read them. Eventually, you'll fill up a case in your mind and remember every bottle in it.

Cantina Foresi wine cellar in Orvieto, Umbria, Italy

Que Syrah Shiraz

FIRST, LET'S STRAIGHTEN out a bit of confusion generated by the spelling of this grape's name. Is it Syrah or Shiraz? That depends on where you buy the wine, and where the grapes grow. Simply put, it's all the same grape, just spelled differently.

In the United States, the grape is primarily called Syrah. (Do not confuse this with Petite Sirah, an entirely different grape mostly grown in California.) In Australia, the grape is called Shiraz (see Day 65 for its history), and it's the dominant red grape in that country. Then there are U.S. producers who capitalize on the popularity of this wine by making "Australian-style" wines and calling them Shiraz.

For all intents and purposes, Shiraz is Syrah. And it is known for its spicy blackberry, plum, pepper, licorice, and bitter chocolate notes.

A Shiraz sign at Pepper Tree winery in Hunter Valley, Australia

Wine Suggestions: Shiraz/Syrah

Paringa Shiraz, Australia
You can feel the wonderful weight of this wine as soon as you take it into your mouth. It's dark red, dense, and deep with a low center of gravity and flavors of wood, fig, date, and plum. On top is bright, sunny Australian fruit, full of delicious cherry and pomegranate juice.

Ravenswood Shiraz, United States (California)
This Shiraz is juicy and fresh, bright and radiant, with blueberry and raspberry. The grapes all come from the Barossa Valley and McLaren Vale, two big wine regions in southern Australia famous for big-boned reds.

Recipe: Strawberries in Wine

SOMETIMES, LESS REALLY IS MORE, especially in the case of this deceptively simple recipe pairing wine and fruit. Substitute your favorite fruit for strawberries—kiwi, melon, blackberries, almost anything will work—and use almost any white wine on hand, whether it's something dry left over from dinner or the sweet Riesling that is suggested below made for dessert.

2 pounds (450 g) strawberries

½ cup (96 g) superfine sugar

⅔ cup (160 ml) dry white wine

Rinse and hull the strawberries. Sprinkle with the sugar and let stand for 1 hour. Pour on the wine just before serving. If there's wine left, drink it with dessert!

YIELD: Serves 6 (½ cup [75 g] each)

Wine Pairing: Markus Molitor Riesling Spätlese
GERMANY

Spät is German for "late," and this designation means the winery harvested the Riesling after the main harvest, when the grapes are higher in sugar. At only 7.5 percent alcohol, this wine is perfect for that after-dinner sipping that calls for light, low-alcohol wines. It tastes sweet but not sugary.

Carneros Drive-By

DRIVING NORTH FROM SAN FRANCISCO into wine country, you arrive at a fork in the road. Just at the top of San Pablo Bay, you can bear left (west) toward the Pacific Ocean and cool Sonoma, or bear inland toward Napa. This intersection—where Napa and Sonoma meet—is called Los Carneros. Translated from Spanish as "the rams," it is named for the sheep that grazed there more than a hundred years ago. It is both Sonoma and Napa, and neither all at the same time.

Because Carneros is located so close to San Pablo Bay, it has the coolest climate of both Napa and Sonoma. It produces California's best Pinot Noir, super sparkling wines, and great cold-climate-style Chardonnay.

Wine lovers visiting these well-known wine regions in northern California often overlook Carneros: it's the first place you arrive, maybe too early in the day, and it's the last place on your way out after a day of wine tasting. Because of this travel quirk, Carneros doesn't experience the winery lines and traffic jams familiar to Napa Valley (and to a pleasantly lesser degree, Sonoma Valley). Don't miss it.

Mark Occasions with Wine

REMEMBER THE YEAR you met your spouse, the year you said, "I do," or the year you said, "We're done"? There's the year you took an adventurous European backpacking trip. How about the year of the birth of your first child, or the year you started paying a mortgage rather than rent? Graduation, promotion, or life change—countless occasions call for a special bottle of wine to share. Here are a few:

HOUSEWARMING

Choose a local wine, or if gifting the bottle to a friend far away, seek out a winery in his or her area and attach a map with directions to visit the winery.

WEDDING ANNIVERSARY

Select a wine with a vintage year that matches the couple's wedding year. Or choose a bottle from the region where the two were married. Some wineries recommend a dessert wine for a first anniversary, a Champagne for the fifth year of marriage, and a port to celebrate year ten. But Champagne is appropriate any year, and will remind the partners of their toast and commitment.

BABY SHOWER

Create your own label through companies that provide this design/printing service. Check online for suppliers. Then provide a personalized bottle for each guest or serve the "baby bottles" at the shower. (Of course, mom will have to wait to uncork hers until the birth day, but how sweet it will taste then!)

BIRTHDAY

Choosing a bottle with a vintage year on your, or a friend's, birth date could get pricey after the age of, well, ten. So the budget-conscious might prefer plan B: Choose an artsy label that will entertain the guest of honor (or you if you're treating yourself to a birthday indulgence—and why shouldn't you!?). Another approach involves purchasing a collector's bottle and wrapping it with instructions to open on a certain landmark birthday. If you do this, just be sure to bring a drink-now bottle as well so you don't spoil the party.

Plan a Wine and Chocolate Party

WINE AND CHOCOLATE are natural partners. Whether you decide to host a wine and chocolate tasting party, or you are choosing a sweet treat to complement a favorite bottle, here are some suggestions for pairing these two indulgences.

Note: Pairing dark chocolate and red wine gives you a super dose of heart-healthy antioxidants. You can hardly call it an indulgence! *Bon apétit!*

Sweet Choice: Choose wine that is sweeter than the food; a wine that is drier than chocolate will not bring out the flavor of your cacao. White wines rarely complement the richness of chocolate, but if you're looking for a wine to carry over from dinner to dessert (chocolate dessert, of course), try a Zinfandel.

Go Red: Chocolate is a strong flavor, and it needs a wine that can stand up to its richness. Dark chocolate and red wines are a match; sweet dessert wines go better with milk chocolates.

Add Sparkle: Try a sparkling Shiraz with chocolate to tickle the taste buds. Your red choices aren't limited to plain reds, and that sparkling Shiraz will pair far better than Champagne will.

Complementing Chocolate Notes: A wine that contains chocolate notes may compete with chocolate desserts. Look for flavors such as raspberry, cherry, and nuts in a wine to pair with chocolate. Think complementary.

Don't Be Afraid to Fail: In addition to tasting wine and chocolate pairings that work and setting off fireworks in the pleasure centers of your brain, make sure to taste and learn from the un-pairings—the failed combinations that everyone hates. Sometimes, we will actually try, on purpose, to find the worst wine and chocolate pairing of the night. Ironically, that's often the one people really remember and learn from, even if it's in a negative way.

Feeling the Chocolate: Besides the many varieties of flavors and intensities chocolate can possess, it also expresses a range of textures. On one end, Lindt is always exceptionally smooth—Rodolphe Lindt himself invented conching (whipping and smoothing) for chocolate in 1879—and on the other, organic Taza is bracingly gritty and unconched. Try them both along with everything in between.

The Two Faces of Wine:
Dionysus (and Bacchus)

YOU MAY HAVE HEARD OF the Greek god Dionysus, or his Roman counterpart Bacchus, without giving him much extra thought. But given a second glance, Dionysus is a complex character, as complex as the most revered bottle of wine. Dionysus represents the two faces, or natures, of wine. He represents fertility and agriculture—the caring of grape vines and the harvesting of their fruit—as well as joy, passion, and festivity. He also represents a darker side—escape from humanity and daily life through spiritual and physical intoxication, and an impulsive temper.

His split nature may be attributed to having none other than Zeus as a father and a mortal mother, Semele, a Thebian princess. He is the only Greek god to have this mixed parentage. He has no definite shape or form, unlike other gods. He appears at one time youthful and effeminate, at other times aged and masculine.

The Roman story of Bacchus recounts his tales of wandering in madness until cured by Rhea, the Titan, considered the "mother" of the gods. Enlightened, he wandered through India and Asia, teaching the people how to cultivate grape vines. He returned to Greece hoping to be worshipped once again, but the princes reigning there feared him for the madness and disorder he was known to bring with him. (It is true that his festivals were some of the largest and wildest ever seen.) In the stories of Bacchus (and Dionysus), he maintains the love and respect of many of the people and the fear and hatred of those in power.

It seems only fitting that wine should be embodied by a god as complex as Dionysus—no age could define him, nor could he be completely identified by gender. He brought out the best and the worst in people, and he is at once a symbol of passion and festivity contrasted with intemperance and escape.

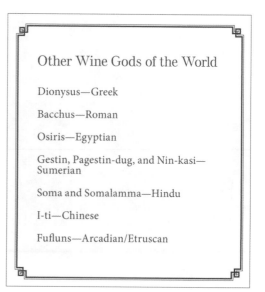

Other Wine Gods of the World

Dionysus—Greek

Bacchus—Roman

Osiris—Egyptian

Gestin, Pagestin-dug, and Nin-kasi—Sumerian

Soma and Somalamma—Hindu

I-ti—Chinese

Fufluns—Arcadian/Etruscan

Photo Credits

© Daniel Acevedo/Alamy, 174

AFP/gettyimages.com, 142

© All Canada Photos/Alamy, 255

Jonathon Alsop, 18; 23; 34; 56; 59; 62; 65; 68; 83; 98; 102; 104; 120; 124; 219; 312

© Jon Arnold Images Ltd/Alamy, 237

© Aurora Photos/Alamy, 225

© Brent Bergherm/agefotostock.com, 293

Bloomberg/gettyimages.com, 90

© Bon Appetit/Alamy, 2; 17; 44; 52; 107; 140; 167; 181; 240; 299

© Pitu Cau/Alamy, 281

© Cephas Picture Library/Alamy, 108; 152; 155; 217; 260; 273; 274; 285; 294

© Rob Cousins/Alamy, 95

© DEA/G BERENGO GARD/agefotostock.com, 151

© Danita Delimont/Alamy, 7

© Emilio Ereza/agefotostock.com, 41

Nancy Falconi/gettyimages.com, 8

Michele Falzone/gettyimages.com, 263

Dennis Flaherty/gettyimages.com, 163

© Derek Gale/Alamy, 72

© Paolo Gallo/Alamy, 301

© Norma Jean Gargasz/Alamy, 233

© Garry Gay/Alamy, 47

Getty Images, 147; 201; 230

© Tim Graham/Alamy, 310

© ICP/Alamy, 185

Image Source/gettyimages.com, 113

iStockphoto.com, 43; 48; 60; 66; 69; 71; 74; 77; 81; 97; 100; 117; 130; 131; 139; 157; 168; 171; 177; 189; 195; 196; 202; 208; 222; 227; 234; 245; 247; 249; 265; 277; 287; 291; 303

© Per Karlsson, BKWine.com/Alamy, 135; 289

© Jo Katanigra/Alamy, 27

© Stuart Kelly/Alamy, 159

© LOOK Die Bildagentur der Fotografen GmbH/Alamy, 5; 266

© Alan Majchrowicz/agefotostock.com, 205

© Melba Photo Agency/Alamy, 87

Camille Moirenc/gettyimages.com, 269

Luciana Pampalone, 10

© Malcolm Park/Alamy, 253

Nicholas Pavloff/gettyimages.com, 129

© Doug Pearson/agefotostock.com, 31

© Photononstop/Alamy, 314

© Radius Images/Alamy, 110

Rolph Richardson/Alamy, 198

© Mark Sadlier/Alamy, 221

© Stephen Saks Photography/Alamy, 206

© Trevor Smith/Alamy, 282

© Inga Spence/Alamy, 228

© STOCKFOLIO®/Alamy, 39

© Johnny Stockshooter/Alamy, 211

© Martin Thomas Photography/Alamy, 309

© Peter Titmuss/Alamy, 305

© E. D. Torial/Alamy, 191

© Frank Tschakert/Alamy, 258

© Jim West/agefotostock.com, 37

Index

Acknowledgments

Thank you to everyone who has supported and reinforced my dream to write about wine over the years: my parents and family, friends and daughters, Eve especially for visiting so many vineyards and wineries with me when she was a little girl. I will never forget it. Thanks to my best friend, Jay Fedigan, for teaching me how to take a photograph. Thank you, Pam and Kim, for never cooking a bad meal. Thanks to Dr. Raoul Bronner, Ph.D., for thinking up this whole crazy wine angle in the first place.

Special appreciation to wine legend Burt Miller and the Miller family for all their help and encouragement to the Boston Wine School.

Authors say all the time they "could not have done it" without their editors, but I never really knew what they meant until working with editor Rochelle Bourgault. Special thanks to her for really helping me write, and turning my phrases around the right way. Thanks also to Jen Grady for her perfect production, and to Kristen Hampshire for giving this book the boost it needed to cross the finish line.

About the Author

JONATHON ALSOP is a wine writer who has been writing about wine, food, and travel since 1988. He is author of the wine column and blog In Vino Veritas (www.InVinoVeritas.com) as well as many articles for the Associated Press, *Frequent Flyer*, *La Vie Claire*, *Beverage Business Magazine*, Mobil Travel Guides, Fodor's Travel Guides, the *Boston Globe*, and many others. Jonathon is founder and executive director of the Boston Wine School where he has been teaching wine and food classes since 2000.